Spiritual Care

Spiritual Care

The Everyday Work of Chaplains

WENDY CADGE

OXFORD
UNIVERSITY PRESS

Oxford University Press is a department of the University of Oxford. It furthers the University's objective of excellence in research, scholarship, and education by publishing worldwide. Oxford is a registered trade mark of Oxford University Press in the UK and certain other countries.

Published in the United States of America by Oxford University Press
198 Madison Avenue, New York, NY 10016, United States of America.

CIP data is on file at the Library of Congress
ISBN 978-0-19-764782-0 (pbk.)
ISBN 978-0-19-764781-3 (hbk.)

DOI: 10.1093/oso/9780197647813.001.0001

1 3 5 7 9 8 6 4 2

Paperback printed by Lakeside Book Company, United States of America
Hardback printed by Bridgeport National Bindery, Inc., United States of America

For Risa, Nate, and Deborah, with love.

Contents

Acknowledgments ix

1. Introductions 1
2. Chaplaincy in Greater Boston: A Short Historical Overview 20
3. Becoming a Chaplain 47
4. Brokers With(out) Authority? The Improvisational Work of Chaplains 69
5. The Value Added of Holding the Space 92
6. Brokering Deaths: Chaplains as Midwives and Escorts 111
7. Engaging Religious and Spiritual Differences: Organizational and Individual Approaches 127
8. Conclusions Can Be Beginnings 148

Appendix: Initial Glimpses and Focused Attention: A Methodological Approach at Mid-Life 165
Notes 175
References 207
Index 229

Acknowledgments

This book was a long time in the making, enabling me to accrue gratitude to a great many people and institutions in the process. I am grateful first to the chaplains who talked with me, allowed me to shadow them, and shared their stories. What I learned from them is at the center of this book. I appreciate the institutions that have employed these chaplains and the historians and archivists that saved records and helped me find my way through some of them. Archival staff and volunteer historians at the Archdiocese of Boston Archives, the *Boston Globe*, Beth Israel Deaconess Medical Center Archives, Brandeis University Library and Archives, the Boston Fire Department, the City of Boston Archives, Congregational Library & Archives, the Episcopal Diocese of Massachusetts, Harvard Divinity School, the Jewish Chaplaincy Council of Massachusetts, and Massachusetts General Hospital Archives were invaluable.

While initial glimpses came before a year of research leave in 2016–2017, much of the data shared here was gathered during that time. Thank you to Brandeis University for a semester of paid academic leave and a Senior Faculty Research Semester that enabled me to have twelve months of research time. The Work and Organizational Studies Group at MIT's Sloan School was an ideal place to spend this year, and I am deeply grateful to Erin Kelly, Sloan Distinguished Professor of Work and Organization Studies, for making that possible. The opportunity to meet and work with Mary Rowe, Adjunct Professor of Work and Organization Studies, and Katherine Wong, then a student at Wellesley College, through MIT's UROP program was an unexpected and exciting surprise.

Many, many undergraduate and graduate students at Brandeis University worked with me as research assistants on this and related projects. I learned from and thank each of them, including Adah Anderson, Jennifer Cañas Alegria, Philip Bonmassar, Daryl Cabrol, Alison Cantor, Olivia Combs, Cynthia Crispiano, Rebecca Hersch, Savannah Jackson, Nan Jiang, Jung Kim, Ben Katcher, Sarah Karan, Sophia Koolpe, Mariah Lewis, LiJun Lin, Markia Neufville, Zoe Pringle, Tali Rychik, Jessica Shenkel, Teresa Shi, Weijian Shi, Simona Shuman, Caty Taborda, and Amanda Votta. Swarthmore College students Juliane Ding, Laura Hirai, and Sophia Peterson were also amazing short-term research assistants. Thanks to the College and the SwatWorks program for the opportunity. Undergraduates Helena Buckman (the College of William and Mary), Lily deLaRue (Clemson University), Claire Dettelbach (Carleton College), and graduate student Elena van Stee (University of Pennsylvania) were also enormously helpful on this and related projects.

The staff and advisors of the Chaplaincy Innovation Lab have been and remain key intellectual partners. A special thanks to Trace Haythorn and Michael Skaggs for helping the Lab launch in 2018 and for ongoing conversations, sometimes every day, since then. To Helen McNeal and Shelly Rambo for their continued wise counseling and seemingly boundless energy, to current and previous staff Aja Antoine, Steve Dahl, Jiaying Ding, Shirah Hecht, Bethamie Horowitz, Grace Last, Amy Lawton, Jasmine Okafor, Darra Sweetser, and Grace Tien for all your amazing work. And to Cheryl Giles and the Lab's Advisory Committee for what you have taught me along the way.

The writing of this book was facilitated by continued encouragement from Trace Haythorn and Michael Skaggs, amazing editorial skill especially in the final stretches from Sophie Trachtenberg, and comments on parts or all of the manuscript from Nancy Ammerman, George Fitchett, Trace Haythorn, John Schmalzbauer, Michael Skaggs, Winnifred Sullivan, Jim Wellman, and Robert Wuthnow. While the mistakes are mine, the manuscript is stronger thanks to their feedback and insights. Portions of this work were presented at meetings of the American Academy of Religion and the Society for the Scientific Study of Religion as well in talks at the Center for the Study of Religion and American Culture at IUPUI, Center for the Study of Religion at Princeton University, Indiana University, Pew Forum, RAND, University of California-San Diego, University of Nebraska-Lincoln, and a range of professional chaplaincy associations meetings across the country. Faculty and administrative colleagues at Brandeis University supported me over the past fifteen years and enabled me to work across research questions and disciplines in creative and energizing ways for which I am grateful.

This book and my creative intellectual energy are daily fed by the outdoors and by my personal circles of support. I am grateful to Kathy D'Agostino and David McLoon for their friendship, childcare, and ongoing support. Friends and companions in the journey Beth Freed, Katie Klingensmith, Dana Lehman, Estelle McCartney, and Sara Shostak made a huge difference to me. My human and animal family here in West Newton are my miracle, and whom I am most grateful for daily. Nate and Risa, you have lived with this book for your whole lives. Your energy, goofiness, and questions fuel me, my hope for you, and for the world. Thank you for being your amazing creative selves and for keeping me going. Deborah Elliott, you are my all and without whom our family would not be. This book is for the three of you with my abiding thanks, respect, and hope. It was made easier by snoring pugs Gus and Thelma (sometimes under my desk), cats Max, Graham, Whiskers, and Slippers, and various other creatures who came into and out of our lives during its writing. For my parents and sisters and in memory of my grandparents who paved the way and continue to teach me about the in-between places, thank you.

1
Introductions

"Chaplain Braves Guns of Convicts to Aid Hostages" the *Boston Globe* reported on January 19, 1955. Frustrated with the long sentences delivered by criminal courts in Massachusetts and the lack of hope that went with them, four armed prisoners took eleven people hostage at the Charlestown State Prison. No stranger to prison riots, Catholic prison chaplain Edward Hartigan was there. In 1952, he had spent a night with barricaded prisoners in another standoff, helping bring about the release of two guards. "We knew we had a chance as long as Father Hartigan was working on our behalf," one of the guards said after that conflict, "if anyone could save us, we knew he could."[1]

So it was then that the *Boston Globe* called Father Hartigan one of the most popular men at the state prison and described how he talked with the hostages (five guards and six other convicts), the four ring leaders, and then with the attorney general, public safety commissioner, and prison warden in January of 1955. Catholic priest and prison chaplain Father Hartigan was born in Lowell, Massachusetts, educated at St. Francis Xavier University in Nova Scotia and St. John's Seminary in Boston, and ordained in 1942. He served two local parishes before becoming a chaplain at the prison in 1951 while directing the Guild of Our Lady of Ransom, a group founded by Boston-born Archbishop Richard Cushing to support rehabilitation for current and former prisoners.[2]

During the three-and-a-half-day standoff at Charlestown State Prison, Father Hartigan accompanied state officials into the prison, cared for the hostages and the ring leaders, and—along with prison physician Samuel Merlin and Protestant chaplain Howard Kellett—was granted free access into the Cherry Hill cell block where the hostages were held. With Dr. Merlin, he listened to the prisoner's concerns about long sentences. He told the *Globe* he remained optimistic about a peaceful settlement even as the state police brought in an Army tank and prepared machine guns, riot guns, shotguns, tear gas, carbines, and bazookas.[3]

Spiritual Care. Wendy Cadge, Oxford University Press. © Oxford University Press 2023.
DOI: 10.1093/oso/9780197647813.003.0001

After eight-five hours, the prisoners surrendered to a seven-man citizens committee—convened by Father Hartigan at the direction of the ring leaders—that included the president of the Boston Bar Association, the editors of the *Christian Science Monitor*, and Boston's Catholic newspaper the *Pilot*, the prison physician, the Protestant chaplain, and a member of the Governor's Council. This group met with the prisoners who, according to the *Globe*, "admitted to committing bad crimes and knew they had to be punished" but had grievances including long trial delays and poor living conditions before trial in addition to their long sentences.[4]

As the prisoners turned over their weapons and released the hostages, the citizen's committee agreed to work as a group to improve prison conditions. Tired the evening of the release, Father Hartigan told a *Globe* reporter, "The prisoners still trusted me, and that means everything to me." He also told the reporter that he preferred to stay in the background, calling the support he offered for the "welfare of prisoners, their hopes and fears" his life's work.[5]

Fifty-eight years later, chaplains were (much more) quietly on hand at another moment of crisis in the city of Boston—the Boston Marathon bombing. As first responders rushed to Boylston Street moments after the bombs exploded on that sunny Monday in April, chaplains and spiritual care providers began their work in the city's hospitals, fire and police departments, and civic responses teams. A National Guard chaplain was present in the bunker with the city and state's crisis leadership team and activated other chaplain teams across the state.[6] A community chaplain called trauma specialists from the Boston Public Health Commission. She remembers telling them that "we have a group of chaplains that are prepared to support in any way needed." After submitting training certifications to the Commission, this chaplain served in a dispatching capacity; "We need two people in Dorchester at the park, people are gathering to mourn Martin Richard. . . . We need people down at the castle to be there for the runners who are coming to collect their things, OK dispatch five chaplains over there."[7]

News reports described chaplains who were active in the city's hospitals in the days that followed. The Huffington Post described patients and staff members at Boston Medical Center talking and praying with chaplains who also provided for things as seemingly mundane as finding outlets to charge phones.[8] Bombing victims and the suspected perpetrators were all rushed to Beth Israel Deaconess Medical Center, where staff—including chaplains—cared for them. Gratitude and determination were central to what Rev. Julia

Dunbar, then director of Pastoral Care at Beth Israel Deaconess Medical Center, heard in many conversations—that and a lot of questions. "For many there's a whole other level of heartbroken, life-changing, 'Where do we go from here' type questions," she told a reporter. Hospital staff—from environmental service workers to trauma surgeons—were all impacted. "Some started talking about previous trauma that they hadn't actually identified as trauma . . . some talked about just incredibly strong faith and that was their complete focus," and another person talked "about cleaning—mopping and cleaning, mopping and cleaning. . . . Bottom line," he said, "it's got to be clean for the next patient. . . . Got to take care of the next patient."[9]

In the days and months that followed, chaplains joined local clergy and trauma experts across the state as they publicly and privately supported first responders, victims, family members, and many private citizens. Robert Randolph, then chaplain at the Massachusetts Institute of Technology led prayers at the memorial service for slain MIT police officer Sean Collier.[10] The Red Cross also deployed chaplains they call "disaster spiritual care providers" in Boston. There were interfaith services and comfort dog ministries, crying and singing and talking and listening.[11] Chaplains at Spaulding Rehabilitation Center were available to victims through their months and years of recovery, and caregivers supported many across the state with the anxiety, transitions, and the public and private questioning that followed the bombing.[12] To the extent that he is treated like other federal prisoners, convicted perpetrator Dzhokhar Tsarnaev likely has access to a chaplain in the federal prison where he resides.

* * *

Father Hartigan, Rev. Dunbar, and chaplains with the National Guard, Red Cross, hospitals, and rehabilitation facilities in Boston are a few of the thousands of people that work as chaplains and spiritual care providers across the United States. Required in the military, federal prisons, and Veterans Administration medical centers, chaplains also work in two-thirds of hospitals, most hospices, many institutions of higher education, and a growing range of other settings.[13] While few are in situations as public as the 1955 Charlestown Prison riot, some—like Barry C. Black, the sixty-second chaplain to the U.S. Senate, and Rev. Margaret G. Kibben, the seventeenth chaplain to the House of Representatives—regularly engage with national leaders through public prayer and private conversation.[14] Chaplains have also been present at national protests ranging from Standing Rock to the Occupy Movement to racial justice protests that took place across the country in 2020.[15]

A national survey conducted in the United States in March of 2019 found that 21% of the American public had contact with a chaplain in the past two years, more than half in or through healthcare organizations.[16] These numbers increased during the COVID-19 pandemic as chaplains were described in the early months as "Run[ning] Toward the Dying" in the *New York Times*, responding to "Shifted Spiritual Care" in *U.S News and World Report*, and "bridging the gap between patients and grieving families who can't stay by their bedside during the coronavirus pandemic" on CNN.[17] Chaplains facilitated calls (and too often goodbyes) between patients hospitalized with COVID-19 and family members not permitted to visit. "COVID-19 brutalizes bodies, but it also disempowers families who are unable to see their loved ones," wrote Bridget Power a chaplain resident at Brigham and Women's Hospital in Boston in June 2020. "Most of the families that I have supported over the past three months have been people of color. Their first language is often Spanish or Creole. . . . Physicians rotate through the ICU, so families often wonder if their loved ones are receiving as good care this week as they did the last. I assure them they are."[18]

Rocky Walker, a staff chaplain at Mount Sinai Hospital in New York City echoed these sentiments in the national media. "I spend a lot of time trying to make sense of things that just don't make sense," he told a reporter, "the fact that you can't be next to your loved one, the fact that so many of our patients that are dying." He reported feeling closer to death in the midst of COVID-19 than he did thirty years ago when serving on the front lines of Operation Desert Storm in Iraq. "I feel like I'm much closer to death now than I was then. Back then I was a field artillery lieutenant," Walker explained, "With the COVID deaths today . . . these are all not just Americans, but these . . . are [also] innocent people."[19]

COVID-19 thrust chaplains—especially those in healthcare—into the national spotlight as they cared for patients, family members, and exhausted and traumatized medical staff fighting the pandemic in real time.[20] COVID-19 and the national media spotlight on chaplains was new in 2020, but the work of chaplains was not. I step back from the spotlight in this book to ask who chaplains are, what they do across the United States, how that work is connected to the settings where they do it, and how they have responded to and helped shape contemporary shifts in the American religious landscape.

Photo 1.1 Rev. Lindsay Popperson visits Sherrill House in Jamaica Plain, Massachusetts, during the pandemic. Photo credit: Eunny Kim.

I consider these questions aware that in some regions of the United States traditional religious organizations and affiliations are declining while the existential issues we face—from climate change to political polarization to mass causality events to the life and death challenges of being human—are not and, if anything, are on the rise.

I find that chaplains—who have shifted from being mostly Protestant men to people from a range of genders and religious backgrounds in the last fifty years—have a long, largely overlooked history at the edges of American religious life and institutions. Those who become chaplains today arrive along multiple paths. Those who stay see themselves making a difference, appreciate the flexibility the positions allow for religious leadership, and in some cases strategically utilize the title of chaplain as religious entrepreneurs. The work itself varies significantly by setting. All chaplains seek to engage with people holistically and remind them of bigger picture questions, what one chaplain described as reminding people of their peripheral vision. Regardless of setting, all chaplains work around death and help individuals and institutions negotiate religious differences, including with people who are not religiously affiliated.

Photo 1.2 Martin Mugerwa studied to become a chaplain at Boston University. Photo credit: Sian Richards Photography.

While most chaplains work outside of formal religious organizations, their work is often made possible by historic and current relationships between religious groups and the organizations where they work. The separation of church and state in the United States prohibits formal intermingling, and chaplains as religious professionals have long been employed by the military, federal prisons, the Veterans Administration, and by many states across the country. In the military and prisons, frameworks of institutional mandate dominate as chaplains invoke the first amendment and free exercise of religion to explain and motivate their work. In most other settings, frameworks of interpersonal care are most common as chaplains draw on principles of personal or moral responsibility that motivate them to hold space and provide care to all.[21] The educational and—in some settings—financial support of religious organization continues to quietly underlie the work chaplains do.[22] Chaplains are not distinct or divorced from local religious ecologies; they have been and remain an important part of them.

An Approach

To write about chaplains and begin to understand their largely undocumented histories and lineages, it was important to first define the term and role. One of the central challenges in writing this book was that there is no commonly agreed-upon definition of "chaplain" in American public life or culture. Chaplains are not licensed or institutionally regulated by the state, which means a range of people call themselves chaplains and seek work or volunteer opportunities as such.

The federal government uses a specific (Christian-informed) definition of chaplain to hire individuals with graduate theological education and the endorsement or support of their religious organizations into positions in the Veterans Administration, federal prisons, and the military.[23] Truckstop Ministries, founded in 1981 in Georgia, also uses the term to describe their evangelical Christian staff and volunteers who serve truck drivers across the country.[24] People called chaplains work in NASCAR pits, the National Science Foundation's base in Antarctica, the Olympics, and traveled with the Ringling Brothers Barnum and Bailey Circus until it closed in 2017.[25] In healthcare, most people called chaplains have a graduate degree, completed clinical education, and, like in the federal government, are endorsed by their religious organizations.[26]

The *Oxford English Dictionary* (*OED*) helps with the history of the term "chaplain" but does not begin to address the wide variation in how it is used today. The *OED* defines chaplain along very narrow, historical lines, calling a chaplain first "the priest, clergyman [*sic*] or minister of a chapel" and second:

> Clergyman [*sic*] who conducts religious services in the private chapel of a sovereign, lord or high official, of a castle, garrison, embassy, college, school, workhouse, prison, cemetery, or other institution, or in the household of a person of rank of quality in a legislative chamber, regime, ship, etc.

The term "chaplain" is connected historically to the original *cappellani* that described those "who had charge of the sacred cloak of St. Martin." The term was used in Latin or Old Norman French and dates to the Middle Ages.[27]

In the United States today chaplains are people who describe themselves as such. They range from volunteers with limited formal training in religion to highly trained professionals with multiple degrees. In some settings, like the military, there is more homogeneity in who uses the term, while in others, like social movement organizations, there is not. A colleague and I conducted short exploratory interviews with members of the general public to help us write survey questions about the term "chaplain." We quickly determined that most people think chaplains have something to do with religion, but beyond that, there is little agreement.[28]

Definitional and conceptual questions about the term "chaplain" have only become more complicated—or perhaps more interesting—in recent years, as some institutions began to name the Christian history of the term and move away from it. Instead, they moved toward "spiritual care provider" or "spiritual caregiver"—phrases they find more religiously inclusive. "We're not called chaplains here," one who works at a university in Boston told me. "The new lingo is spiritual advisor because [her supervisor] decided early on that in some traditions the word chaplain doesn't resonate. Spiritual advisor is more generic."[29]

I took the lack of a clear and consistent definition of chaplain as a challenging starting point when I began the research for this book. I approached the term inductively, knowing that who uses it and how its use has changed is an important part of the story. Because settings like healthcare organizations and prisons tend to have their own internal definitions of chaplain, I cast my analytic net wider, aiming to catch as broad a set of people using the term "chaplain" as possible to inform my understandings.[30] Also anticipating that the use of the term and concept varies based on the demographics and religious histories of different regions, I focused geographically on a single city: Boston.

The View from Boston

I consider Boston as a case study in this book, aiming to capture and historically contextualize who describes themselves as chaplains and how that has changed particularly since 1965. Though not a historian, I combed through the archives of major Boston institutions, including the city government, police and fire departments, hospitals, universities, rest and rehabilitation centers, the Catholic Church, and several Protestant denominations. I also worked with Katherine Wong, then an undergraduate at Wellesley College, to review the *Boston Globe* and read articles about chaplains published every five years between 1945 and 2015.[31]

To describe the current landscape, I identified every institution and group in the city of Boston during the fall of 2016 and spring of 2017 that might have a chaplain. I focused primarily on chaplains who work inside Boston's city limits, including hospice chaplains who serve patients within these limits but are staffed through offices outside of them. I worked through existing professional and personal networks, local rabbinical and theological schools, and public records—primarily the *Boston Globe*—to locate these chaplains and organizations. I met and interviewed over one hundred chaplains who work in greater Boston and include the sixty-six who work in the city in the analysis here. I also shadowed chaplains whenever possible, boarding container ships in the port, walking through homeless shelters, and attending religious services at local prisons as described in more detail in the methods appendix.

In interviews and the archives, it quickly became clear that chaplains are not new in Boston or across the country as evident in figure 1.1 which shows the presence of the words "chaplaincy" and "spiritual care" in books between 1965 and 2019. They have been largely overlooked by scholars and the general public. Historically, many were clergy of local congregations. A request was submitted to the Boston City Council in January 1902, for example,

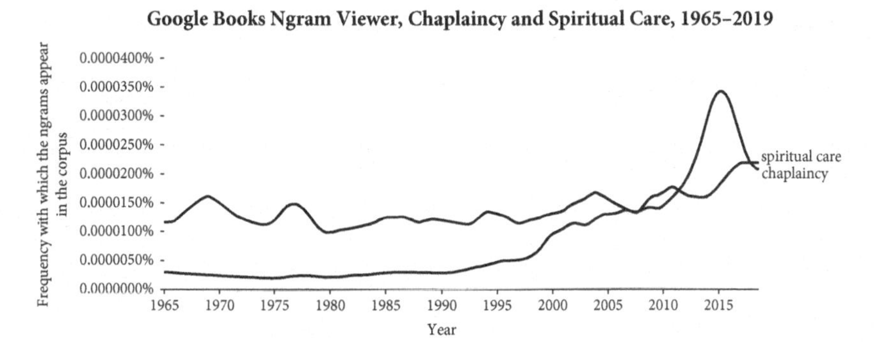

Figure 1.1 Shows the Google Books Ngram Viewer for the terms "chaplaincy" and "spiritual care" from 1965 to 2019. Figure credit: Google Books Ngram Viewer, 2021, http://books.google.com/ngrams.

that two chaplains—one Catholic and one Protestant—be appointed to the Boston Fire Department with the same rank and compensation as the captain. They were to attend all fires and provide spiritual care to ill or injured department members.[32] The first department chaplains were local clergy appointed in 1906 to these additional roles.[33] More chaplains were appointed to the Department of Public Welfare, the Massachusetts House and Senate, and Boston's Logan airport in the 1940s and 1950s.[34]

Data about how many chaplains currently work or volunteer in the United States would help me situate Boston as a case study compared to national patterns and allow me to think about how to generalize from it. This data has not been gathered. Federal records indicated that there were about 5,600 chaplains in the military, federal government and Veterans Administration in 2020.[35] Researchers estimate 10,000 chaplains work in healthcare organizations—many in hospices—and there are professional associations for chaplains in the following settings: healthcare, the military, airports, seaports, corrections, corporations, higher education, crisis and disaster, police, fire, NASCAR, and sports.[36] Data from the Bureau of Labor Statistics shows that the number of clergy working outside of congregations has been increasing since the 1970s, with the largest increase in clergy working in healthcare. Some of these clergy are chaplains.[37] About a quarter of theological schools have also started degree programs with chaplain or spiritual care in the title in the last few decades, but whether this says more about theological education or about a demand for chaplains is an open question.[38]

If Boston is any indication of national trends, people calling themselves chaplains work in traditional settings, as well as in more surprising places, and their numbers are on the rise. I found chaplains in Boston in local health centers, trauma organizations, community groups, police and fire departments, retirement facilities and nursing homes, airport and ports, social change organizations, and homeless shelters. Some have long histories, like in the Department of Youth Services where there have been chaplains since before 1960, while others work in newly founded nonprofit organizations. While the largest and most consistent groups of chaplains over time worked in healthcare, colleges and universities, and prisons, some people calling themselves chaplains in Boston are religious entrepreneurs who have continually adapted the term for use in new contexts.

I do my best to situate Boston in broader trends in chaplaincy, spiritual care, and American religious life. Because so little about the work of chaplains has been synthesized by scholars looking across the settings or over time, I encourage colleagues to generalize from these findings with care. Local factors shape much about how and where chaplains work. Boston with its historical Puritan/congregational establishment, Catholic influence, and more recent religious diversification is today among the least religious cities in the nation. More research is needed across the United States and around the globe to fully tell the story I begin here.[39]

Scholarly Considerations

Winnifred Sullivan, one of the few scholars who had chaplains in her sights before the COVID-19 pandemic, examined how chaplains shape and are shaped by the law. Calling them "secular priests" or "ministers without portfolio," Sullivan argues chaplains are ubiquitous and "largely invisible to most Americans." Following legal and demographic shifts, chaplains have become "strangely necessary figures, religiously and legally speaking in negotiating the public life of religion today."[40] Pushing against simple distinctions between church and state, Sullivan focuses primarily on government-supported chaplaincies to show how they normalize religion and make it more widely accessible in particular forms. Supreme Court decisions have shifted norms away from a high degree of church-state separation, creating a regulatory framework Sullivan calls spiritual governance. The chaplain is the very person required to make this situation work—the one to whom questions of meaning and purpose are outsourced who can meet people where they are.

Sullivan's analyses focus on the legal positions of chaplains based on readings of case law and historical documents. I offer a companion analysis of who is doing the work of chaplaincy, what that work is, and how it connects to local religious ecologies. My analysis draws not from the law, but from the practice, and from evidence I gathered from chaplains doing this work daily.

In the classic *Hospital Ministry: The Role of the Chaplain Today*, Lawrence Holst described how hospital chaplains work "between worlds." He sees the "tension" or "enigma" of this positioning shaping the work; "each world, or structure, has its own domain and demands, its assumptions and mission."[41] In their work between worlds, chaplains seem to have fallen between the scholarly cracks. The COVID-19 pandemic brought them back into the public eye, reminding scholars that chaplains have long been a part of local and religious ecologies and they need to broaden their empirical and analytic lenses to see them.

I begin aware of the shifting demographic realities of the American religious landscape and with the fact that the vast majority of chaplains historically have been Christian, specifically Protestant, male, and white. The number of adults who identify as Christian continues to decline, while those who describe themselves as atheist, agnostic, or "nothing in particular" continues to rise. The latter group grew from 16% of the American public in 2007 to 21% in 2014. Surveys conducted by PPRI reported that 24% of the American public was unaffiliated in 2019.[42] These changes are present among all age groups, particularly for those under the age of thirty, one-third of whom are not religiously affiliated. A majority of adults continue to believe in God, although those who are absolutely certain about their beliefs declined, from 71% in 2007 to 63% in 2014. During this same period, those who weekly experienced a sense of spiritual peace and well-being increased from 52% to 59%, and those who felt a sense of wonder about the universe grew from 39% to 46%. More than half of adults continue to pray daily, and about 40% meditate at least once a week according to recent surveys.[43]

Congregations, traditionally the bedrock of local religious life, have been changing over the past twenty years, and attendance at some local congregations is decreasing.[44] A report issued by the How We Gather project in 2015 described millennials gathering not in traditional congregations but in groups like athletic and activist organizations with similar goals—to build community, support personal growth, and cultivate a sense of purpose.[45] Increasing pressure on people with low incomes working multiple jobs to make ends meet leaves little time for traditional religious memberships. Skyrocketing incarceration rates make in-person religious memberships and participation impossible for those in prison.[46]

This deinstitutionalization of American religious life, or at least the shift in the kinds of institutions in which people connect around existential questions of meaning and purpose, is taking place in the midst of deep divisions in other aspects of American life and culture. Emotional debates about immigration, repeated mass shootings, environmental threats, tensions around the appropriate role of policing, and growing inequality in the United States contribute to an atmosphere of stress and tension that many people experience in daily life. Many in the United States—whether on the right, left, or somewhere in between—are emotionally raw from the tenor and ferocity of public debate, the pandemic and the grief and economic despair it brought, as well as from the daily challenges of work, caregiving, and the like.

While some in previous decades turned to religious leaders during such difficulties and gathered in congregations for mutual support, the deinstitutionalization of American religion raises the question of whether this is still the case today. Many people in my grandparents' generation called their local rabbi, priest, or minister when they needed support. To the extent that people in my generation and that of my children are in contact with any religious leader in the midst of difficulties, that person may be a chaplain. They might meet a chaplain in a hospital emergency room, a hospice as a loved one is dying, the military, or with the Red Cross in an emergency situation. Theological schools and clinical training programs are likely to continue to expand their training for chaplains (as described in figures 1.2 and 1.3). Whether business models will emerge apart from congregations to support the work of chaplains financially and recipients will find it beneficial are open questions. Stated boldly, the in-between roles chaplains have occupied on the fringes of religious ecologies and the settings where they work are likely

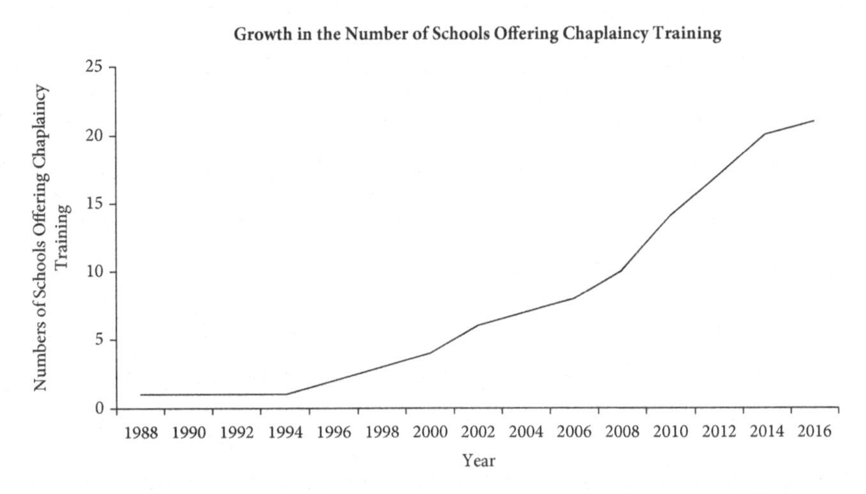

Figure 1.2 Growth in the number of schools offering chaplaincy training from 1988 to 2020 based on a sample of twenty-one schools. Figure credit: Wendy Cadge et al. "Training Chaplains and Spiritual Caregivers: The Emergence and Growth of Chaplaincy Programs in Theological Education." *Pastoral Psychology* 69 (2020): 187–208.
Note: The only change made to this figure was shifting from color to black and white. The article where it was originally published is licensed under a Creative Commons Attribution 4.0 International License, https://creativecommons.org/licenses/by/4.0/.

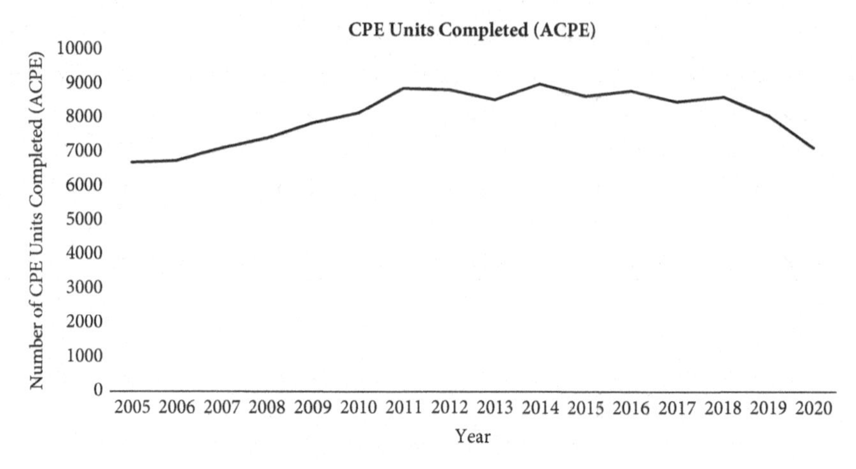

Figure 1.3 Shows growth in the number of units of CPE being completed annually by students from 2005 to 2020. Figure credit: Trace Haythorn/ ACPE: The Standard for Spiritual Care & Education.

to become more central in the coming years as religious demographics continue to change.

Chapter Outlines

I begin, in the next chapter, with a historical overview of chaplains in greater Boston. Historically, Boston has been known for its Puritan history and then heavily Catholic presence. Large waves of Irish Catholic immigrants fleeing the potato famine arrived in the mid-1800s, diversifying the largely Protestant makeup of the city. By the 1840s, the first Jewish congregation was formed in Brookline, establishing an early, yet much smaller, Jewish presence. Islam was first introduced by descendants of formerly enslaved people. Immigrants continued to diversify the city religiously after 1965.[47] Today, people who identify as Christian—specifically Catholic—and those without religious affiliations are the largest groups in Boston. The Pew Research Center's Religious Landscape Study reported that 67% of the population in Boston identified as religious in 2014. Just over half (57%) were Christian with the largest group (29%) Catholic. Another 10% of adults belonged to non-Christian faiths, including Judaism (4%), Islam (1%), Buddhism (1%), and Hinduism (1%). About one-third said they were unaffiliated, or a religious "none," with 20% saying they belonged to no religion in particular, 9% identifying as agnostic, and 4% atheist.[48] PRRI reported similar numbers in 2019.[49]

Those calling themselves chaplains in the city have historically been white Catholics, Episcopalians, and congregational clergy in what is today known as the United Church of Christ. More have been ordained than laypeople over time with slow racial, religious, and gender diversification since 1980. In addition to slow diversification, this overview illustrates the broad range of people—from full-time religious professionals to those with little training—who have used the term "chaplain" to describe their work. It also shows continuing ties between local congregational clergy—some of whom have simultaneously been chaplains with police and fire departments—and those for whom chaplaincy is a full-time job. Financial support from the state, religious organizations, and healthcare organizations has made the work of some chaplains possible in greater Boston and probably beyond.

In chapter 3, I turn to how those working as chaplains in Boston came to the work. Almost all those I interviewed—close to 90%—have some theological education though the ways they came to the work and their specific details of their training varies. Most came through personal connections, commitments to social justice, or the simple need for a job. Some—because of their gender, family situations, or sense of vocation—did not fit into the jobs people with their credentials typically obtain, and chaplaincy positions were a good alternative. While the largest group work in healthcare, many also work in colleges and universities and community settings, with one-quarter working across multiple sectors. Just under half are full-time employees, and close to 90% are paid for their work. The stories chaplains tell in that chapter confirm the breadth of people in the field and show the challenge of efforts to professionalize it in simplistic, universal ways. They also show how chaplains are connected with local religious organizations, less through institutional connections and more through personal relationships they have with the clergy who lead them.

The next four chapters describe the work of chaplains. In chapter 4, I conceive of that work along a continuum from tasks requiring less to more integration in the institutions in which they take place. I find chaplains in healthcare organizations do the broadest range of tasks and are most integrated or embedded in their settings. They are followed by military chaplains, those working in higher education, and those in municipal settings. Prison chaplains—arguably the most physically embedded—tend to be more restricted to rituals, ceremonies, and limited counseling and bearing witness. I show in their work across settings the ways chaplains negotiate their in-between roles relationally. I listen in chapter 5 to what chaplains see themselves most contributing to the organizations and individuals with whom they work. While I expected to hear them helping people wrestle with existential questions of theodicy—why bad things happen and what role, if any, God or the sacred has—such talk was relatively rare. More often they spoke about the spaces they help people create and hold in the midst of difficult moments rather than any content they contribute to those spaces. They code switch, or move between traditional religious languages and more broadly accessible emotional languages, when describing their contributions.

Chapters 6 and 7 focus on two areas central to the work of almost all the chaplains I interviewed. All chaplains, regardless of their settings and backgrounds, work around death, the focus of chapter 6. I describe how chaplains engage when a death is sudden or more expected, and then I pay particular attention to how they broker death through relationships, mostly improvised ritual, and reflective listening. I show how the institutions where chaplains work shape their engagements around death and how they broker end-of-life issues serving as midwives to death and first steps in chains of memory that help loved ones and institutions remember those who are lost. As they help people die, most chaplains care for those who are religiously alike and different from themselves in diverse settings comprised of staff and family members who are pluralistic in spirituality and religion as well as race, ethnicity, age, and other factors.

Most chaplains work across religious differences in life as well as death and the institutions where they work negotiate those differences in varied ways. In chapter 7 I consider three case studies—the New England Seafarer's Mission (NESM), the Boston Fire Department (BFD), and Massachusetts General Hospital (MGH)—to show how chaplains and the organizations they serve responded to religious diversity over time. While some organizations—most notably prisons and the military—offer clear guidance about religious diversity, chaplains in most other settings improvise by neutralizing religious differences and/or code switching (as mentioned, moving between different religious and spiritual languages and registers depending on who they are engaging with and to what end). I show how they learn to do this in their training and daily work, and how they negotiate personal boundaries around authenticity in the process. Although the majority of chaplains I interviewed make space for everyone—even if their personal beliefs and practices challenge their own—a few do not, pointing again to variation among chaplains as a group and the space these roles allow for individual improvisation.

I reflect on the implications of these findings in the conclusion before offering methodological reflections, including on my positionality in this research in the appendix. A work of social science, I leave questions of theology—including of the chaplains' personal theologies—for exploration by others. In the conclusion to the book, I consider factors that might lead chaplaincy and spiritual care to expand or to contract in the coming years and how that relates to broader changes in the American religious landscape. I then offer specific, practical recommendations for theological educators and religious leaders, chaplains, and scholars. I call on theological educators and religious leaders to ask bolder questions about the shape of religious leadership—not just for the future of chaplaincy but also for the future of their religious organizations. I encourage them to ask bigger structural questions about what chaplains and spiritual care providers need to know, how they are uniquely prepared to train in those ways, and how they are related to "third-spaces" efforts like the Daring Compassion Movement Chaplaincy Project at the Faith Matters Network whose efforts include training people unable—financially or educationally—to attend theological schools. I also encourage chaplains to claim their spaces at the table and name their value while continuing to learn from chaplains in different settings and from growing bodies of research about their work and its impacts. I encourage scholars of religion to look for the chaplains around the edges. The flexibility of the title, the improvisational nature of the work, and the ways both have changed yet been continuous since the earliest years of the republic, again reminds scholars of the cultural space for religion (and things marked as such) in the United States.

Broader Implications

Historically on institutional edges, the chaplains I met and describe in this book are a motley crew. Their predecessors were as well—a mix of congregational clergy, part-timers, and people, particularly in the military and healthcare organizations, for whom chaplaincy was their life's work. Some sought out the work and others ended up there because they did not fit well in congregations or had histories that made them difficult to place in congregations. In recent years, some religious entrepreneurs, with and without formal religious training, have also taken up the term "chaplain." Members of religious minority groups and those in majority groups formally excluded from religious leadership have also adapted the role and formal institutional space it facilitates for professional (paid) religious work.[50] The term "chaplain," then, remains flexible with a largely Protestant history that is inconsistently used and easily adapted in the American religious marketplace characterized by free exercise and limited regulation.

Chaplains have been, and remain, however an important part of institutional religious ecologies locally and nationally. I encourage scholars, religious leaders, and educators to step back and look broadly enough that they can see chaplains and integrate their histories and work into their analyses and thinking about American religion. While it is easy to conceive of chaplains as distinct or divorced from local congregations, most are trained alongside congregational clergy and are doing some of the same work in different organizational containers.

Carefully considering the work of chaplains and keeping it on the radar of scholars and religious leaders may be a source of continuing insights into the future of religious life in the United States. While local clergy mostly serve those who join their congregations, it is chaplains who regularly interact with people where and as they are in a broad range of settings. The work of chaplains has the potential to extend and suggest ways of enlivening the more traditional work of religious leaders with people with whom those leaders are unlikely to have contact. It can show how out of date and old-fashioned some traditional delivery systems of religious content are and point provocatively to new approaches. And especially for those from more liberal religious backgrounds, it demonstrates, in its doing, the core values of the historical religious traditions from which it was birthed.

Whether the work of chaplains will continue as fewer people are religiously affiliated and less often belong to local congregations is an open question. The chaplains people meet in hospitals, hospices, higher education, the military, and other settings may pick up and occupy the space that remains when members of the public are not connected to local religious leaders. Or that space may decline or change in such a way that religious leaders are less relevant.

"We're not, you know, living through a great awakening," a military chaplain in Massachusetts told me, while sharing his doubts about the future of his work. "I think it [the work of chaplains] is just going to become increasingly strange to people . . . our flexibility is helpful . . . . We're there for people regardless of their faith outlook, but it is just an odd situation. We're tied to religion, and religious expression is not important to millennials." He went on to talk about high-status military leaders he interacted with "who frequently articulate that they appreciate the chaplain apart from their religious role—just the fact that they would even say that, right?" The role of chaplain increasingly does not translate, he concluded, which "goes back to some of the work that I'm doing—articulating the role of the chaplaincy . . . telling the story about them as religious leaders . . . thinking about how I can be a chaplain to these seniors. These are the things I'm trying to sort out."

The pandemic showed us that religious institutions can pivot. In addition to the religious leaders from whom some found support, people reached out to family, friends, new neighborhood support associations, co-workers, and other community connections through the long difficult months. Clergy were moral and practical leaders for some people, but not others; chaplains like Bridget Power and Rocky Walker played key roles at bedsides and with exhausted healthcare staff. Not having a common language or scholarly frame for the work chaplains do is not an excuse for not seeing it and integrating it into our understandings of American religious life, past and present. If I do my job well, this book will help.

2

Chaplaincy in Greater Boston

A Short Historical Overview

Boston's Catholic Archdiocese today includes parishes from the Worcester line to the eastern border of Cape Cod to the Massachusetts–New Hampshire border. There are about seventy hospitals within its jurisdiction as well as twenty-two prisons and more than fifty colleges and universities. While about one-third of hospitals in the diocese hire their own Catholic chaplains (who, if they are priests, must have permission from the archdiocese to practice), the diocese staffs full- and part-time chaplains in many of the rest, including through the use of local parish priests. The diocese also places Catholic chaplains in most of the prisons, some as staff and some as volunteers. Local parishes pay a kind of tax, a deacon responsible for chaplains in the diocese told me, to financially support this work. Given fewer priests available, growing numbers of Catholic chaplains are deacons, laypeople and women religious.

Chaplaincies in Boston have a long history. They are profoundly different today than they were a century ago and face dramatically different challenges. While the history of Boston's religious institutions has been written many times over, rarely are chaplains, in Boston or other cities across the country, included in how scholars conceive of local religious ecologies.[1] Sometimes viewed as second class or marginal because their work takes place outside of traditional parishes and congregations, the number and range of places chaplains work seems to be on the rise nationally. In Boston, chaplains are no longer only in prisons, higher education, and healthcare. They are also present in a growing number of social service organizations, community groups, sports teams, and other venues. Nationally, growing numbers of clergy have been working outside of religious organizations since the 1970s, a trend that makes it even more important to consider those serving people where they are, as they are, in a broad range of settings.

This chapter offers a short overview of chaplains in greater Boston in the context of broader changes related to the religious ecology of the city.[2] How

Spiritual Care. Wendy Cadge, Oxford University Press. © Oxford University Press 2023.
DOI: 10.1093/oso/9780197647813.003.0002

chaplains have changed and adapted to these challenges is the focus of this chapter. From 1906—when the Boston Fire Department welcomed its first chaplain—to the present, the demographics of chaplains, the range of settings where they work, and what that work consists of, all reflect changing demographics and cultural dynamics. I focus primarily on the years after World War II.[3] The colonial Protestant history of Boston and Protestant establishment through the early twentieth century are the backdrop against which the Catholic population grew exponentially in the early postwar years. Cardinal Richard Cushing, a giant figure in Boston Catholicism and much loved by liberal Catholics, fostered greater understanding among Catholics from different ethnic backgrounds and between Catholics and non-Catholics in the city.[4] Protestant congregations were strong in the early postwar years and declined later, even as some welcomed new immigrants and others tried to hold on to their establishment histories.[5] The Jewish population grew and suburbanized in postwar Boston and the range of settings in which Jewish chaplains worked slowly expanded.[6] As the number of Muslims, Buddhists, Hindus, and people with no religious background increased in greater Boston, they were only slowly reflected among those calling themselves chaplains in the city. The large (and growing) number of people in Boston who have not been religiously affiliated in recent years has surely shaped the experiences and work of chaplains in ways different from more religiously affiliated regions of the country where chaplains likely interact with more traditionally religiously people.[7]

I piece together this overview from the records of major religious and civic institutions in Boston, articles in the *Boston Globe*, interviews with key leaders, and secondary sources.[8] Those calling themselves chaplains in Boston have historically been white Catholics, Episcopalians and/or congregational clergy. More have been ordained than lay. They were predominantly men until the early 1980s when slow racial, religious, and gender diversification began to take place. While people of color and those from non-Christian backgrounds have long done the work of chaplaincy, the history of the term and racialized ways it has been used emerge throughout this chapter. This overview also illustrates the broad range of people who have and continue to use the term "chaplain," ranging from full-time religious professionals to those with little training. It also shows ties between local congregational clergy—some of whom are simultaneously chaplains with police and fire departments—and those for whom chaplaincy is a full-time job. Perhaps most importantly, this chapter demonstrates how financial support for chaplaincy positions from the state, religious organizations, and healthcare organizations made the work of chaplains possible in greater Boston.

A Short National Overview

Boston, like towns and cities across the country, is shaped by the national history of chaplaincy and spiritual care. While religiously motivated people have long cared for those in need, the notion of chaplaincy being a distinct kind of work, and defined and labeled as such, is a relatively modern concept. In *A Ministry of Presence: Chaplaincy, Spiritual Care and the Law*, Winnifred Sullivan traces the history of chaplaincy in Christian contexts, to military chaplains working for Frankish kingdoms and then to a range of secular organizations.[9] Chaplains have occasionally been present in literature; a prison chaplain appears at the end of Franz Kafka's *The Trial* and in Herman Melville's *Billy Budd*.[10]

Scholars have rarely included the work of chaplaincy and spiritual care when thinking about local and national religious ecologies in the United States.[11] Perhaps it is the organizational in-between-ness of chaplains, the ephemeral notion of presence, or the improvisation chaplains often do within and across settings that led them to be largely off the radar of scholars. Historians and social scientists that have written about chaplaincy focus in single settings—usually the military, prisons, healthcare organizations, or higher education—rarely if ever stepping back to compare and contrast multiple settings where chaplains work or ask how that work is a part of American religious life and institutions.[12] The limited synthesis that has been conducted focuses on the betwixt and between roles chaplains occupy and on the notion of presence that many emphasize as central to what they bring. Few scholars ask what I call "demand-side questions," that is, wanting to know how the demand for chaplains—or the skills that chaplains bring—has changed over time, how those who interact with chaplains experience them, and what—if any—effects the time chaplains spend with people has on the recipients of care.[13] More attention focuses on "supply-side questions" about how chaplains are or should be trained, though answering those questions is difficult without more demand-side evidence from recipients of care.

In the United States, chaplains likely have the longest history in the military dating to before the Revolutionary War.[14] The Ancient and Honorable Artillery Company of Massachusetts (the oldest chartered military organization in North America) had chaplains in place in the seventeenth century.[15] Military chaplains support military efforts, help maintain troop morale, and provide spiritual and religious rituals and services. They move among military and religious frames, languages, symbols, and ceremonies in their daily work that requires engagement across people from different religious backgrounds, including none as well as across ranks and other markers of difference. Military chaplains are uniformed, noncombatant, commissioned officers who have rank but not command and are usually unarmed.[16] They are supported by chaplain assistants.

Nationally, chaplains were fully integrated in the military in the twentieth century, sometimes called "force multipliers," or figures that expand the capacity of their units to be successful. Military chaplains have long been responsible for serving everyone, regardless of religious affiliation, and not proselytizing. While the military has slowly welcomed more non-Christian chaplains, tensions surround the appropriate role of military chaplains, whether chaplains evangelize despite rules to the contrary, and whether humanists can be chaplains to support the nonreligious have been and remain heated.[17]

While chaplains in different branches of the American military traditionally support one another, there are historical and demographic differences. The Army has the largest chaplain corps and has been the quickest to adapt to racial and religious diversification. Army chaplains are deployed to battlefields alongside their units. Chaplaincy in the Air Force looks more like congregational ministry because they do not go on aircraft and mostly work out of chapels on base. In the Navy, the chaplaincy corps has a formal and traditional culture. Navy chaplains tend to be the most liberal and cosmopolitan.[18] In addition to serving members of the military, chaplains have been asked—especially in the last twenty years—to serve as cultural and religious brokers with local populations when deployed.[19] Current estimates suggest there were about 2,900 active-duty chaplains in the U.S. armed forces in 2020 in addition to those in the reserves.[20]

In prisons, colleges and universities, and healthcare organizations, the work of chaplains often emerged from the religious founding of these institutions and then morphed over time. The role of religious figures and institutions in historically shaping corrections is well known, and the Federal Bureau of Prisons today employs about 250 chaplains.[21] In prisons, chaplains typically combine ministry to prisoners with support for the behavior modification outcomes sought by prisons, making in-between-ness a structural part of their positions.[22] State and local correctional facilities manage chaplains and/or religious volunteers in ways as varied as the settings themselves. A Pew Forum survey of state prison chaplains conducted in 2011 estimated that there were close to 1,500 state prison chaplains. The majority (90%) have one-on-one contact with inmates, and two-thirds say that leading worship, educational sessions, and counseling is central to their work.[23] Many also serve staff.[24] The work of prison chaplains is strongly shaped by law and legal precedent as Sullivan explores in her work.[25]

In higher education and healthcare, the work of chaplains can often be traced to the religious founding of organizations. Chaplains and campus ministers (the distinctions are blurry at best) have worked in some colleges and universities since at least the late nineteenth century.[26] Over time, some were paid by the colleges and universities, and many others were supported through Protestant groups, Catholic Newman Centers, Jewish Hillels, and parachurch organizations including InterVarsity Christian Fellowship. Today, the presence of Muslim—and to a lesser extent, Hindu—chaplains in higher education has become increasingly common.[27] Interfaith efforts and exchanges are common on many campuses leading sociologist John Schmalzbauer to call today's chaplain something of an "interfaith traffic director."[28]

Local religious leaders were present in the early years of American hospitals, especially those that were founded by religious organizations.[29] Healthcare chaplaincy, as a distinct field and profession, began in the 1920s in Boston out of efforts to reform Protestant theological education. As educators tried to get seminarians out of classrooms, they experimented with bringing them into contact with patients. Richard Cabot, a prominent Harvard physician also known as the father of medical social work, played a key role in this process as did Anton Boisen who was appointed the chaplain of Worcester State Hospital in Massachusetts in 1924.[30] With Austin Guiles and Russell Dicks at Massachusetts General Hospital, Cabot and Boisen played key roles in what developed into the clinical pastoral education (CPE) movement. Out of these efforts, more hospitals hired CPE-trained chaplains in the 1940s and 1950s at first alongside and eventually, in some settings, instead of the local religious leaders that served them.[31] Hospital chaplaincy worked to professionalize throughout the twentieth century.[32] Today, healthcare chaplains are a part of protocols in some healthcare institutions and more peripheral in others. They are most often present at the end of life, itself a liminal or in-between time.[33] Chaplains are usually endorsed or formally supported by their own religious traditions while being paid by the institutions where they work.

Those who became chaplains were mostly trained in theological and rabbinical schools alongside colleagues who became local clergy.[34] Christians typically completed a master of divinity degree (an MDiv), which has become the "gold standard" for religious professionals and is required in some religious traditions for entrance to ordained ministry.[35] Some Jewish chaplains were rabbis and others completed degrees in Jewish education and other fields.[36] Most had a class or two in counseling or pastoral theology but little education specifically geared toward their future work as chaplains. This began to change in the 1990s when theological schools began to develop degree programs in chaplaincy and spiritual care. More than a quarter of theological schools—including rabbinical schools—currently have such programs though they were developed independently of one another and do not share learning goals or outcomes.[37] In some settings, including federal positions, chaplains are also endorsed or certified for specialized ministry.[38] Until recently, theological schools gave little formal thought to how to prepare chaplains, focusing instead on how to prepare people for congregational ministry. Declining enrollments and fewer congregational positions in some areas have undoubtedly motivated some of this reorientation.[39]

Some of the curricular development in theological schools was motivated by growing numbers of people interested in becoming chaplains. That said, not all of them enroll in degree-granting programs, often for reasons of cost, access, and time. Numerous groups train chaplains online, some in courses as short as a week.[40] The Faith Matters Network in Nashville recently began training social movement chaplains and advocates training opportunities outside of degree-granting institutions, particularly for people that have not historically had access to them.[41] In the open religious context of the United States, all of these people can—and do—call themselves chaplains with badges, vests, certificates, and other credentials signifying as much. In greater Boston, people calling themselves chaplains have—and continue—to include full-time chaplains with formal degrees and education, local clergy who do chaplaincy work on the side, and those trained in short non-degree-granting programs.

Chaplains in Boston's Religious Ecology

Before 1945: Routine Work in Hospitals, Prisons, and Universities

Before 1945, the majority of chaplains in greater Boston were white men who worked in hospitals, prisons, and religious schools. Most were Catholic or Protestant.[42] A few Episcopal leaders did this work full-time in area hospitals that they described in reports to the diocese. "I have carried on the work of visiting the hospitals in the city every week, visiting patients in the private as well as the public wards and at the same time distributing Testaments, magazines, tobacco, fruit and toys and picture books in the children's department," George Ponsonby Bentley wrote in 1920.[43] Another described the work of chaplains as the "Cheer-up Men" in hospitals in 1925.[44] They offered sacraments as well as friendly visits, Christmas cards, and other connections to hospitalized patients to boost spirits by simply caring for one person at a time. "Personally, I am strongly convinced that there are distinct advantages really gained by concentrating on this 'one by one' direction," G. DeWitt Dowling wrote in 1930. "And right here in this direction there are many quiet opportunities which could come in no other way that are constantly being presented for rendering the most deeply helpful service."[45] Major Boston hospitals that had or welcomed clergy as chaplains before 1945 included Boston City Hospital, Boston Children's Hospital, Long Island Hospital, Massachusetts General Hospital, New England Baptist Hospital, Peter Bent Brigham Hospital, most of the government hospitals, several tuberculosis facilities, and many psychiatric facilities.

Clergy were also present as chaplains in many prisons, jails, religious schools, and some colleges and universities during these years. In jails and prisons—including Charles Street Jail, House of Correction in Cambridge, House of Corrections for Men, Massachusetts State Prison, Prison for Women at Deer Island, Reformatory at Concord, Suffolk School for Boys at Rainsford Island—they offered sacraments, visited with inmates, and offered counsel and encouragement. Catholic Directories list priests as chaplains at most of the Catholic schools in the region.[46] Many colleges and universities also had chaplains connected to their religious origins. Representatives from the Boston City Mission—called chaplains in some years—served fishermen and seafarers in the port of Boston.[47] Six different Catholic chaplains served the Boston Fire Department between 1906 and 1945.[48]

While some hospital and prison chaplains worked full-time before 1945, most were local clergy who served area institutions alongside their congregations and parishes. In their chaplaincy work, many worked beside religious leaders from other backgrounds. Henry E. Edenborg was the Episcopal Church's representative at Boston City Hospital and the Homeopathic Hospital area in the 1930s where he worked part-time. He described a call in an annual report; "Early one morning, recently," he wrote in 1935, "I received a telephone call from the City Hospital. The woman speaking reported that her brother was dangerously ill, and there was no hope for his recovery, and she did not want him to die unbaptized. Immediately I went to the hospital and baptized him. In a few hours he was dead, but she was comforted and by God's grace he was blessed before he went."[49] Edenborg served alongside Catholic chaplains writing, "Needless to say this ministry is not restricted to our own church people alone, and some of the most helpful contacts I have been able to make have been with people of other religious affiliations. It is a pleasure to report, also, that the most kindly feelings exist between the Roman Catholic chaplain and our own representatives."[50]

The majority of chaplains did not have training different from that of local clergy, though that slowly changed in some settings. Records show growing numbers of Protestant theological students completing short stints alongside chaplains to learn about the work into the 1940s. Episcopal priest George E. Keith was appointed the official chaplain of the Deer Island House of Corrections in November 1940. Records noted, "it represents the first appointment in this state that has come as a result of specialized training for this work. It is not essential that every person who does chaplaincy work be a specialist in this field, but it is important for the work that there be a few clergy in the Diocese whose major concern is the development of this ministry and who from special training have acquired a real knowledge of the whole field of penology."[51] The military has long had their own training for chaplains, and reports from the *Boston Globe* noted in 1945 that more than one hundred chaplains graduated from Fort Devens Army Chaplain School.[52]

Many of the people chaplains served—especially in prisons and public hospitals—were those without resources who were on the margins of society. "Visiting the sick in a great institution like the Boston City Hospital," a hospital chaplain wrote in 1940, "indicates that the church feels special responsibility for the spiritual ministry to the large numbers of the city's poor who must perforce seek treatment in such institutions rather than in private hospitals."[53] Another serving in the city's almshouse wrote, "I am the friend for those who have no friend."[54] The religious motivations for this work are clear in the New Testament texts some cite in their reports and the ways they described themselves as representatives of the church, doing the work of the church in service to the community beyond those settings.[55]

1945 to 1960: Ecumenical Work Post–World War II

World War II raised the profile of chaplains nationally as many members of the military returned to the states familiar with chaplains from their military service.[56] More than one hundred articles in the *Boston Globe* made substantive mention of chaplains in 1945 and again in 1955, many in relation to the military and veterans affairs. Army chaplain and Catholic priest John Dugan describes his experiences as a Japanese prisoner of war in the Philippines in sections in the *Boston Globe* in 1945.[57] Military, veterans, and civic organizations such as the Veterans of Foreign Wars, the American Legion, fraternal lodges, the Massachusetts State Grange, and the Knights of Columbus had chaplains in the immediate postwar years who opened meetings and provided other ceremonial functions.[58] Nationally, healthcare chaplains slowly began to professionalize in Boston during these years. A few chaplains working in industrial settings—including with the independent Longshoremen's Union and the Caritas Licensed Beverage Guild—were mentioned in these years.[59]

By the postwar era, suburbanization was well underway and the Protestant-Catholic-Jew framing of American religious life had reached its apex. In Boston, postwar religious life was transformed by the appointment of Richard Cushing as the Catholic archbishop following the death of William Henry Cardinal O'Connell in 1944. Born in a working-class Irish Catholic neighborhood in Boston, Cushing attended Boston College and was ordained in 1921. An excellent fundraiser with commitments to workers, he launched an ambitious building program across the city that included chapels for workers at Logan airport, South Station railroad terminal (see photos 2.1 and 2.2), the Fish Pier in the seaport, and other venues. Postwar religious mixing, the declining significance of denominationalism, and Cushing's charismatic approach to leadership also led him to forge ties with religious leaders across traditions pushing against sectarian differences. Cushing preached to Protestant groups, built strong relationships with Jewish groups, and pushed strongly against anti-Semitism in many forms.[60] His work was

Photo 2.1 Our Lady of the Railways Chapel at Boston's South Station under construction. It opened in 1955. Reprinted with permission of the archives of the Boston Archdiocese. Photo number P647.

acknowledged on a much larger scale when he was created a cardinal by Pope John XXIII in late 1958.

In part due to Cushing's ecumenical orientation, charismatic leadership, and political savvy, the range of places chaplains were present and the religious traditions they represented seems to have expanded in the late 1940s and 1950s. While chaplains continued their work in hospitals, colleges and universities, and prisons, they were also present in Catholic schools, social service organizations, and the state government. In 1946, the state ruled that "at every public institution under the control or jurisdiction, or both, of the department of public welfare and of the department of mental health there shall be a Catholic chaplain, a Protestant chaplain and a Jewish chaplain."[61] In 1952 this expanded to stipulate that at each institution under the jurisdiction of the Department of Corrections or Youth Services there must be a chaplain "who shall provide for the spiritual needs and religious teachings of the inmates."[62] The Boston Fire Department welcomed its first Protestant

Photo 2.2 A service inside Our Lady of the Railways Chapel at Boston's South Station. The chapel was built in a space previously used as a movie theater. Reprinted with permission from the Boston Archdiocese archives. Photo number P646.

chaplain, Howard E Pomeroy, in 1945, and the Jewish Chaplaincy Council began to organize in the mid-1950s to serve Jews in hospitals and nursing facilities.[63] The Institute for Pastoral Care, a key training organization for healthcare chaplains nationally, was established at Massachusetts General Hospital in 1945.[64] In a more unusual locale, the *Boston Globe* even reported on a local minister in Cambridge who also served as chaplain with the Circus Fans' Association of America.[65]

Chaplains from Catholic, Protestant, and Jewish backgrounds worked together during these years. Catholic chaplain Lt. Vincent B. Lavery and Protestant Lt. Paul C. Morton, for example, offered the invocation and benediction at a memorial service at Fort Devens for the late President Roosevelt on April 15, 1945.[66] In 1955, Catholic, Protestant, and Jewish chaplains commemorated the oft-told story of the 1943 sinking of the SS *Dorchester* when four Army chaplains (two ministers, a priest, and a rabbi) gave their life jackets to others and went down with the ship reportedly arm in arm.[67] Catholic, Protestant, and increasingly Jewish chaplains continued to work alongside one another in area hospitals. In 1955, Jewish chaplains distributed food packages donated by the Jewish Welfare Board for Passover. The *Globe* reported Christian chaplains assisting in facilities where Jewish chaplains were not available.[68] Chaplains representing similarly diverse religious backgrounds participated in college and university baccalaureate and graduation ceremonies during these years across the city.[69] Father Christopher Griffin, chaplain of the newly opened Catholic chapel in South Station and chaplain to the Massachusetts Senate and House, offered a prayer later published in the *Globe* calling on Jews, Protestants, and Catholics to love one another.[70] The majority of chaplains in Boston remained white through the 1950s even as more people of color and non-English speakers began to move to into the area.[71]

Many of the workers' chapels Archbishop Cushing built were dedicated in greater Boston in the 1950s alongside others with more multifaith orientations. Protestant, Catholic and Jewish chapels were dedicated at Brandeis University in 1955.[72] The George Howard Monks Memorial Chapel was opened for Protestants and people from Orthodox backgrounds at Boston City Hospital in the 1950s, and the Beth Isaac Memorial Chapel was dedicated for Jewish patients, families, and staff.[73] MIT opened its famous 1,200 seat auditorium and cylindrical windowless chapel in 1955 designed by renowned architect Eero Saarinen (see photo 2.3).[74] Ground was also broken for a nonsectarian chapel at New England Deaconess Hospital in 1955 (see photo 2.4).[75] The built environment reflected growing relationships among people from different religious backgrounds in the city facilitated by community leaders, local clergy, and chaplains during these years.

The 1960s and 1970s: Chaplains Protesting and Then Declining

The ecumenical work of earlier years continued in hospitals and prisons into the 1960s and 1970s in Boston as chaplains—particularly in higher education—took more public roles in the 1960s and quieter ones into the 1970s. The Catholic Directory of 1960 continued to list almost one hundred priests serving forty different institutions in the city ranging from hospitals and psychiatric facilities to schools, cemeteries, prisons, and reformatories

Photo 2.3 MIT opened its famous 1,200 seat auditorium and cylindrical windowless chapel designed by renowned architect Eero Saarinen in 1955. Photo credit: Randall Armor.

as well as military installations outside of the diocese. Father Edward Hartigan continued to serve prisoners, see photo 2.5. Almost all these priests were the chaplains of these facilities along with their assignments in local parishes. The Episcopal Convention Journal from 1960 similarly noted some full-time chaplains serving hospitals and prisons as well as "the willing cooperation of parish clergy who not only follow their people to the hospital, but also answer the calls to minister to our brethren who come from afar and are patients at our smaller hospitals that have no regularly assigned chaplains."[76]

Photo 2.4 Nurses in Arthur T. Dooley Chapel at New England Deaconess Hospital. Groundbreaking ceremonies for the chapel were held on September 12, 1955. The chapel was dedicated on June 28, 1956. Reprinted courtesy of the Ruth and David Freiman Archives at Beth Israel Deaconess Medical Center.

The Episcopal Diocese directed more of their resources to chaplains in colleges and universities in the 1960s purchasing large houses close to Boston University and MIT that allowed for private counseling and larger gatherings without disrupting (traditional) family life.[77] A range of chaplains in higher education were centrally involved in civil rights advocacy, including Howard

Photo 2.5 Father Edward Hartigan visits with a prisoner in 1964. Reprinted with permission of Northeastern University Archives and Special Collections.

Thurman who had been the dean of Marsh Chapel at Boston University since 1953 and played a central role as a kind of chaplain to the civil rights movement.[78] In addition to preaching about these issues, chaplains such as Rev. John Russell at MIT were local organizers for the Southern Christian Leadership Conference and reported that close to 1,000 people were interested in traveling to Alabama to join the march from Selma to Montgomery led by Martin Luther King Jr. in 1965.[79] Reports from the march named Boston religious leaders, including chaplains, and called them "top figures on college campuses" and "campus heroes" for the examples they set for students.[80]

Clergy, including chaplains, continued to advocate in Boston in 1965. In June, a group interrupted a Boston School Committee Meeting to press the issue of racial imbalance in school integration championed by a larger group of Boston clergy through the Greater Boston Committee on Racial Imbalance.[81] In October, sixteen chaplains including Protestants, Catholics, and Jews affiliated with the United Ministry at Harvard and Radcliffe wrote to U.S. President Johnson, U.S. and Massachusetts attorneys general, U.S. congressional representatives from Massachusetts, the governor, and others arguing "against labeling anti-Viet Nam policy protestors as 'communists'" and making statements about draft procedures.[82]

Pastorally, chaplains continued caring for people across the city and working across religious lines to do so. The Boston Fire Department now included Protestant, Catholic, and Jewish chaplains supporting firefighters and their families (while still serving local congregations) who were mourning five firefighters killed in the line of duty in October 1965.[83] Rev. Patrick J. Tague was named chaplain of the Massachusetts State Police by Public Safety Commissioner.[84] Richard Caples, and the Department of Youth Services had a full roster of chaplains from Protestant, Catholic, and Jewish backgrounds, some working full-time and some much more part-time.[85] Hospital chaplains, including those supported by the Jewish Chaplaincy Council of Massachusetts, continued to support patients across the city in a range of capacities. And prison chaplains continued to work in prisons in the state, even as the Report of the Governor's Committee on Jails and Houses of Correction in 1965 argued that they were not paid enough.[86]

Several Protestant denominations also worked together in the 1960s to support a Protestant chaplain in the Columbia Point Housing Project, home to nearly 7,000 people (including 800 children).[87] The extent to which this was a missionary versus a social service effort was blurry, as was also the case in the port. Protestant organizations had offered ministry and social services to seafarers in the port of Boston since the late nineteenth century. In the 1960s, these port chaplains continued to board vessels, offering scriptural tracts, magazines, and friendly visits as well as lodging, meals, and sometimes religious services in their inns for seafarers needing a place to stay on land. Forest Cleveland Higgin of Boston Seamen's Friend Society and Reverend Wallace Cederleaf of the New England Seafarers Mission gathered small Christmas gifts—including through calls in the *Boston Globe*—and delivered them to sailors annually with support from a wide range of congregations in greater Boston.[88]

The public activism and energy of chaplains in the 1960s declined in the 1970s, even as they continued to quietly serve people across the city. Chaplains financially supported by Catholic and Episcopal Dioceses continued in hospitals, prisons, schools, and universities across the state—many in addition to their work in congregations—and an act was passed stating that a committee consisting of a Protestant, Catholic, and Jewish chaplain would advise about chaplains in state institutions and confer with the religious bodies of those represented.[89] Peter Gomes began to serve at Harvard University's Memorial Chapel, and chaplains in higher education saw their work begin to expand from traditional Catholic-Protestant-Jewish communities as campus demographics began to shift.[90] Chaplains continued to officiate at local ceremonies and services, including funerals for city leaders.[91]

The work of chaplains was not without conflicts. In the 1970s, a political skirmish erupted around Catholic priest George V. Kerr who had been the chaplain of the Massachusetts House of Representatives since 1959 and coordinator of the chaplain service in addition to his role as a parish priest. Perhaps as a result of decline in membership in the Catholic Church and an increase in the Protestant Church in the city, members of the House questioned his annual salary of $8,400 and called for a system through which clergy from a range of religious traditions could offer the opening prayer. He was made the "chief chaplain," and a rotating schedule established.[92]

Fire and police chaplains—who typically wore department uniforms and received small stipends from the city—made the rounds of fire houses and police department offices and were called through internal phone systems when needed for support or ceremonial functions. They played important roles at two disasters in the city in the 1970s—the Hotel Vendome fire on June 17, 1972, and an airline crash at Logan airport in 1973. The hundred-year-old former Hotel Vendome on Commonwealth Avenue in Boston was being remodeled when it caught fire. Firefighters battled the blaze all afternoon when an adjacent building unexpectedly collapsed killing nine firefighters and injuring nine others. Reports described Catholic chaplain James Keating crawling into the rubble to administer last rites to two firefighters whose bodies could not be quickly recovered.[93] Another Fire Department chaplain, Father Dan Mahoney, was also on the scene and later received a commendation from the commissioner for the support he offered. Father Mahoney also offered support after Delta Flight 723 from Burlington, Vermont, crashed on approach to Boston's Logan airport killing all eighty-nine occupants, as did Boston's first police department chaplain Rev. James Lane.[94]

While the racial composition of Boston continued to slowly diversify after 1965, this was not reflected among chaplains, who remained predominantly white and male across sectors. The Catholic Archdiocese began outreach to Spanish speakers from Puerto Rico in the 1950s and then to Cuban, Haitian, Vietnamese, Chinese, and Korean immigrants under the Office for Ethnic Apostolates established in the late 1980s. Ministries established for outreach to nonwhite groups did not consider themselves to be providing "chaplaincy" as they did for hospitals, fire departments, and the like.[95] A number of evangelical churches grew because of immigration, but there are no records of them calling their leaders "chaplain" or those leaders also serving in public chaplaincy roles in the city. While leaders in immigrant communities certainly offered the support chaplains provide, in the documents I reviewed there is no evidence of the term "chaplain" being used outside of white Catholic, Protestant, and increasingly Jewish communities in the city.[96]

Quieter Years: 1980–2000

From 1980 through 2000, chaplains quietly continued their work in greater Boston. The demographics of chaplains (very) slowly feminized and became more religiously diverse. While some hospitals, prisons, and institutions of higher education had full-time chaplains, the majority of people identified as chaplains remained Catholic, Protestant, and Jewish leaders who also led local congregations. Federal, state, and local financial support for these positions was channeled to members of these religious groups through positions in the military, jails and prisons, and the Veterans Administration. Some of them operated from a largely Christian-centered approach. Part-time positions with city and state government seem to have slowly phased out during these years. So called "banquet chaplains," those who show up to pray at banquets and ceremonies but do little more, continued to have a role in civic associations and some city events—particularly for veterans—that often had strong patriotic and civil religious themes.[97]

Catholic priests, numbers of whom were then on the decline in Boston and elsewhere, continued to be assigned as chaplains to organizations across the city alongside their parish work as were clergy in several Protestant denominations. Women and deacons were listed, for the first time, in the 1990 Catholic Directory as supporting Catholics in area hospitals while the number of priests continued to decline.[98] The Episcopal Church continued to support a few full-time chaplaincy positions in higher education and used a pager system so the diocese could react to needs in hospitals. The Episcopal Church also made a point to serve mental health facilities, including Solomon Carter Fuller Mental Health Center where Rev. John Douglas supported patients, families, and staff. An Episcopal canon who served as chaplain also celebrated the Holy Eucharist on holidays and major church festivals in the chapel at the Lindemann Mental Health Center in Government Center.[99]

Much of the work of chaplains was improvisational during these years. Catholic priest Bernard P. McLaughlin—chaplain at Boston's Logan airport—for example, continued to serve at the airport chapel, which was one of the workmen's chapels Archbishop Cushing built in the 1950s and 1960s. He celebrated about twenty weddings per year in that chapel, according to a 1984 *Boston Globe* article, and led twelve well-attended Masses per week.[100] Rev. Walter J. Martin SJ was named Catholic chaplain for Boston's waterfront. In the early 1980s, a *Globe* reporter claimed that the unorthodox had become the norm; "Crowds fill his chapels for a Saturday midnight Mass for night workers, and for his special Masses for fishermen, police, the rights of children, Ireland and its hunger strikers, mothers, parents, grandparents, Friendship Day, the burned-out St. William's Church in Dorchester or other people, issues or events."[101] By the end of the decade, these events were no longer reported in the *Globe*.

Chaplains continued to play pastoral and advocacy roles in other settings. Father Dan Mahoney continued as Catholic chaplain with the Boston Fire Department. In 1982 he rescued Torah scrolls from Temple Tifereth Israel in Everett during a fire.[102] The Boston Police Department also appointed its first Jewish chaplain in 1984.[103] Black clergy continued a push—which started in the 1970s—for more African American prison chaplains, particularly important given rising incarceration rates of Black men.[104] And chaplains remained present at funerals and annual memorial gatherings across the city.[105] Congressional chaplains in state government continued to fade away in the 1990s, and positions in public hospitals were frequently threatened, leading salaries to be paid by coalitions of religious groups rather than the state.

In area hospitals, the work of chaplains became decidedly more multifaith between 1980 and 2000, with chaplains increasingly staffed by unit and responsible for seeing all the patients in that unit rather than only those with whom they shared a religious background. Growing religious diversification was partially responsible for this shift. Limited resources were another factor as well as that many chaplains were clinically trained in multifaith groups, tended to be more religiously liberal, and were open to finding ways to be flexible and connect with patients from a range of religious traditions.[106] This transition was particularly evident at Hebrew Rehabilitation Center, now Hebrew SeniorLife, where an Orthodox Jewish rabbi was replaced by a liberal Reform rabbi and a nonordained Jewish leader. Long Jewish services were replaced by groups focused on Jewish music or Jewish sports. The nonordained leader remembered, "my job was as he [the rabbi] would do these groups on Jewish music or Jews in sports . . . they were more uplifting groups rather than a Torah study or a Talmud study. I would identify the people in the room who clearly wanted to talk a little more, I would take them out . . . and then they could ask the questions of, what has my life meant? And so I developed those kind of relationships with people and their families." This chaplain's job focuses entirely on these relationships today with residents and staff.

> I'll go and do a visit, Where are you today? How are you today? What's on your heart? And have those kinds of discussions. I'll leave with a blessing or a prayer and then in between those, I'll try and make connections with people who might like a visit, someone new to the floor or someone with a birthday or someone with some kind of anniversary that I know is coming, be it good or bad, you know, the death of someone or the birth of a great grandchild, and I will go and offer them a blessing or a prayer. . . . And my office door is always unlocked, and I have staff from all over the building coming in to just sit in that chair.[107]

Chaplains also appeared in a few new places in response to local and national events. In the 1990s, the Episcopal Diocese assigned a half-time chaplain to the AIDS wards of Lemuel Shattuck Hospital, the public hospital largely responsible for serving people who were incarcerated. They also assigned a chaplain to Victory Programs of Boston that managed residencies for people in recovery, many of whom were HIV-positive.[108] Two articles in the *Globe* named a resurgence and diversification in spiritual and religious life on area campuses in the mid-1990s. The number of students involved in religious activities at Northeastern University doubled between the late 1980s and early-to-mid-1990s, and non-Christian students were increasingly vocal. "I think there is a real spiritual hunger," Rev. Scotty McLennan, then chaplain at Tufts University was quoted saying.[109] With the arrival of the cruise ship industry in Boston in the late 1980s, port chaplains also began providing services for cruise ship staff in the terminals, offering banks of telephones, ways to send money home, and other opportunities for workers to communicate with their families outside of the United States.[110]

More women served as chaplains in greater Boston after 1980 than before. More Catholic women moved into these roles as fewer men were training for the priesthood, and in later years, the sexual abuse scandal began to rock the church.[111] The number of immigrants from Central America and the Caribbean continued to grow in the region during these years. Like African

American and Asian Americans already living in greater Boston, the newly arrived did not readily adapt the title or role of chaplaincy in the spiritual work they did or enter the ranks of existing chaplains in the city, although many did the work informally. Black clergy centrally involved in the Ten Points Coalition, a partnership between Boston police and clergy to reduce youth homicides, for example, did pastoral and advocacy work common to municipal and community chaplains but did not use the label chaplain.[112] It was not until the late 1990s and early 2000s that Muslim, Buddhist, and Hindu chaplains were first visible in the city.

Edges and Some Reimagining: 2000–2020

Since 2000, the religious backgrounds of chaplains in greater Boston have expanded and include many more women than in the past. The priest shortage—made more acute by the fall-out from the clergy sexual abuse scandal—meant that the majority of Catholic chaplains were laypeople and women as the archdiocese assigned the few priests they had to local congregations. The Episcopal Diocese continued to financially support chaplains (almost all women) during these years in a handful of area colleges and universities. More evidence is needed to document the feminization of chaplaincy positions in Boston and nationally and the reasons for it.[113] More women may have opted for chaplaincy positions because they were in line with their beliefs and values or because they allowed more set hours or flexibility. Women may also have come to these positions because of glass ceilings in congregations and other labor market factors that reflected implicit and explicit discrimination against them.

In 2005, the Episcopal Diocese charged a College Work Committee with identifying eight new sites for campus ministry in Massachusetts.[114] MIT hired Robert Randolph as the first "Chaplain to the Institute" who explained, "My job will be to help knit together the fabric of faiths that already transcend our community."[115] Amy McCreath, the Episcopal chaplain at MIT, also led the Technology and Culture Forum, launched there in the 1960s, featuring speakers delivering lectures on ethics and public policy. "Serving Episcopal students through worship, Bible study, and doing pastoral care is important, but it's not enough" she was quoted in the *Boston Globe* as saying. "To really join God and what God is about at a place like MIT necessitates being out in the midst of the academic and technical life of the institute."[116]

Growing numbers of Buddhist, Muslim, and Hindu chaplains worked in area institutions during these years particularly in higher education.[117]

The events of 9/11 led several chaplains to reorient toward caring for Muslim constituents. The Catholic priest-chaplain at Logan airport who served airport staff and the families of victims throughout the events of 9/11 was particularly concerned and added Muslim prayer mats to the otherwise traditional Catholic chapel at the airport. As he told a *Boston Globe* reporter, "'Many people still today are filled with anxiety and are overwhelmed when some Muslims are present. . . . There is a stigma right now, and it's a tragedy.' The image of travel comes naturally. Believers of all stripes, he says, share a search for the divine: 'It's a journey that we're all on.'"[118] In the port, chaplains who had long emphasized hospitality over explicitly religious aims reported that after 9/11 most Muslim seafarers were not permitted to leave port gates so chaplains served them where they were.[119] While some institutions, like Children's Hospital, had Muslim chaplains, many more hired them after 2000.[120] Tufts University, for example, hired Shareda Hosein, its first female Muslim chaplain in 2007, and area hospitals opened Muslim prayer rooms for patients, staff, and families.[121]

Chaplains continued to support members of the military and veterans speaking the language of civil religion.[122] They were present at annual gatherings, at Hanscom Air Force Base, and through Veterans Administration medical facilities. Daniel R. Sweeny, a fellow at Boston College and an Air Force Reserve chaplain created a Catholic prayer/catechism booklet in 2005 for military personnel designed—with water- and tear-resistant pages—to be carried in combat. It was paid for by the Knights of Columbus, and more than 300,000 copies were distributed to military personnel.[123] In 2007, Chaplain Jeremy Bastian even performed a service to honor dogs being honorably discharged following their work sniffing out bombs in Iraq.[124]

Staff and volunteer chaplains also continued to serve in city, state, and federal prisons across the state as well as in hospitals and hospices. In the late 2000s, the *Boston Globe* reported that thirty-two staff chaplains recruited and oversaw more than 1,000 volunteers in state prison facilities. Half were slated to be laid off in 2009 but were not.[125] The state continued to move toward one chaplain providing services to people of all religious backgrounds.[126] Boston's Catholic leadership celebrated Mass in state prisons on Thanksgiving or Christmas, a practice that continued during these years.[127] Chaplains also continued working in local facilities like at the Nashua Street Jail where chaplains included a Spanish speaker, a chaplain of color, and a Muslim chaplain. Local congregations also organized programs including Alcoholics Anonymous and Narcotics Anonymous in some facilities and led services.[128]

In hospitals, palliative care programs grew nationally and in Massachusetts and almost always included chaplains in their work. Massachusetts General Hospital has one of the oldest palliative care programs in the country, for example, and has long included a chaplain.[129] Community-based hospices long included chaplains and were frequently the settings in which there were the most chaplaincy job openings. As in hospitals, chaplains in hospice offered interfaith support accessible to patients and families from a range of spiritual and religious backgrounds including those with no religious backgrounds.[130] In a 2014 *Boston Globe* article, hospice chaplains described their spiritual care work to include conversation, relaxation techniques, poetry, and family support. Several described removing religious-specific items of clothing before making visits and drawing on aspects of their personal religious backgrounds that are universally accessible.[131]

Chaplains also continued to work quietly with police and firefighters across the state as well as with seafarers. Police chaplains continued to attend swearing-in ceremonies, funerals, and services on Memorial Day, honoring police officers who died that year.[132] A Catholic priest who was a chaplain with the Boston Fire Department during these years described how his chaplaincy role narrowed given priest shortages and his other commitments: "I see my role first as a priest and then in assistance to the police or fire. I'm not the type that is going to jump in a fire truck all the time . . . I don't see that as my role. . . . There are not as many priests as in the past." He went on to explain that he is responsible for a parish, a school of 400, and serving as a chaplain to the police and fire departments. "The priest is there to assist, not be at every fire, we just can't do that anymore—physically or emotionally or spiritually."[133]

Chaplains affiliated with Seafarers Friend and the New England Seafarers Mission continued to serve seafarers and cruise ship workers, helping them communicate with loved ones abroad, send money home, have a cup of coffee while in port, and very occasionally attend religious services. In the words of Steve Cushing, executive director and chaplain of the New England Seafarers Mission, in the *Boston Globe* in 2006, "One of the thrusts we're working at this year is to really hone this term 'hospitality,'" he said. "As you and I think of it, we think of the Sheraton or the Ritz. . . . We're looking at a larger picture of hospitality, even as Christian scripture looks at it, which is you take in the stranger who asks for help as he's on his travels or on her travels through this world. When they cross your path, you provide kind of a safety zone where they can receive help, receive comfort, receive rest, and then you send them on their way to continue their journey."[134]

Glimpses of the 1960s activism were evident in clergy, including chaplains, demonstrating in front of the state house about anti-Muslim rhetoric in 2010.[135] Boston University chaplain Rev. Cameron Partridge spoke in front of the City Council in 2013 to support school policies to better protect transgender students.[136] And chaplains were among the clergy and activists rallying against casinos in the state, arguing that they take advantage of the poor.[137] Increasingly the work of chaplains was described as spiritual care rather than chaplaincy or pastoral care to recognize its openness to all.

Chaplains and spiritual care providers emerged in new places in the 2000s, including with the Red Sox, the Patriots, at a truck stop, a pet hospice, and a range of community groups. In 2005, Rev. Walt Day, an affiliate of the evangelical Christian Baseball Chapel which sends chaplains to major league baseball teams, held a service for Red Sox players, staff, and coaches before an August game.[138] Day also served as occasional chaplain to the New England Patriots supporting evangelical Christian players and staff.[139] In 2008, a truck stop chaplain set up a trailer chapel in Shrewsbury, a town outside of Boston, owned by Pennsylvania-based Transport for Christ International. Transport for Christ, a nondenominational evangelical effort to help truck drivers avoid sin, has more than thirty mobile chapels for truck drivers in the United States and abroad.[140]

More religiously progressive religious leaders also used the term "chaplain" to describe their work in new places. Rev. Eliza Blanchard, a Unitarian Universalist minister and chaplain of New England Pet Hospice, cared for humans and animals through pet-loss circles, worship services for people and their pets, and related educational programs.[141] Still Harbor, a nonprofit organization started in 2008 to serve global health workers, also came to describe portions of its work as chaplaincy (as described in the next chapter). More chaplains also started working with the homeless after 2000. Leaders with Common Cathedral, a community including the unhoused that gathers weekly to worship, began to do chaplaincy work in related social service organizations in Boston. A similar organization in an ethnically diverse suburb also started in the late 2000s with a local Protestant minister walking the streets and connecting with those who are unhoused. The work continues, often in McDonald's restaurants, as religious leaders calling themselves chaplains support and talk with people who are unhoused. "We live out our mission," their website explains, "by building trusting relations with people . . . who are experiencing homelessness and struggling with mental health and/or substance use issues. We offer a ministry of compassion and companionship through life's struggles and triumphs, welcoming all into relationship and loving community."[142]

Some local religious leaders were invited to settings new to them and came to describe their work there as chaplaincy. Leaders of a local health center that serves large numbers of elders approached a local minister about offering a regular memorial service to recognize those who died. He started offering the service that led staff to "recognize that there were some participants in the program who would come in—who had real spiritual depth and history—and may want and need a pastoral visit."[143] The staff introduced him as a local pastor. Gradually he asked them to use the word chaplain instead, explaining, there is confusion "in people's heads—when they hear pastor they think that person represents a church—and no thank you, they're not from that church." Being described as a chaplain made it easier for him to meet and talk with elderly patients even as the work he was doing with them did not change. "I am a reverend. I am a pastor," he explained, but in this setting, "I don't represent my church. I represent the health center. That just takes it in another direction. I think it puts it in a place where people are more comfortable." Laura Everett, the executive director of the Massachusetts Council of Churches and an avid bicyclist even sometimes calls her work with bike communities in greater Boston "bike chaplaincy."[144]

As in earlier years, chaplains improvised to meet the demands of those they served. One who served as a prison chaplain alongside her work as the pastor of a local church was described in the *Globe* caring for people from church to shelters to gravesides. She also conducted many funerals for young victims of homicide.[145] Another ordained minister and community leader organized people to train as chaplains through short courses offered through the International Fellowship of Chaplains, a Christian organization. "As I began to talk to people about the initiative," she explained, "I found that a lot of, what I'll call second career chaplains, . . . were interested in being trained in chaplaincy. . . . They were retired lawyers, retired nurses, retired educators . . . who really were feeling a sense of wanting to serve in chaplaincy as minister in the workplace but did not want to go back to school to get a Masters of Divinity . . . because they're feeling like, who has time for that?"[146] A group of them started the Greater Boston Community Collaborative, a "volunteer ministry dedicated to preventing violence in the city."[147] One of the first ordained was Tina Cherry, mother of Louis Brown a 15-year-old killed by stray gunfire in 1993. She created the Louis D. Brown Peace Institute in the city to further her vision and brought her new chaplaincy credentials to her work there.

In these and other examples, tensions between those trained for chaplaincy through degree programs and clinical work and those prepared in short online courses remain, as do questions about who has access to these paths. Sometimes—like in the Boston Police Department—people with different preparations for chaplaincy work alongside one another. In addition to the local clergy that receive stipends for their work as police chaplains, at least one person trained through the International Fellowship of Chaplains also does this work. The new places chaplaincy emerged in Boston in the 2000s demonstrate the continued flexibility of the term and ways people are using it to describe their work with the unhoused, international aid workers through Still Harbor, and others likely described in different ways in the past. While the backgrounds of those calling themselves chaplain in Boston have diversified some in the past twenty years, there are still few chaplains of color overall and very few from the city's vibrant immigrant communities.

Conclusions

Chaplaincy—increasingly called spiritual care—has taken many forms in greater Boston since 1945 as this chapter begins to show. The concept of chaplaincy has shifted from being used to describe the work of religious professionals in established organizations, like hospitals, prisons, and the military, to also describing this work in nonprofit organizations, community settings, and other less structured contexts. Spurred by the presence of chaplains in the military who became known to more people during the two world wars, the role has expanded and shifted alongside growing numbers of religious leaders working outside of congregations and the broader deinstitutionalization of American religious life in Boston and beyond.

In greater Boston after World War II, the majority of chaplains were white men. That slowly expanded to include women and people of color, mostly in the 1980s. While some institutions, like the Boston Fire Department, Boston City Hospital (now called Boston Medical Center) and most other large hospitals, most major universities, and state prisons, have long histories of chaplains, the term and concept have also been used flexibly by others in the years since World War II.[148] Those describing themselves as chaplains have always included local religious leaders working as chaplains on the side and those—particularly in hospitals and some prisons and universities—doing the work of chaplaincy full-time. The Christian—particularly Protestant and in Boston Catholic—history of the term is strong even as it has been adapted by religious leaders from Jewish, Buddhist, Humanist, and other backgrounds. While people of color have certainly done the work of chaplaincy, few in Boston used the term to describe their work—at least as evident in the *Boson Globe* and local archives. Additional research with Black and Asian American newspapers as well as with non-English sources is needed to explicate this history in Boston and nationally.

Rather than being fully distinct from local congregations, some chaplains in Boston over time were supported by them, as well as by state-funded positions. As chaplains and spiritual care providers emerged in new places in recent years, the financial support for them from religious organizations and the state has declined. I turn to the present in the next chapter by asking who chaplains are in greater Boston today, how they came to the work and prepare for it, and how it connects to the city's current religious ecology. It is personal relationships chaplains have with local clergy rather than formal connections between religious institutions and the organizations where chaplains work that are a defining feature of Boston's religious ecology, as explored—alongside the financial bases for the work of chaplains—next.

3
Becoming a Chaplain

Father Joe Bagetta, a young-looking seventy, is the real name of the only chaplain who until recently worked in Boston's Department of Youth Services.[1] Wearing a fleece jacket with a "Department of Youth Services" logo over a collared shirt and dark pants, he sat and talked with me in his office inside the youth detention facility where he spends his days. Neat stacks of papers and Bibles sat on government-issued bookshelves across from Father Bagetta's desk and computer. This facility houses sixty kids aged fourteen to twenty-one while their cases weave their way through the state courts. There used to be several chaplains in the department as well as in the courts themselves. When their positions were eliminated in the 1970s, Cardinal Richard Cushing used his political ties—or so the story goes—to maintain this one.

Father Bagetta moves freely through this facility with keys for everything. He is responsible for the religious needs of all sixty kids and making sure their religious rights are respected. He understands this in terms of formal state policies and handed me a document while we spoke with excerpts from Chapter 265, Section 37 of the General Laws of the Commonwealth underlined which read, "No person . . . shall by force or threat of force, willfully injure, intimidate or interfere with, or attempt to injure, intimidate or interfere with, or oppress or threaten any other person in the free exercise or enjoyment of any right or privilege secured to him by the constitution or laws of the commonwealth or by the constitution or laws of the United States."[2]

After the excerpt is an underlined summary not in the section, "The free exercise of religion is a right guaranteed by both the First Amendment of the U.S. Constitution and Article II of the Declaration of Rights of the Massachusetts Constitution. Moreover, Chapter 272, Section 38 of the General Laws states" and then a quoted (and underlined) piece from that section, "Whoever willfully interrupts or disturbs an assembly of people met for worship of God shall by punished by imprisonment for not more than one year or by a fine or not more than one thousand dollars."[3] A passage from Chapter 434 or the acts of 1990 related to hate crimes is also quoted on the handout.[4]

Spiritual Care. Wendy Cadge, Oxford University Press. © Oxford University Press 2023.
DOI: 10.1093/oso/9780197647813.003.0003

Father Bagetta offers unconventional Mass with rap music once a week in each unit as well as communion services. He brings Protestant clergy in and consults with an imam who works with adults at another Department of Corrections site as needed. Ten volunteers do faith sharing with the kids, and a group of older women he calls "the grandmothers," come in every six weeks to check on the girls.

He does a lot of pastoral counseling and grief work especially when the kids first arrive. "I explain who I am and what to expect in this institution," he told me, telling the kids "that you are totally safe, that no harm will come, that you will be well taken care of, you will eat well, all of your needs will be taken care of." He spends time eating and watching television with the kids on their units and hands out Crest toothpaste and Irish Springs soap—better than the state versions—to build rapport. He and the volunteers play Pictionary and Family Feud. "Even though they are committed, they are still just kids" he explained, saying, "the best parts [of the work] are when kids laugh and are having a good time." Pressure from gangs has increased over time, he said, which makes it even harder to encourage kids to accept each other for who they are.[5]

Before our conversation concluded, Father Bagetta also gave me a second handout with quotes from Massachusetts General Laws Chapter 233 Section 20A that allows him, as a clergy person, to keep conversations with kids confidential. "A priest, rabbi, or ordained or licensed minister of any church or an accredited Christian Science practitioner shall not, without the consent of the person making the confession, be allowed to disclose a confession made to him in his professional character, in the course of discipline enjoined by the rules or practices of the religious body to which he belongs."[6] Because of this confidentiality, his job rarely involves being called to court, but instead allows him to spend time with the kids, get to know them, and be present to support their needs in real time. Born in the North End of Boston, Father Bagetta worked as a corrections officer before he became a priest and a chaplain. Several years ago, he built a Catholic chapel on the side of this state facility in a single-wide trailer with financial support from the Knights of Columbus.[7]

Father Bagetta's workplace is quite different from that of Perry Dougherty (also her real name) and her colleagues at Still Harbor: Chaplains for Social Justice who, a few miles away, support programs and services that "create a network of fiercely loving and compassionate spiritual leaders for social change."[8] The organization was founded in 2008 out of a sense that people were seeking meaning and purpose through social justice work and that spiritual formation and accompaniment might be a support in that work. The founder, Ed Cardoza, worked in global health, which led to one of Still Harbor's first major partnerships: the Global Health Corps Fellowship Program. "We helped them design training and provide support to fellows throughout the year, and in 2010 we started calling it chaplaincy for the first time. We framed it around this being not spiritual accompaniment generally but chaplaincy embedded in the organization," Perry told me. "We called ourselves chaplains and began that framing . . . as chaplains to nonprofits."

Since its inception, Still Harbor has worked with people in a range of social movements and organizations—many of them highly secular. "There's no space in a lot of the organizations we work with for people to process just the ethical questions, the spiritual questions, the personal questions that come up in a neutral and confidential way. And a lot comes up when you are on the frontlines of witnessing suffering," Perry explained. Still Harbor offers accompaniment to folks locally and around the world; they connect through phone and video calls. Some work is one-on-one and others are more group focused. Some are in the form of one-off workshops and others in long-term partnerships. "We're highly customized," Perry explained, "our long game is always to be able to do more transformative chaplaincy work that often happens first individually and then in groups. . . . Workshops are an opportunity to build the contemplative muscle for folks."

Since 2008, Still Harbor has been a 501c3 nonprofit supported through partnerships and philanthropic contributions. Still Harbor has evolved over time, making transformative changes in their organizational leadership structure and choosing to focus primarily on offering spiritual accompaniment to activists and organizers while training people to accompany individuals and groups who are engaged in movement work. The organization is not affiliated with any faith tradition or institution, and Perry, who now serves as a senior partner, was ordained as an "Interspiritual Minister" by One Spirit Interfaith Seminary in New York. "Our collective quest for justice and peace cannot be accomplished by intellectual or professional training *alone*" their website reminds us, "Still Harbor believes that spirituality cultivates the depth of **imagination**, **courage**, and **resilience** we need to create a more **kind**, **equitable**, and **sustainable** world. Our programs and services seek to create a network of fiercely loving and compassionate spiritual leaders for social change."[9]

* * *

Father Bagetta and Perry Dougherty are two—of many—who have historically and still today use the term "chaplain" to describe their work. Ordained by the Catholic Church and working as a long-term employee of a state institution, Father Bagetta offers ritual support and counseling as he aims to serve all with the assistance of volunteers. His position grew out of historical relationships between the Commonwealth of Massachusetts and the Catholic Church, or its leaders, and may remain today as a remnant of that relationship. In contrast, Perry Dougherty and Still Harbor came to chaplaincy as a container or frame to describe the work they were already doing helping individuals explore questions of meaning and purpose in their work for social change. They saw in the term and concept of chaplaincy a way to communicate their work, emphasizing the importance not of ritual or religion but of ethical questions of suffering, meaning, and purpose in ways that might expand the potential that individuals and organizations have for social change. Not affiliated with any state or religious organization, Perry and her colleagues are religious entrepreneurs who not only raise the funds for their work but also name and seek to communicate that work and its value to potential clients locally and around the world.

Viewed from a distance, Father Bagetta and Perry Dougherty both seek to relieve suffering and support people through relationships informed by their understandings of religion and spirituality. Viewed up close, their differences come into relief: a state employee and a religious entrepreneur, someone with religious training through a long-standing established religious organization and someone trained through a newer, much smaller organization; one chaplain with a literally captive audience and another who creates and gathers her audience; one where religious ritual is central and another where the work is more improvisational. While Father Bagetta and Perry Dougherty both call themselves chaplains, their work may be best conceived of as overlapping circles that share a small amount of area.

This chapter describes who—in addition to Father Bagetta and Perry Dougherty—call themselves chaplains in Boston today, how they came to that work, and where they do it.[10] It is the first scholarly attempt to look at chaplains working across settings in a single geography and to focus inductively on those using the title. I ask how those doing this work came to it, the kinds of institutions (including multiple different settings) in which they do the work, how they were trained, and whether they are compensated. As a group, these individuals illustrate the breadth of people using the term "chaplain" today, as well as patterns in their paths to the work and the organizations in which they do it. These stories also demonstrate variation in the training and preparation of chaplains and how they connect to greater Boston's broader religious ecology. They confirm that, in practice, "chaplain" is a flexible term and the people using it are quite distinct from one another. These findings challenge simple efforts to develop or professionalize the field of chaplaincy by showing the true breadth of the field. Perhaps most importantly, these stories help us begin to see how chaplains interact with the religious institutional field in Boston—spiritual and religious organizations in the city that range from congregations to social service organizations to faith-based nonprofits. Most chaplains who are not local clergy connect with other religious organizations not through formal relationships between their workplaces but through personal relationships they have with the people who lead them.

Evolving Titles

Everyone I describe here identifies as a chaplain or spiritual care provider, though some hold that title more tightly than others. While people working in the military, prisons, and municipal contexts like police and fire departments clearly identify as chaplains, the language used to describe this work is shifting in other settings. One of these individuals is called a "university chaplain" by the Episcopal Diocese (which pays her), even though she is described as a "spiritual advisor" at the university where she works.[11] A hospice chaplain, described a similar evolution in language. "We use the term spiritual care provider here," she explained, though she uses a variety of terms to describe her work when she talks with patients and families. "Depending on who I'm speaking to—to a Christian patient I would use the word chaplain because they get it right away." She also does bereavement work and sometimes describes herself as the "Bereavement Care Coordinator" saying she basically does "ad hoc chaplaincy" for the whole company.[12] In these and other examples, the language used to name this work is institutionally situated and constrained by relationships and settings.

A number of people described what it means to call themselves a chaplain by comparing that title and work to the work they do or used to do in congregations. A National Guard chaplain who also works in a congregation spoke of "going into a phone booth" to change from his congregational to his chaplaincy hat. "I find myself going back and forth, but I think when it comes sometimes to advice where I'm advising a commander or something like that . . . I'm funneling my rabbinic Jewish training in answering even though it is not in Jewish terms." He described how chaplains need to "speak universal[ly]" even while being "true to your denomination or your specific faith group . . . I think the key is you have to be open, especially in military chaplaincy."[13] Several prison chaplains spoke of the chaplaincy role saying they have to follow more guidelines than in congregations and serve a broader range of people, including the officers. "I'm not only the pastor for the inmates," one said, "but I'm also the pastor for the officers who are willing to share with me. They share different things."[14]

Those who came to chaplaincy more recently had the most to say about evolving descriptions of the role and title and the need for new language about it. "I've wanted to use words like chaplaincy and ministry," explained a Buddhist chaplain who was raised Jewish and works in higher education. "I kind of like the power of coming into a label that already has an authority in the Christian tradition and broadening that invite." But then, he reflected, "the whole religious landscape is shifting . . . so the verbiage will need to change, I'm not sure to what—like 'coaches' is already here, but it's not the same thing exactly."[15] A municipal chaplain remembers when chaplains used to wear uniforms. They do not anymore because people were confused and thought they were officers, he told me. He made a similar argument seeing the work as ecumenical and the term "chaplain" as not up to date with the work as it continues to evolve.

Coming to the Work

Amidst the nuance and discussion of the title of chaplain are five broad paths through which the people I interviewed came to the work. Each path combines personal, relational, and institutional factors to highlight patterns that brought people to this work. Like growing numbers of clergy nationally, many of the chaplains I met came to the work as a second career. One group came to chaplaincy primarily through *personal experiences*. A second group was *asked* to add a chaplaincy position to their work as a congregational leader and/or was *assigned* to such a position by leaders in their religious hierarchies. A third saw in the work opportunities to live out their commitments to progressive understandings of *social justice*. The fourth group was simply *looking for a job*. And the final group saw in chaplaincy the opportunity to do a kind of work or to find a position of religious leadership in a *system that otherwise did not have an obvious place for them.*

Several in the first group were already working as religious leaders and shifted to work in chaplaincy after *personal experiences* caring for loved ones through long illnesses. Others had experiences—like the birth of a premature baby or struggles with addiction—that led them to want to offer better support to others than they had received. A second group were *invited* to become chaplains as a result of their positions in the community as local clergy. A Catholic priest, for example, was invited to become a fire chaplain by a member of his congregation who was the local fire chief. A Protestant minister received a phone call asking if he could do some work as a hospice chaplain alongside his work with his current (small) congregation. And another religious leader was asked, through personal networks, to serve patients at the Veterans Administration. Episcopal and Catholic priests and deacons were often *assigned* to chaplaincy positions while others tended to make freer decisions.

Many of the people who came to chaplaincy through personal experiences or through positions as religious leaders in their communities connected the opportunity to broader themes in their personal biographies and senses of vocation. A National Guard chaplain, for example, heard that the Guard was looking for chaplains and reflected, "I just had this sense of call to that . . . I hadn't really had a plan for chaplaincy. I do have a lot of military people in my family, so it wasn't an alien concept. . . . The church came looking, and I decided to go with it."[16] Another, who works with the police, was a police officer for many years and a minister at his church on the side. He retired from formal police work and fully stepped into the chaplain position, seeing himself as uniquely positioned to help. "As a chaplain and police officer you are able to look at and understand their [police] perspective and what they are dealing with better."[17] He does a lot of crisis work and debriefing and lets police officers know about supportive services within the department. He feels most rewarded when he helps people get back on track.

In addition to those who came to chaplaincy through personal networks or were asked or assigned—mostly without planning to do so—a third group came to the work through progressive *commitments to improving the lives of others and addressing systematic inequalities.* These individuals worked in homeless shelters, volunteered with prisoners, cared for AIDS patients, and/or trained to be social workers before finding work as chaplains. One worked with women who were incarcerated, "I'd go over and visit them, see if they're OK . . . just give them a word of encouragement, so I think that is what sparked it. I never thought I'd be a chaplain, never thought I'd be a pastor, never thought I'd be a minister."[18] Another ran a housing program for ten years and was looking for a change, "I was wanting something that integrated my faith into my work in a more direct way. . . . I thought chaplaincy might be something that I would enjoy and be good at."[19] And another worked in a soup kitchen and raised her children before becoming a Unitarian Universalist working as a chaplain with people who are unhoused. While a few of these people were in seminary or theological school before discovering chaplaincy, most enrolled after learning about chaplaincy explicitly to do that work.

The fourth, and largest group, came to work as chaplains while *looking for work* after completing graduate training. A few were interested in chaplaincy, while others were seeking work in line with their education and training. A rabbi was the part-time Jewish chaplain at a local medical center and the part-time rabbi at a university for several years before shifting to full-time hospital work. Chaplaincy, in his words, "works with my model of being a rabbi who doesn't work on Shabbat" and fulfills his deep interest in "interfaith stuff."[20] Others saw chaplaincy positions advertised while job searching and were hired. Chaplains that supervise or educate other chaplains in their workplaces typically came to those positions through work as a chaplain in the same organization (i.e., they were promoted internally). When the director of chaplaincy at one hospital retired, for example, the current director applied telling me, "I couldn't possibly imagine somebody else getting it, and I just had all these ideas about how things could be better. . . . So I put my hat in the ring and was on fire for this job. It was really kind of like what I'm meant to do. It is fun to feel that kind of passion."[21]

The final group, like Perry whose story was at the beginning of the chapter, saw in chaplaincy the opportunity to do a kind of work or to find a position of religious leadership in *a system that otherwise did not have an obvious place for them*. Perry and her colleagues at Still Harbor thought paying attention to spirituality might enlarge the capacity of individuals and institutions to do the work of social justice. A Catholic woman who wants to be a priest saw in chaplaincy an alternative approach to religious leadership in a tradition that does not ordain women. A man who left the Catholic priesthood, got married, and had children got a job as a hospice chaplain saying, "my education has been primarily as a Catholic priest for ministry, and I kind of fell into chaplaincy and found it a wonderful fit in a lot of ways."[22] Several other chaplains also did not fit the employment boxes for which their training prepared them. One was a Southern Baptist who moved away from the tradition for theological reasons and found in hospital chaplaincy a way to use his religious training. Another could not get a job in a congregation in his denomination following a geographic relocation to care for elderly parents because of the ways his denomination places clergy. He also found work as a hospice chaplain.[23]

While individual stories include many components, these five general patterns broadly capture how the chaplains I interviewed came to the work. Languages of call and the notion that they were somehow destined to do this work runs through the stories of about half the chaplains (all Christians) shared about how they came to it. "When God puts something on your heart, you can't shake it," a community chaplain explained while describing how he received online training to prepare himself for the work.[24] "God doesn't tell you why, it was just right" explained a prison chaplain.[25] Others used similar language to describe "God's tugging at my coat" and "developing a hospice heart" as part of what led them to this work. While the stories some chaplains told about their paths start within religious institutions or existing religious roles, the stories others told did not—beginning instead from work with the homeless and desire to make broader systematic changes in the world.

Where Do Chaplains Work?

As they traveled along these five broad paths, the people I interviewed came to work in a range of organizations. According to our historical analyses of chaplains mentioned in the *Boston Globe* between 1945 and the present, the largest fraction in greater Boston worked in healthcare, higher education, and prisons. Significant numbers also worked with civic organizations over time.[26] As described in the methods appendix, I aimed to maximize the number of different organizations where chaplains work in gathering a sample of people to interview in Boston rather than the number of chaplains working for the same organization. The demographics of chaplains I interviewed are, therefore, more suggestive than representative of all chaplains in Boston.

These demographics suggest, as described in more detail in the appendix, that a large group of chaplains continue to work in healthcare, including hospice. Many also work in higher education and in prisons. The number of

Photo 3.1 Pictured left to right: Chaplain and Cantor Nancy Sargon, Chaplains Ylisse Bess, Jaime Riggs, Fr. Jim Nunes, Rev. Katie Rimer, Fr. Ignatius Nze, Nancy Smith, Jessica D'Angio, ACPE Educator Rev. Burkhard Weber, and Chaplain Interns Amy Russo and Yonatan Gorin at Beth Israel Deaconess Medical Center. Reprinted with permission of BILH Media Services. Photo credit: James Derek Dwyer.

chaplains working in the community seems to have increased the most over time to include those who work in community centers and social service organizations. About a quarter of chaplains interviewed work in more than one setting, most commonly in municipal, crisis, and federal institutions. Some of these people, like one recent graduate of theological school, are stringing together part-time positions to make ends meet, while others are employed in one setting (usually a congregation) and working or volunteering in another (usually the National Guard and/or a municipal setting). There is clear clustering by sector with municipal, crisis, and National Guard chaplains most likely to move across these three settings. Chaplains in healthcare and higher education typically do not also work in other settings with the exception of some healthcare chaplains who volunteer with the Red Cross on disaster relief work.

Photo 3.2 Army Captain Chaplain Roger Gordon stands outside a forward operating chapel in Camp Arifjan, Kuwait, on March 1, 2021. Forward operating chapels are temporary or fixed tents that provide religious services to all soldiers several times a week. Captain Gordon graduated from Boston University and began serving as an active-duty army chaplain in 2019. Photo credit: U.S. Army photo by Sgt. Aimee Nordin, mass communications specialist, 101st Division Sustainment Brigade.

Close to 90% of the chaplains I interviewed are paid for their chaplaincy work—pay that ranges from a full-time salary to a small annual stipend like that received by the Boston fire and police chaplains. Just under half (45%) work full-time as chaplains with the remainder working part-time. Healthcare, hospice, and higher education chaplains are those most likely to have full-time positions. About one-third of the chaplains are connected to congregations where they do full or part-time work. About one-third are or were state or city employees through their work with state prisons, the National Guard, or municipal services. Full-time federal and state employees are usually the most highly paid chaplains with healthcare, retirement, and vacation benefits, though I did not collect salary and benefits information in this work.

Chaplains are differently integrated into the organizations where they work as described in more detail in chapter 4. In healthcare, including hospice, chaplains usually report to a director of Chaplaincy or Spiritual Care, who then reports to the director of Social Work, Psychiatry, Patient Care

Services or occasionally the CEO of the organization. Quite a few hospice chaplains also have formal positions as bereavement coordinators providing care to loved ones in the six months to a year after the patient dies. College and university chaplains similarly report to a director of Spiritual Life or Chaplaincy who usually reports to a dean of Students or director of Student Life.

Chaplains in the military and National Guard have formal reports but are officially outside the chain of command that allows—and in fact requires—them to maintain complete confidentiality with those with whom they work.[27] "If you ask to speak to your platoon sergeant or company commander privately," a National Guard chaplain explained, "it is not one hundred percent private. You say that to a chaplain and unless it is a national security risk it is confidential. That's huge."[28] In the words of another National Guard chaplain who talks with a lot of people who stop by his office on their way to or from work, "You're outside the chain of command. You're outside the line of the supervisor, and you have a way, hopefully, to solve some problems below the radar and it does help."[29] In the words of a military chaplain, "That confidentiality is something that is unique for chaplains because any other helper is mandated to report certain activities or thoughts, like I said: suicidal ideation, harm to others, that kind of stuff."[30] The fire and police chaplains I interviewed officially report to the chief but most are not supervised. One laughed when I asked about this in an interview saying he reports to God. Most of the community chaplains report to someone in their organization, are freelance and do not really report to anyone, or report to the Board of Directors of the organization where they work.

While military chaplains are clear about their place outside the chain of command and the requirement of confidentiality, some chaplains in other settings experience tensions between their identities as clergy that allows them to guarantee people complete confidentiality and confidentiality policies of the organizations where they work.[31] In the words of one Protestant university chaplain:

> I have always held that my priestly confidence is sacrosanct and that's given a little shelter that, for example, it doesn't give a lay person. Because the university rules are that they have your allegiance for everything . . . when the document goes around I put in parenthesis, secondary to church confidentiality, and I initial it. If someone tells me something under the stole, I'm not going to lose my vocation and be defrocked trying to report to the school

something they think is reportable. My understanding is that the attorney of the diocese and the attorney of the school would work it out and tell me what I could say.

With very few exceptions, chaplains I interviewed maintain complete confidentiality unless someone they are working with is threatening harm to themselves or others. In the words of a municipal chaplain, "If the person says they're going to hurt themselves or hurt someone else, we have to report it. Otherwise, everything is kept between us."[32] Incidences include reporting elder abuse, as several chaplains who work with older people noted. These tensions are particularly evident on college and university campuses around Title IX issues that, among other things, require organizations that receive federal funds to report suspected sexual misconduct. Some chaplains, like therapists and other mental health professionals, are not mandated reporters in their organizations while others are. In the words of another university chaplain, "Like counseling centers, ordained chaplains, ordained ministers, ordained rabbis—anyone who meets the requirements of their faith tradition—does not have to report as a mandated reporter in the technical sense of the Title IX terms."[33]

All the chaplains I interviewed work in Boston by design. Some of them also see themselves as part of larger networks that can be mobilized nationally, as needed, to do crisis work and counseling across the country. The Red Cross and the International Fellowship of Chaplains (IFOC) are the main mobilizers. The Red Cross works mostly with healthcare and disaster chaplains who are usually also ordained clergy, while the IFOC mobilizes the individuals, mostly evangelical Christians, trained through their programs. Chaplains in Boston have been mobilized by the Red Cross for tornadoes, hurricanes, mass causality events, and other disasters across the United States. Referring to a colleague trained through the IFOC, a chaplain explained, "she's more of a national chaplain, so if something happened outside of Massachusetts and there's a need for the chaplain, she will get called in."[34]

Training for the Work

Like the paths they took to the work, the training people received for it varies. There is little agreement nationally about how chaplains should be trained, and much discussion about certification, endorsement, and credentialing—what I call supply-side issues. There is very little information about what I call the demand side—how chaplains are received by the people they serve and the most effective ways they can serve them. This leads to a gap between the demands of employers and possibly the people chaplains serve, and the ways they are trained in theological schools, clinical settings, and a range of shorter online training programs.[35]

Historically, the training chaplains received was no different from local clergy, as large numbers of them were local religious leaders.[36] Today, chaplaincy positions with the federal government require a graduate degree, work experience, and the endorsement or support of a recognized religious organization. Some have age and physical fitness requirements. Positions in the Veterans Administration require two units of clinical pastoral education (CPE), a clinical form of experiential education that teaches people the basics of spiritual care, including to be aware of their perspectives, make emotional space for those they serve, and engage across religious and other differences.[37] Chaplaincy positions in other healthcare organizations typically require one or more units of CPE, with hospitals increasingly requiring up to four units and board certification.[38]

Ninety percent of the chaplains I interviewed had master's degrees or PhDs, mostly in theology.[39] While most did not earn these degrees with chaplaincy work in mind, a few did. One who came to chaplaincy through social justice work went to seminary specifically to prepare to be a chaplain. "I joined the Unitarian Universalists," she explained, "and started doing a lot of volunteer work, including pastoral care at a hospital. They have a really good training program. And one time I came from this amazing visit with somebody, and I said to the chaplain, 'Is there a place that you can learn more about this, that you could study this kind of stuff?' She sent me to her mentor . . . and there I was going to seminary."[40] Another went to theological school where he tried chaplaincy internships in different settings because "as someone training in Buddhist chaplaincy, I was not out to become a pastor or parish minister."[41] In the words of an older university chaplain, "The whole reason I wanted to go to divinity school was to be a college chaplain," which was unusual at the time but she figured out a path. Nationally, about a quarter of theological schools have developed training programs geared at chaplains, mostly since the year 2000.[42]

Several of the military and National Guard chaplains I interviewed came to chaplaincy through the chaplaincy candidate program that aims to recruit and begin to train future chaplains while they are in master of divinity (MDiv) programs.[43] "The vast majority of our chaplains come through the chaplain candidate program, so we get them while they're still in seminary," a military leader explained.[44] While the programs vary by branch of the military, candidates typically continue their religious education and also take military-led courses in leadership and other topics while receiving financial support toward completing their degrees. Increasingly, the military is looking for chaplains who were trained in in-person degree programs rather than online and have gone through the holistic developmental and training experiences theological schools call formation. They are most challenged to recruit Catholic priests whose numbers are dwindling and who are the only Catholic leaders the military will recognize as chaplains. A rabbi who completed the candidate program reflected on how he learned to transition between rabbinical schools and military training. Following graduation, he worked for a congregation and in the National Guard, finding great satisfaction in moving between the spheres.

Many of those who became chaplains following a theological degree completed clinical pastoral education. There are several CPE programs in the greater Boston area, mostly at large academic medical centers. There are groupings with almost all the chaplains who work in healthcare institutions having completed CPE, often the full four units required to be board certified as a healthcare chaplain. Those who work in the Veterans Administration and National Guard usually completed the required one or two units. Few of the individuals I interviewed who work as chaplains in college or university settings, prisons, municipal settings, or community organizations had completed any CPE—likely because CPE is not required for these positions.

Some chaplains also receive sector-specific training. "To be a chaplain" in a Massachusetts fire department, a leader told me "you have to be picked by the chief and take two classes—an introduction to chaplaincy and an introduction to critical incident stress management (CISM), which is the gold standard for caring for first responders."[45] The Mass Corps of Fire Chaplains offers these courses which are the main training that local clergy—who hold the majority of these positions—receive for chaplaincy. Most chaplains working with the police or other emergency management officials also do CISM training, often alongside non-chaplains on the force. "I've taken a long list of different courses," one remembered, "all the basic stuff, all the advanced stuff, all the peer to peer, dealing with children, dealing with suicide, all of those experiences." He has used all these skills, he explained, "I became involved with a team of volunteers—police, fire, EMS, and clinicians that would go out and debrief emergency responders who had been through a very critical or bad call—loss of a child, a victim known to a responder, a fellow responder, mass causality situations—my team was involved with all the teams in the state."[46] Some made a point to say this training is inadequate: "If they [police leaders] do continual training for . . . the police officers, and for all the different units, they could put something in there for their chaplains because it benefits the law enforcement if the chaplains are better trained and better resourced."[47]

The chaplains I interviewed who do not have theological degrees mostly completed classes and certificates through the International Fellowship of Chaplains (also IFOC); what their website describes as "a Christian Chaplain Ministry that provides practical community support and spiritual counsel to emergency service workers, those in crisis, secular society and those persons in transition by meeting their needs."[48] This short-term Christian-centric training makes resources available to those who do not have the financial resources or educational credentials required to attend theological schools. LeSette Wright, an ordained minister who herself completed an MDiv, flew from Boston to North Carolina to complete her first training with the IFOC and then helped build partnerships between the IFOC and Boston-based organizations including Gordon Conwell, a local evangelical Christian seminary. "This was definitely the spirit of God saying this is a pathway that needs to be opened up so that my people can do what I'm calling them to do in the various sectors of society," she explained. Many of the people she helped train as chaplains were retired and brought rich skill sets, she argued, "to be able to walk alongside people and also just had the ministry and presence and the compassion needed to you know walk alongside others." LeSette explained, "as far as the skills necessary for chaplaincy. I don't agree that it has to come through a traditional academic pathway."[49]

Several people trained through the IFOC belonged to local African American congregations. The majority were women who felt they had something to contribute and saw in IFOC trainings a way to be credentialed and recognized in that work. In 2015, the *Boston Globe* reported on the ordination of seven members (pictured in photo 3.3) by the Greater Boston Community Chaplaincy Collaborative following a forty-seven-hour training week. "'We believe in having a preventative presence in all communities," one leader is quoted as saying. "'We're working in nursing homes, working in prisons, working in homeless shelters . . . there is no task that we consider menial."[50]

Photo 3.3 Pictured left to right: Chaplain LeSette Wright (GBCCC Founder), Chaplain Patricia Washington, Chaplain Connie Robinson, Chaplain Clementina Chéry, Chaplain George Guyon, Chaplain Catherine Miller and Chaplain Shelton Miller receive their certificates of ordination on June 21, 2015, at the Historic Tremont Temple Baptist Church in Boston. The chaplains proudly serve as disaster response/community chaplains with the Greater Boston Community Chaplaincy Collaborative and the International Fellowship of Chaplains. Photo credit: Harrison Hill/Boston Globe/Getty Images.

Regardless of how they were trained, a number of the chaplains I interviewed described being hired even though they thought they were not qualified for the position—pointing again to the flexibility of who is hired as chaplains outside of positions in the federal government. A chaplain in a Catholic care facility said she had no experience with the patient population and was hired a few years ago based on her teaching and chaplaincy experience in other settings. Another, who has worked with elderly people at her facility for more than twenty years, described writing a letter to the hiring manager (before people routinely emailed) saying that she was unqualified but asked for an interview anyway. She received the interview and, eventually, the job.

Quite a few chaplains, particularly those who work in prisons or with people from low-income neighborhoods, made strong arguments about life experience—not training—as what enables them to do their work. A chaplain who had her first child when she was sixteen, buried both of her parents when she was young, and grew up in a low-income neighborhood told me, "I literally walked into this because of my life experience . . . everything just fell into place. There are some things you can't explain—that what you got from God. . . . Education is great and that's fine, it just didn't fall in line for me to do that."[51] A chaplaincy leader at one of the main trauma centers in Boston made a similar argument when they hired a new chaplain: "The candidates we were getting . . . some of them were board certified, or they had done units of CPE somewhere, and yet I could tell they wouldn't be able to hack it here." I asked what they were missing, and she explained that "some social analysis—some ability to understand the reason that this nineteen-year-old African American who was shot and now is having trouble adjusting," as well as "some degree of racial, ethnic, gender analysis," and the life experience to put that into practice.[52]

Despite ongoing, lengthy discussion and debate among chaplaincy leaders nationally about training and certifications, only a third of the people I interviewed were certified. Twelve were certified by one of the professional organizations of healthcare chaplains that requires a graduate degree, 400 hours of CPE, the endorsement of a religious organization, and membership in a professional association. Five were recognized by the military. And three were certified through the International Fellowship of Chaplains on the basis of in-person or online classes usually lasting less than a month.[53] This variation points again to the openness of the market around who counts as a chaplain, what chaplains need to know, and who is prepared to teach it and certify chaplains as such.

It also points to the need for more attention to the demand side of chaplaincy—the experiences of people who receive services from chaplains and spiritual care providers—to truly understand the breadth of people calling themselves chaplains, what they are offering, how it is received, and how that information can inform leaders looking to continue to strengthen the profession. If less than a third of people calling themselves chaplains are certified nationally—as is the case in Boston—this information also contextualizes debates about certification by pointing to bigger picture questions about who is inside and outside of that group, why, and what the implications are for both training and care. It confirms that chaplaincy is very much what sociologists Rue Bucher and Anselm Strauss called a "profession in process," or a professional group with many segments in transition.[54]

Institutional Connections

Scholars who write about the religious ecologies of cities rarely, if ever, include chaplains, spiritual care providers, or other religious professionals (or volunteers) who work outside of religious organizations as part of that ecology.[55] You can imagine networks of spiritual care providers helping to connect an elder, for example, as they move from a hospital to a rehabilitation facility and then maybe transition to a nursing or retirement home, all the while helping them stay connected to their local congregation (if they have one). However, that is not how it works in greater Boston or other localities across the United States. Chaplains in one setting are rarely, if ever, connected to chaplains in other settings and rarely collaborate to care for particular people moving across institutions. Occasionally they refer. A military chaplain, for example, who is not authorized to conduct baptisms for children through his own religious tradition, described reaching out to the minister of a local church who assisted him. "There's local clergy that I occasionally need to reach out to," he explained, "I'll reach out and explain and the circumstances, and I've gotten support from all of these different individuals."[56]

Chaplains who also work as the leaders of local congregations tend to be connected to other clergy through their congregational work. Most of the fire and police chaplains I interviewed—as well as some of the chaplains who work with the National Guard and Veterans Administration—led local congregations alongside their chaplaincy work. A few others also do part-time work for local congregations around youth ministry or other topics. While they certainly know other chaplains that work within their settings in Boston, most of their connections are with other congregational leaders.

Few of the organizations where chaplains work are formally connected to congregations or other religious organizations in greater Boston or to other secular organizations that help the people chaplains serve but in different ways.[57] This means that chaplains who work in higher education do not know chaplains who work in healthcare and vice versa, and the networks that might provide support for people moving across organizations do not exist. The exception is some African American chaplains who gather with other African American clergy and chaplains through Black clergy networks in Boston. Rather than being connected to religious or other secular organizations institutionally, most chaplains who do not also work in local congregations are connected to religious leaders through friendships, colleagues they met in theological school or CPE, or broader interfaith or local groups of religious leaders. It is primarily these personal relationships that connect them to local religious ecologies rather than formal or informal institutional relationships between their workplaces and religious organizations, like those between the Catholic Archdiocese of Boston and some city institutions as described in the history of chaplains in Boston in chapter 2.[58]

As the people chaplains serve move across organizations, chaplains sometimes find themselves in tricky positions negotiating their different roles on the ground. A chaplain who leads a local congregation and also serves as a chaplain at a public health facility and with a local trauma team explained, "If a young person was killed in East Boston, the trauma team would be prepared to reach out to address the trauma of that." While he is a pastor to the members of his congregation who live in East Boston, he would be a chaplain to those he meets through his work with the trauma team who live in the same neighborhood.[59] A police chaplain who also leads a congregation reflected on these identity tensions saying, "Sometimes as a chaplain you have to be conscious of how you present things. You are also a local clergy and to do what you do, you have to have a relationship with the community." He went on to explain how being both a local clergy member and a chaplain requires negotiation because as soon as you seem to "sell-out" to one group or favor one identity over the other, you can no longer do your work.[60]

These tensions were particularly acute for prison chaplains who are forbidden, by policy, from keeping in touch with inmates once they are released but, in several examples, live in their neighborhoods. One told me a story of going to the grocery store and having a clerk tell her that he worked in the prison and knew her. She did not remember the individual, who said she really made a difference to him. While this exchange was in passing, another former prison chaplain leads a congregation several former inmates attend. This pastor is no longer a chaplain and questions the idea that she can ever separate her work as a chaplain from that of a local pastor. Some former inmates, she explained, "they're going to join your church, you can't tell them they can't," pointing again to role tensions.[61] Such tensions are less common for chaplains in other settings who sometimes keep in touch with people after they graduate or leave the hospital and in some cases, like in hospice, conduct memorial services for clients after they die.

People who work as chaplains in greater Boston are connected to the area's religious ecology primarily through personal rather than organizational relationships among the institutions they serve. They work for or attend local congregations. Some—especially African American clergy—gather for support and networking. And they occasionally help one another as needed around specific situations. While some institutions, most notably prisons, try to separate chaplains from local communities by prohibiting them from staying in touch with people they serve, such prohibitions are not always successful.

Conclusions

A broad range of people call themselves chaplains, spiritual care providers, or other related, evolving titles in Boston. As was the case historically, they work in healthcare organizations, including hospice, higher education, and prisons, with growing numbers working in community settings. Smaller numbers work in the military, at the Veterans Administration, in fire or police departments, at the airport, or in the port of Boston. While the interviews I conducted do not offer definitive numbers, they suggest that chaplains continue to work in a broad range of settings and include people with backgrounds and experiences as varied as that of Father Bagetta's and Perry Dougherty's, whose stories began the chapter.

While the majority of people working as chaplains have theological education—which may be unique and reflective of the broader educational demographics of Boston—just over half completed some CPE. Just over 80% are ordained, including as deacons, and just under one-third are formally certified as chaplains by a professional association of healthcare chaplains, the military, or the online International Fellowship of Chaplains. These data points illustrate the breadth of people working as chaplains, the range of places they work, how they prepare educationally for the work, and the continued presence of local congregational clergy alongside those who work only as chaplains.

Those working as chaplains have slowly become more diverse in Boston and nationally. Just under half the chaplains I interviewed in Boston were women—possibly continuing the gradual feminization described in chapter 2. The majority remained white, less than 20% were people of color, and almost none were immigrants. Nationally, almost nothing has been written about chaplains of color, a significant omission given shifts in American religious and racial demographics and the overrepresentation of people of color in some of the settings chaplains serve.[62]

In Boston, the role and influence of the Catholic Church shrunk following the sexual abuse scandals, priest shortages, and the need for the priests in the diocese to serve more as local parish priests than as chaplains. I suspect religious diversification across the city also weakened informal relationships between the Catholic Church and central Boston institutions like the police and fire departments. Nationally, the majority of chaplains likely remain Protestants, including evangelical Protestants, who tend to be overrepresented in the military, and mainline Protestants, who are overrepresented in healthcare. The number of chaplains from non-Christian backgrounds is on the rise, supported by growing numbers of educational programs, many at historically Christian theological schools.[63]

If observers step back and open their field of vision widely enough, they will see that chaplains—historically and in the present—are a part of the religious and broader institutional landscape of Boston and other cities and regions across the United States. Some, like Father Bagetta, are formally state employees, while others, like Perry Dougherty, are religious entrepreneurs paying their own salaries and occupying niches at the edges of the traditional institutional religious ecology. The majority are chaplains in healthcare, including hospice, higher education, and other mostly private organizations paid as full- or part-time employees whose connections to the religious ecology are primarily through personal rather than institutional relationships with other religious leaders. The work of chaplains has often been overlooked—perhaps only brought into the public eye with national and global challenges like the COVID-19 pandemic, mass casualty events such as wars and school shootings, and other catastrophes that raise existential questions for large numbers of the public. They are present outside of those catastrophes, however, often quietly serving the sick, the vulnerable, and people far from home. The next two chapters describe what it is that chaplains see themselves doing in their work and how they understand their central contributions.

4

Brokers With(out) Authority?

The Improvisational Work of Chaplains

It was a rainy spring morning as I sat at a Catholic spiritual retreat center outside of Boston with twenty members of the Massachusetts Corps of Fire Chaplains. While their work dates back more than one hundred years, the group was officially founded in 1999 to bring fire chaplains across the state together for community, support, and continued education. All but a few attendees were older white men, and most wore jeans and dark jackets or vests with "Fire Chaplain" or "Mass Corps of Fire Chaplains" on the back. Catholic saints and statues decorated the room, though most of the men attending were Protestant clergy who led local congregations alongside their work as fire chaplains.

The meeting opened with discussion about upcoming trainings, talk of the website, and a few people noting their need for more education about working with dogs. The convener invited me to say a bit about my earlier research on healthcare chaplains, and then I listened as the group shared with me and one another perspectives on their work. The role of fire chaplain develops organically, one chaplain explained. "In your twenty- or thirty-year career as a firefighter," he explained, "you are going to have a train wreck. You don't know when it will come, but when it does, you want—as a firefighter—to have someone with the spirituality or skill set or attributes to come to about it." This chaplain spends his time developing relationships with firefighters so when that "train wreck" comes, he is there. He talks with the men about their cars, fishing trips, really whatever they want "so you can get that thing going so that when that train wreck comes it is a wide-open door." He then shared with the group stories of some of those train wrecks.[1]

Listening to the train wreck stories—and every fire chaplain has one if not a whole handful—illustrates how these chaplains serve firefighters and victims in the midst of crises and trauma. They generally report to and take orders from the chief, who asks them to do different things by department: "He [the chief] is hoping I will keep my eye on the firefighters," one

Spiritual Care. Wendy Cadge, Oxford University Press. © Oxford University Press 2023.
DOI: 10.1093/oso/9780197647813.003.0004

chaplain explained that morning. "Firefighters are notorious for wanting to stay on the scene and in the buildings, and, I say this respectfully, there are a lot of health issues. . . . These guys don't think of their health, but when they come out huffing and puffing, the chief is expecting me to take care of them, make sure they have their oxygen on or whatever." This chaplain also does a lot of rituals. "We are expected to be there to serve the men. I have done probably a dozen or more weddings. A lot of these guys don't go to their local priest or parish to do that. They want to be married by the chaplain, keep it in the family so to speak. And funerals." Another chaplain reflected, "We have to be diverse in what we do. . . . We have that full range of anywhere from being counselors to be a presence to being safety, being rehab officers, and it is all combined in that one office called chaplain." Most fire chaplains are clergy of congregations in the towns where they work. Some come from fire families—they have or had relatives on the force. The majority are volunteers, and none are required by state or local policies.[2] A few also work as volunteer firefighters. Empathy and personal connections with firefighters are the foundations of their work.[3]

As I listened to these men talk about their work, I reflected on a conversation I had with a young Catholic woman several months earlier who is paid to work as a chaplain by a healthcare organization and also volunteers (and is passionate about her chaplaincy work) in a local prison. She started volunteering in prisons by serving communion to inmates as a Eucharistic minister when she was a graduate student. She now supervises the volunteers who organize three different communion services that take place over two hours in three different buildings in one prison. "A communion service," she explained to me "is like a Mass without the consecration so any layperson can give communion and give a communion service. We have the readings of the day, and we have a shared homily that is led by the presider, and then if there is time, we'll say the words that are similar to what is said at Mass during the consecration. If not, we just kind of go right to the Our Father communion and sign of the peace." She brings the host for communion with her as well as pretend candles (no flames are allowed in the prison), a cross, and the readings of the day in English, Spanish, and Portuguese. These services are held in common areas, the library, or the chapel depending on the prison and unit.

In addition to providing religious services for inmates, as is required by state policies on the free exercise of religion, she also engages with some individually. On a recent visit to the prison, she talked about bringing a booklet from a national prison ministry group to an inmate. "I walked down the hall to his unit," she remembered, "he was standing right there by the door." She apologized for not having been by recently, and he told her that he was getting out in ten days. "I said, well, that's awesome, can I give you a blessing? He said yes, and we're standing right there. He didn't mind. . . . I have been praying with him for months, so I just said whatever came to me in the moment. I put my hands on his shoulders and said, 'I'll be praying for you. I really wish you well. I hope I never see you here again.' "

In addition to the inmates, this woman sees herself as a chaplain to the corrections officers (CO). "They're stuck there too—if not enough people show up they can be ordered to do a double [shift] or if it is snowing. They don't really have control over their lives or their situations either." Occasionally, she reflected, a CO "will come up to you and say they'd like communion—that's really brave, I think, especially in that environment. Most COs don't like showing their human side to inmates."

She studied Christian scriptures as part of receiving a graduate degree in theology, and says her most central skill in prison chaplaincy work is listening. "I can listen to you, and I can empathize. But I don't really know what it is like, so all I can do is be there to listen. . . . It's really about accompanying people and telling them they're valuable. The main message that I tell people is . . . that they're loved and they're worth something and they're wonderful and God loves you just the way you are. That is the same everywhere, so it is just how you deliver it."[4]

* * *

The work chaplains do, like the paths that brought them to it, is varied and often improvisational. Even in settings—like the military—where chaplains are required by law or policy, they usually have some latitude in how they spend their time day to day, and many develop that latitude relationally over time. Scholars have developed various typologies to describe the work of chaplains in individual sectors, usually the military, prisons, or healthcare.[5] I analyze the work of chaplains in institutions across the city of Boston in this chapter to describe what it consists of and how it is shaped by the settings where it happens. I also consider questions of authority, asking on whose authority chaplains do their work. A minority of chaplains are required by state or federal policy. Most look to religious organizations, historical precedent, and the needs they see in the people they serve as sources of their authority and justification for their presence and work.

Chaplains are formally positioned between the religious institutions that train and credential them and the mostly secular organizations where they work.[6] This marginality, or organizational "in-between-ness," has been described as a defining and consistent characteristic of their work.[7] They also often meet people in transition—in in-between or liminal times, giving the phase another meaning. Dutch theologian Heije Faber compared chaplains to circus clowns in a 1971 volume, arguing, "He [the clown] is much more than a joker, a funny guy. He brings home to us an aspect of life which we need to make the world tolerable. He has his own wavelength, his own pattern."[8] While many chaplains do not like this metaphor—seeing their work as much more serious than that of clowns—the improvisational nature of clowning and the in-between spaces it can occupy in life's transitions reflects long-standing conversations among sociologists about the improvisational nature of acts and the ways actors negotiate in situ as chaplains, marijuana users, or jazz musicians in Howard Becker's classic works on the subject.[9]

Regardless of the setting where they work, relationships are at the center of the work chaplains do. They improvise in all the institutions where they work, though there is less room for improvisation in highly structured settings like prisons and the military.[10] Most all develop a grab bag of strategies they use as the basis of their improvisation and as ways to develop relationships and support people in their settings. Chaplains who are full-time paid staff—mostly in healthcare and the military—are more deeply embedded in their workplaces and have opportunities to engage more broadly and deeply in the life of the institution than others. I develop a continuum of institutional embeddedness in this chapter to delineate the range of ways chaplains are connected to the institutions where they work and to show how those settings shape the work. Chaplains who are more institutionally embedded do a broader range of tasks with a wider range of people—be they hospital or university staff, prison guards, members of the military, patients, victims of violence or students—than those who are more peripheral. They are more integrated and fully a part of the institutions where they work. Healthcare chaplains tend to be the most embedded—they engage in the broadest range of tasks with and for the institutions with others in the broadest range of roles. Chaplains in higher education, municipal, and prison settings are less embedded.

The chaplains I interviewed describe their work in four general categories: rituals and ceremonies, individual support, mediating and bridging community, and being present. Those who are the least embedded, meaning they do the most limited range of work in their settings, primarily do rituals and ceremonies. Those who are more embedded also provide counseling and mediate or bridge communities. They all speak about being present. This continuum of embeddedness only moves in one direction, with chaplains who are more embedded almost always also doing the work of those who are less embedded. Organizational structures and culture, more than personal factors, inform where chaplains fall alongside this continuum.

The Work

Rituals and Ceremonies

Almost all the chaplains I met engage, at least occasionally, in rituals and ceremonies. Some of these ceremonies are regular and predictable like commissioning police officers, holding communion and other religious services in prisons, participating in annual memorial services, leading opening and closing prayers at certain meetings, leading regularly weekly worship services, and being asked (at least occasionally) to marry staff members.[11] A military chaplain explained: "I do weddings, I've done burials, I haven't done a baptism yet."[12]

Many of these ceremonies have patriotic or civil religious themes.[13] They link beliefs in God and the nation and reinforce patriotism and nationalism. This was particularly evident in *Boston Globe* articles describing the work of chaplains after World War II.[14] In the interviews I conducted, a municipal chaplain pulled out his official job description as we spoke to show me that among other things, he is to "represent the department at various gatherings and events in the community."[15] A police chaplain was present at the funeral of a state trooper killed in the line of duty where hundreds of police officers stood in formation outside the church and at graveside.[16] Some local congregations in towns outside Boston hold services to honor first responders.[17]

Other rituals are more spontaneous and require chaplains to improvise. One chaplain described his training in a hospital, telling a story of being asked to engage in a prayer ritual with a patient and family. The family called him Father—assuming he was a Catholic priest—and asked him to pray with them. He clarified that he was not Catholic, yet the family asked him to pray anyway: "At that moment, all they [the family] want is to get a message to the big man [God]. Just come on in here and pray for my son."[18]

In some settings—most notably prisons—rituals include chaplains making sure inmates can freely practice their religions. Chaplains who work in prisons spoke of the steps they go through each week to make sure all the inmates know about weekly services, rituals, and ceremonies and have the opportunity to participate.[19] Part of inviting inmates to services is making sure their religious and spiritual affiliations are appropriately registered with the facility and working through changes in affiliation. "The responsibilities of the chaplains inside of the jail," a prison chaplain explained, "is making sure when a person first comes in, that they are able to get whatever they need to practice their religion." The second step is making sure they have the appropriate diet—which, he explained—prisoners often try to change as part of accessing better food. "We had a lot of Catholics that came out to be Muslims because the Muslim meal is better. . . . My job is to go in there and kind of explain the situation." He tries to encourage those looking for better food to request a vegetarian meal unless they are actually converting to Islam. Making sure inmates are invited to the appropriate services is a key piece of this work.[20] Prison chaplains also sometimes provide ritual support to corrections officers. "I've served communion to them," another prison chaplain told me, "I've buried some of them, buried some of their family members."[21]

Individual Support

In addition to rituals and ceremonies, many chaplains provide one-on-one support to the people they work alongside. Most spend most of their time in this relational support work. This includes healthcare and military chaplains as well as—to a lesser degree—chaplains in colleges and universities, municipal contexts, and prisons where they get to know students, soldiers, and inmates. These engagements take different shapes depending on whether they take place inside or outside of emergency contexts.

Chaplains called to emergency situations engage with the people they find there in multiple ways. A chaplain in a children's hospital, who is frequently called to be with people in crisis, explains, "I bring to those situations a non-anxious presence, some calm, an agility of perspective, some deep respect, and also a new person to carry the load for a few minutes."

She sometimes finds that distraction is a helpful spiritual intervention—not small talk about sports but helping a parent walk out of the room for a minute and then walk back in. "Sometimes you see it differently—just change the subject a little bit, just back up. And if nothing else happens, then the parents are diverted and then come back to the situation again with fresh eyes, that's still huge."[22] A number of municipal chaplains serve on critical incident stress debriefing teams that are dispatched to care for first responders during and after crisis situations. They first, as one explained, "diffuse, debrief these emergency responders in a group. We also respond immediately to a scene if we're called to do a demobilization which is to help the responders." They later provide peer-to-peer support or one-on-one conversation, as needed, to those involved in the incident, confidentially and outside the chain of command.[23]

Outside of emergencies, chaplains describe how they offer this one-on-one support in other ways. A prison chaplain who gets to know some inmates spoke of how he sits with them and just listens. "I'm just listening, hearing their struggle, what they're going through . . . giving them that space and some tools in order to process and go through whatever they are dealing with right now." He tries to help people use their spirituality to stay strong, "Here are some tools to kind of exercise your spirituality while you're in here—put that spiritual force to keep focused until that day comes. And everybody has a wrap day. . . . Let's just thank God that you're not going to be in here forever."[24] This work differs from what social workers or case workers do, he says, in the ability to really help people through these processes. Another prison chaplain agreed saying, "I think training as a chaplain is a lot in how to keep your mouth shut and how to let people go through their process."[25] Several healthcare chaplains that work in retirement and nursing contexts also described this listening as at the core of their work. In the words of a military chaplain, "it's just to really be that astute listener."[26]

Some of the time chaplains spend is with those they have just met. In other settings and contexts, they develop relationships over time. A police chaplain says he often does short debriefs with officers, which he can do because he knows them and their situations. "Police officers deal with situations that often end up requiring some kind of mental cleansing—we call it a debrief. As a chaplain and police officer you are able to look at and understand their perspective and what they are dealing with better."[27] Military chaplains similarly talk about people coming to see them when they need support because they already know them. "I do the bulk of my counseling with soldiers who hold on to their stress and then come to me afterwards."[28] Another full-time military chaplain often has people stop by his office on their way in to work in the morning, "They say do you have a minute . . . I have a problem, had a fight with my spouse, kids are making bad decisions. And you help them reframe the problem so they can go to work, and they're still thinking about it but it's not preoccupying them. It helps."[29]

In some of these interactions, chaplains also bear witness. One chaplain described this by saying, "when you bear witness, you are acknowledging the truth of someone's reality, and so I feel like not just hearing but listening. When someone has shared their soul, you're bearing witness. . . . People tell me their truths and being the keeper of that legacy is bearing witness."[30] Bearing witness connects to the centrality of listening in the work and to the fact that many chaplains would argue that a verbal response is not always needed. It includes bearing witness to the fact that someone who is dying has lived, to the realities of a life or a situation someone wants to share, to pain and struggle, to understandings of God, and much more. A young woman who works as a chaplain in a nursing home more explicitly connected bearing witness to the sacred or the holy saying, "I am here to witness that something holy is going on." She says she does not "have to announce it or draw attention to it but be aware of it."[31] These acts of bearing witness assure people they are not alone and name or mark gaps between how things are and how speakers think they should be.

In one-on-one interactions (and occasionally in groups), a few chaplains also teach. One who is both a religious education teacher and the chaplain in a religiously affiliated school runs three or four classes per day as well as after-school bible studies for various groups of students. His main role is as a teacher that lets him "build up a lot of rapport with students in the classroom, and then they kind of trust enough to come and share with me."[32] While some chaplains would experience a conflict of interest in these roles, this one does not. Another chaplain in a religiously affiliated healthcare center for children teaches religious education to patients whose parents have consented. A few hospice chaplains spoke about educating family members, especially around grief and anticipatory grief. One said: "A lot of what I do is educate people on some of the psychodynamics of anticipatory grief. . . . There are all kinds of emotional triggers within the person, the family member. And there are all kinds of emotional land mines in the environment."[33]

Mediating and Bridging

A smaller group of chaplains—those who are most embedded in their institutions—mediate and bridge in addition to their one-on-one work with people and their participation in rituals and ceremonies. Often this involves informally mediating and/or helping members of different teams, or from different backgrounds or communities, understand one another. A chaplain who works with institutionalized elders, for example, described helping nonresident family members and healthcare staff better communicate when there is conflict.[34] Hospice chaplains frequently spoke about supporting family members in conflicts related to the death of a loved one; "When a family member is dying," a hospice chaplain explained, "sometimes it brings out a lot of feelings . . . with family members . . . sometimes we're called in to just kind of diffuse some of that."[35] In a few healthcare organizations, chaplains are also formally a part of the ethics committees that mediate care-related conflicts for the organization.

In describing how they mediate and bridge, chaplains spoke about deep listening and code switching, or speaking in different ways to different audiences to help them understand the other's needs.[36] Often this includes advocacy. A hospital chaplain described advocating for a patient from a religious minority group who was low income and in need of care: "I basically went to my supervisors and said, 'Tell me again why we provide free care for people especially from third world countries who come here?' I explained that I thought this patient needed us." The circumstances of this religious minority community, she argued, led them to live in the United States as if in a third world country without many conveniences and resources of so-called modern life. She said, "I thought they [the hospital] should get serious and fund these families from the bucket of free care." While healthcare executives and members of this religious minority community did not have the language to communicate in this way, the chaplain brokered, aiming to help them better understand one another's situations.

Chaplains also help individuals understand, and sometimes quietly decode, institutional practices. A chaplain with the National Guard, for example, shared a story about how he was passing through an airport when some of the soldiers in his unit encouraged him to quickly come to a gate area. He found a woman and young child—"the daughter's crying, mom is freaking out, and they're looking for an army chaplain." He explains, "I went to talk to the woman, and she shared her story with me. . . . Her boyfriend served in Iraq, the father of the child, . . . he died, and when he died his mom got all the death benefits and his daughter and his girlfriend got nothing, especially since the family didn't like them to begin with." Every time she or her daughter see soldiers, it upsets them. The story continued and the chaplain was able to explain to this woman and her daughter, "the only reason you didn't get the money was because you weren't married. Because the only way we're [the military] able to give you the death benefits is if you're actually married—if you have a marriage certificate in the system." He spent time comforting this woman and trying to decode and explain the practices of the military. "It was literally our fault," he reflected, "we only put family on the insurance paperwork. And she broke down and cried and hugged me, and she told me she was bearing that burden of hurt and pain for over two years."[37]

Occasionally, chaplains are called to help quietly bridge differences and try to solve institutional problems. Police chaplains, for example, are sometimes called to be present when there are community-police disturbances or unrest. A chaplain at a local prison was called by the warden when inmates staged a protest about the food from a new vendor. He said he and the warden were impressed with the thoughtfulness that went into the protest, and when I asked if the warden just wanted the chaplain to know or wanted him to do something, he said probably both.[38]

A healthcare chaplain also described supporting protesting staff and the president over a controversial institutional decision and trying to help them understand the other's perspective.[39] In this and other conflicts, chaplains often name the central ethical dilemmas even if they are not in a position to act on them. A healthcare chaplain, in another situation, described the large amount of money spent to care for some patients with complex medical situations who are then, literally, discharged to homeless shelters. "We spend, and by we, I mean the state and the hospital when the state no longer covers it, we spend generously thousands of dollars on care for children and families that have no resources. Zero. And there are times when we have spent actually millions of dollars, and we have saved lives, and we have turned impossible situations around. And then we'll discharge that kid to a homeless shelter. Makes me crazy."[40] Chaplains are not blind to the ethical dilemmas of their work even when they are not positioned to act on them.

Being Present

As they describe rituals and ceremonies, one-on-one support, and mediating and bridging institutions, almost all chaplains speak about being present. This presence—what Winnifred Sullivan defines as a "minimalist, almost ephemeral form of spiritual care that is, at the same time, deeply rooted in religious histories and suffused with religious references for those who can read them"—is core to what chaplains see themselves most contributing as they hold physical, psychological, spiritual, and emotional spaces for people as described in more detail in chapter 5.[41] It is what Sullivan calls religion "stripped to the basics" without "code, cult, or community."[42]

Presence figures prominently in the work of military chaplains—evident in memoirs with titles like *A Table in the Presence* by Lt. Carey H. Cash, a chaplain who served with the Marines. Chaplains in universities, sports settings, and workplaces also frequently talk about being present with people and accompanying them through a range of life transitions.[43] Chaplains use the notion of presence to mean everything from physically being present with another to indicating or symbolizing divine presence to representing the multiple ways they have been part of the organizations they serve or the sacred has been connected to the lives of the individuals in their care. "As is typical of American religion," Sullivan writes, the notion of presence "both resists specific theological elaboration and is deeply rooted in specifically Christian theology of the Incarnation." She traces the linage of the concept seeing in it multiple unresolved tensions.[44]

In some cases, presence literally means showing up physically.[45] A fire department chaplain remembered showing up at his first major fire and not feeling like he was doing anything. A more senior chaplain told him that just being there with the men gives them strength and comfort, a refrain he has continued to hear over the years. "There is something that a chaplain provides that is calming," he concluded in our interview, "showing up is half the job."[46] Military chaplains also spoke about presence in a physical sense: "We talk a lot about ministry of presence. You know, they hang out with folks, they listen to them, they encourage them, they might do worship with them. . . . Since they're around the unit, they're a trusted person."[47] A municipal chaplain agreed saying,

> I say this humbly. You have to trust the comfort of the presence of the clergy. The people who are either in pain, in sickness, or are struck

Photo 4.1 Rabbi, cantor, and chaplain Oksana Chapman, dancing with a resident at Hebrew SeniorLife. Photo credit: Randall Armor.

> with grief immediately because of a death or a tragedy of a loved one. Sometimes just seeing a clergy person there in their presence, in their midst, brings some comfort. It's not a magical wand. It doesn't solve this or take away the pain. But the presence alone brings some degree of comfort.[48]

More often, presence means something in addition to being physically present. It is short-hand for helping create or support psychological, spiritual, and emotional spaces for people as they are and where they are with difficult issues. This includes chaplains in nursing and retirement facilities who work with people who have cognitive impairments. They speak of presence as making objects and rituals physically present in ways that facilitate spiritual or psychological connection. A nursing home chaplain described residents thinking they forgot how to pray or sing but then doing it when placed in the situation. "A lot of times we try to get to the spiritual through the cognitive," she explained, "and we have to bypass that. Sometimes even for people who aren't verbal just putting a physical thing that cues them back to something."[49]

Photo 4.2 Carlito Ortiz hugs Lisa Loughlin, a Common Cathedral chaplain, after she prayed with him in Back Bay Station. Photo credit: Jessica Rinaldi/ Boston Globe/Getty Images.

Improvisation

Relationships are at the center of all the work chaplains do and require improvisation. As they try to be present, both physically and emotionally, and offer rituals, individual support and brokering—doing what some call "coming alongside" or serving as a "companion profession"—they employ a handful of strategies to build and maintain the relationships central to their work.[50] While there is less room for improvisation in highly structured institutions, there are glimpses of it across settings.

Part of improvising, particularly for healthcare chaplains, involves trying to become part of patient-care teams. "When I first started in chaplaincy, part of my goal was to become a member of the team like everybody else and to just sort of blend in as much as possible," explained one healthcare chaplain. Over the years this blending in has enabled her to see many sides of complex situations and to improvise as she advocates for patients and families: "I would describe it as having the flexibility to move between classes and cultures and power levels in the institution."[51] Some hospice chaplains are particularly skilled at improvising through their work on teams. In the words of one, "I work with the team that includes a social worker, nurses, sometimes our aids, the hospice CNAs, and we all work together in this, you know. Some of these, my colleagues, I've worked with from the beginning you know, almost eight years together."[52] Another hospice chaplain spoke of working with a team of people caring for an older African American patient who had almost no family. "We became this alternative community . . . that was just extraordinary. . . .We were able to have her 102nd birthday in her bed, and we brought her hostess cupcakes . . . we made new memories."[53] They improvised.

Most chaplains improvise to connect with the people they serve. A prison chaplain started a program for inmates focused on what he called "being a man" that, in his words, "opened up the dialogue after showing different videos . . . it began to inspire men to invite other men to come because they saw the richness of the topic of discussion."[54] He was not directed to do this; it seemed the right way to connect with those he aimed to serve. A few others worked with therapy dogs, using them in their daily work to open conversations. Particularly in colleges and healthcare, chaplains say dogs "bring people to a whole different level."[55]

Others consciously code switch or talk about their work in different terms for the different people they serve.[56] A hospice chaplain explained, "Sometimes if they are people of faith, as soon as they hear 'chaplain' they're like, 'Oh absolutely chaplain. Come soon.' " For those who are not traditionally religious, she frames it more as "my piece of the pie is to care for you and your loved one spiritually, emotionally, and intellectually. . . . The intellectual peace is so wonderful for the atheist or the agnostic or for the academic." This chaplain talks explicitly about "soft pedaling" the religious aspect of the work for people for whom traditional religion brings up negative associations or is just not relevant.[57] Chaplains are generally clear that no one has to speak to them, and they try to build relationships slowly, having to improvise and accept when they are not welcome.

Sometimes improvising requires very few words. A fire chaplain described being at a house fire as the crew cleaned up and got ready to leave the scene. "And there is one man who lived there, and he is waiting," this chaplain remembered. "The Red Cross had not yet shown up. He is waiting for the Red Cross to come and suddenly everyone is gone." The chaplain asked the chief who said the Red Cross would be there and then left. "And I sat there and I thought, I can't walk away and just leave this man here by himself. So

I sat there with him for almost two hours before the Red Cross finally came. No one ever really knew I did that. And that is one of the things we do. We are silently there and do what needs to be done."[58]

Improvising also includes being intentional about developing and maintaining good relationships with gatekeepers, high-status individuals in the institution whose approval enables them to do their work. Several of the long-term prison chaplains spoke of relationships with gatekeepers as extending the ways they can work. Saying that she did not want to appear arrogant, one retired prison chaplain told me at the end of our interview that she could go anywhere in the facility she wanted, from the kitchen to the superintendent's office. None of this was permissible by policy. It was because of the relationships she developed with the staff, from the most to the least institutionally powerful.[59]

Continuum of Institutional Embeddedness

As they work and improvise in organizations, there are patterns where chaplains fall on the continuum of embeddedness. This is shaped primarily by the settings in which they work. Chaplains generally move in only one direction along the continuum, with those who only do rituals and ceremonies at one end, those who also support people individually in the middle, and those who also mediate and bridge communities at the more embedded end of the continuum. Healthcare chaplains, including those who work in hospice, tend to fall at the most embedded end of the continuum along with military chaplains. Those who work in prisons, as well as colleges and universities, are most likely to be in the middle to less embedded end. And while there are always exceptions, including some of the fire chaplains whose stories opened this chapter, municipal, some higher education, and some community chaplains are often on the less embedded end of the continuum. Much of this placement reflects structural factors; healthcare and military chaplains are more likely to be in full-time positions than those other settings. Healthcare organizations and the military also tend to be more open to chaplains doing a broader range of work, and chaplains there are likely to have more chaplaincy specific training than those in other settings. Reporting lines and policies also shape this positioning.

Community chaplains are the trickiest to place along the continuum, suggesting that the category of community chaplain may not be especially meaningful and that their work is more improvisational, newer, and perhaps more shaped by the setting in which it occurs than others. One chaplain I interviewed in this group provides occasional ritual support for municipal workers and little more. Another is deeply trusted by police officers and street workers across the city, bridging communities on what seems like a daily basis. This was particularly clear when he described working at a local festival and being asked by the police commissioner to wear a clerical collar because, in his words, "for some reason the commissioner and one of my colleagues think that preachers being out during this festival helps reduce the incidence of violence." He was called to an incident at this event and helped mediate.[60] The notion of community chaplaincy, like social movement chaplaincy, is both very old and very new. People of faith have long supported communities and movements for social change. What is new is chaplains labeling themselves when they do this work. Social movement and community chaplaincy are newer parts of chaplaincy as an institutional field.[61]

Work in the field of spiritual care and chaplaincy remains varied. There is no single situation that, if it happened simultaneously across all the settings where chaplains work in Boston, would lead them all to be called. Municipal and university chaplains are usually involved in ceremonies. Some healthcare chaplains are called in end-of-life situations, especially if there is conflict. Fire and police chaplains are usually called for fires with multiple alarms and for police-related shootings. And chaplains with hospice and the Veterans Administration are called to see new patients within a particular number of hours after their admissions. Military and prison chaplains are also death notifiers, meaning they accompany colleagues notifying loved ones of a death and let inmates know if there was a death in their immediate family. Death is the time chaplains are most frequently called, as described in chapter 6, but the ways this works and the kinds of death-related issues they are called for vary and are institutionally shaped.[62]

On Whose Authority?

In listening to chaplains talk about what they do, shadowing them through many settings, and watching them improvise, I asked in various ways about the authority on which they do this work. Chaplains tend to see "work" in places and around issues that other professionals do not. Their perspective, in other words, raises questions not about who will do particular work as scholars of the professions expect but in what counts as work and needs to be done. Rather than competing with other professionals as Andrew Abbott's approach to professional jurisdiction would suggest, chaplains tend to accompany other professionals as a companion while they articulate the authority or mandate on which they do their work and do it in the day to day. Outside of federal and healthcare contexts, much of the work chaplains do is a kind of invisible religious labor, an organizational extra that will not be done if they do not do it, though that is not always how chaplains see it.[63]

Military and prison chaplains spoke easily of state and federal requirements around free exercise that make their work vital to the institutions where they serve.[64] A chaplain with the National Guard spoke about the challenges of recruiting diverse chaplains, explaining that they are supposed to do three things: "care for the living, honor the dead, and nurture the wounded." They are also to "protect people's first amendment rights to practice their faith," which he illustrated with a story about how he ensured that a specific solider had the space and items he needed to practice his faith when deployed to Iraq.[65]

Prison chaplains are also generally aware of the county, state, and/or federal guidelines that shape their being there, as well as the kinds of confidentiality they can offer individuals. At the county level, a jail chaplain told me, "I tell everyone up front, we can talk about anything as long as you're not going to talk about murdering somebody or you're planning on harming somebody or yourself in the institution."[66] At the state prison level, a chaplain says she was told she can be subpoenaed at the state but not the county level, but, in her words, "I've been in seventeen years, and I've had some stories told to me, . . . but no I've never been subpoenaed, never been called to court."[67]

Healthcare chaplains, particularly those in hospice, are also clear that some aspects of their work that are informed by federal Medicare and Joint Commission guidelines which sets policies that healthcare organizations must follow to receive federal funds. "For example," one hospice chaplain explained, "with every new patient I have to make contact with the family within the first five days of admission, . . . or I would be out if compliance. . . . There are a number of other requirements that are etched in stone that we have to abide by."[68] In the words of another, "Medicare mandates that bereavement counseling be provided to any family members or loved ones who need support so I do bereavement counseling, that's my role at the hospice agency right now."[69] Another hospice chaplain explained, "we [the chaplains] talk about what their [the family's] bereavement risk is. And we have a certain procedure that we do for low, a certain procedure that we do for moderate, and a certain procedure that we do for high. It is all written . . . the Joint Commission reviewed it."[70] Some chaplains in hospitals also mentioned the Joint Commission's policies about spiritual care that set guidelines for institutions receiving federal funds. While these policies do not require chaplains (but some chaplains think they do), they do require healthcare organizations to address patients' spiritual needs.[71] In the words of one chaplain, "We will hear the Joint Commission is in and they evaluate hospitals on safety, surgical success rates, patient infection rates, everything, and so chaplaincy—spiritual support—is something the Joint Commission wants hospitals to have."[72]

Instead of state and federal policies, chaplains in settings outside of the military, prisons, and some healthcare organizations look to religious organizations, historical precedents, and the needs of the institutions where they work to justify their presence and work. Catholic chaplains in Boston (and Episcopalians to a lesser degree) who have been placed in positions by the archdiocese understand their mandate is from the Church. An individual who supports Catholic chaplains for the archdiocese explained the geography of the diocese; the responsibility the Church feels to have chaplains in hospitals, prisons, and some universities; and how placements are made and support is offered to chaplains. "There are seventy-two hospitals" in the archdiocese, he explained, and they place and pay chaplains directly in about a third of them: "In another third of hospitals they [the hospitals] hired their own chaplains, but those chaplains need to have faculties from us. This means they need permission from the archdiocese to practice. To get around this, some of these facilities call the chaplains interfaith chaplains. You can't be a priest though without faculties from the archdiocese." The final third of hospitals are covered by local priests in the mostly small towns where they are located. The archdiocese has also placed Catholic chaplains in all but two of the twenty-two prisons in the archdiocese—many of these chaplains are deacons, a status historically understood by Catholics to be dedicated to practical service. Like in hospitals, he explained, "these chaplains are hired by the state or county and need either endorsement or faculties to practice there."[73]

Many chaplains I interviewed looked to historical precedent to explain the authority or basis on which they do their work, mostly noting that chaplains have always been in the settings where they work. These explanations often include discussion of how the number or ways chaplains have been supported changed over time. A retired Protestant minister, who works part-time as a chaplain in a healthcare facility for people with a chronic condition, said there were always volunteer chaplains and that he is the first paid chaplain working alongside some long-time volunteers. He explained, "There are several former nuns who are in retirement or semi-retirement . . . several of them volunteer for several hours a week . . . I'm the paid chaplain and technically they report to me. I don't really do it that way though."[74] Similar stories emerged at some colleges and universities. One university chaplain recounted the history of her institution, saying that chaplains were sent by a local charity from the 1960s to the early 2000s. "When the charity had to dissolve due to lack of funds" in the mid-2000s, she explained, "the university hired me, and I was the first chaplain they had ever paid."[75] Chaplaincy directors at several hospitals talked about how the archdiocese used to supply them with Catholic chaplains, but those numbers declined or became part-time following priest shortages and the priest sexual abuse scandal, leading some hospitals to hire their own non-diocesan priests or Catholic sisters.

Finally, many chaplains both in the institutions (healthcare, prisons, and universities) where they have traditionally been in greater Boston and in newer places talk about how the people and institutions they serve need their invisible work. A healthcare chaplain who was the only chaplain at the hospital when she started twenty-five years ago and expanded the department from one to seven full-time positions argued:

> If you want to provide care to staff, then you should go with the staff chaplaincy model because when you're in the trenches with doctors and nurses, working elbow to elbow, you build a family relationship, that's one way to put it, you become long-term colleagues and that both enables you to work at a higher level of trust and [develop] a higher level of competency with each year. But it also enables staff to trust you with their own personal concerns, which I think is a critically important part of institutional chaplaincy. Not only take care of the patients and the patient's family but take care of the caregiver.[76]

Other arguments based on need, particularly in institutions with religious histories, emphasized the need individuals have beyond the rituals common in religious traditions. In one elder care organization, for example, trained religious leaders provided ritual needs, but realized they were not meeting the deeper needs of the patients, so they hired a chaplain. The first chaplain, the current chaplain remembered, "really shook the place up. These services were not what the people need, not what the people want. And he [the first chaplain] did fewer groups and a lot more journeying with people and meeting them in their rooms and talking about the things that were on their minds." The current chaplain continues this work, explaining, "You know, age ninety-five, 'I have outlived everybody'. . . . You know you're going to outlive your parents, that's nature. And you outlive your siblings, your spouse, but a lot of our people have outlived their children and that, it's excruciating, and they have religious questions, like 'Did I do something wrong?'" These are the questions this chaplain engages with people around: "we're not activities people. . . . Eighty percent of my job is ministering to people, pastoral care."[77]

Arguments about personal needs were present in other settings. Several fire and disaster chaplains described their importance and authority as stemming from the support they offer around PTSD and morale. In the words of one, "They [the chiefs] themselves, personally have either benefited from it or they've seen how—you know, we're like a morale officer. So when things are getting rough, we get in there and we try to help these guys and gals get their spirits back up again."[78] At a local health center, it was social workers who saw what a visiting minister provided and invited him to become more involved as a chaplain. He explained:

> Some years ago they wanted to start doing memorial services for the participants and the staff when they would have people who died, to just have a way to as a community allow people to deal with that and address that. They asked me to start doing memorial services as a local clergy person, and I started doing those gladly. Then they recognized that there were some participants in the program who would come in who had a real spiritual depth and history and may want and need kind of a pastoral visit. I started doing work, if social workers saw somebody, or recognized somebody, or there was a need, they would refer them to me, and I would start doing those visits.

Eventually these visits evolved into a part-time chaplaincy position. In the words of this chaplain, "I'm not doing anything different than what I was doing before, just having that language . . . puts it on a place where people are more comfortable" and grows out of their needs.[79]

Some arguments were framed in terms of institutional needs. We enable "the institution," a chaplain in higher education explained, "to have more of a warmer side, a space for spirituality to be recognized."[80] At another university, the students wanted a chaplain: "They wanted something for spiritual life" as connected to a range of new institutional multicultural and diversity initiatives the current chaplain explained.[81] And at a healthcare center, chaplains saw the needs not just of patients but also of families and staff when someone is dying, so they created a comfort cart with hand-knit shawls, cookies, muffins, chocolates, a notebook and pen, lip balm, and other things they keep stocked and available when needed. Military chaplains have the strongest institutional focus historically, arguing that they were force multipliers for the units they serve.[82]

In some organizations, chaplains see the need for their work to have arisen organically, while in others—often those where community chaplains are working—they are clearer about the relationship building they did to facilitate access to the people they serve. Following the Boston Marathon bombing, for example, one of the community chaplains who served stayed in touch with staff at the Boston Public Health Commission to advocate for the continuing work of chaplains: "What I found . . . which I'm hoping will change, is that normally after critical incidents people want mental health clinicians. They don't necessarily ask for chaplains. I'm hoping that attitude will change, and we'll see more of a norm towards asking for the clinicians and the chaplains."[83] She continued to work with the Commission, dispatching chaplains when spiritual support was needed after murders in the community. Another community chaplain actively worked with the police to find ways to collaborate. Some of those who work with people who are unhoused actively sought out ways to partner with existing organizations and be invited in to do the work.

Missing from how chaplains explain the authority on which they do their work is evidence and clear organizational and financial models for the work. These silences lead their arguments to, at times, become disconnected to how the organizations or people they serve experience them. Outcome-based studies in healthcare have begun to connect the work of chaplains to individual outcomes like patient satisfaction, decreased anxiety, and/or better coping.[84] A growing body of research documents these connections at the individual level, but the organizational or business models that best facilitate them and support the work of chaplains remain to be articulated.

Demand-side approaches that consider the work of chaplains from the perspectives of users and their institutions must come next and then be used to train and inform not only the work chaplains do but also how they articulate the authority on which they do it.[85]

Healthcare chaplains, who were among the most organizationally embedded chaplains I interviewed, looked to Medicare and Joint Commission policies, historical precedents, and the needs of their institutions when describing the authority on which they do their work. In a pilot study of healthcare executives in three similarly sized cities across the United States before the COVID-19 pandemic, however, executives emphasized the work chaplains do with staff in tragic situations and during organizational change as central to their value.[86] These are the demand-side arguments of institutional leaders that are absent from how the chaplains I interviewed saw the authority or explanation for their work. In higher education, chaplains similarly make a range of arguments about their value but have little to no empirical evidence to illustrate the impact they have on students or other members of campus communities, as well as information about how other staff who serve students see their unique contributions.[87] It is this kind of evidence—and the broader organizational perspectives it represents—that the chaplains I interviewed mostly lacked, even those most embedded in their settings.

Conclusions

No matter where they work and what that work consists of, the chaplains I met in Boston see relationships at the center. "The heart of a chaplain," a prison chaplain told me, "is to really have a heart for the people."[88] That work includes ceremonies and rituals, individual support, and in some cases mediating and bridging communities, which I describe along a continuum of institutional embeddedness. While in some settings, like prisons and the military, the role is more defined and space more regulated, chaplains improvise in all the settings where they work as they build and maintain relationships. How they enter rooms, who they bring with them (like therapy dogs), how they introduce themselves and speak of their work, or how they try to become a part of teams are all part of the improvisational strategies central to doing this work.

This chapter charted patterns regarding where along the continuum chaplains fall, which is shaped largely by the structural settings in which they work. Healthcare and military chaplains tend to fall at the most embedded end of the continuum. Those who work in prisons and college and universities are most likely to be in the middle. And while there are always exceptions, municipal, some higher education, and some community chaplains are often on the less embedded end of the continuum. Structural factors, including whether they work full- or part-time and whether they are paid or volunteer, strongly shape where they fall on the continuum. Those who are physically present more typically have opportunities to move along the continuum and do more mediating or bridging communities than others. Chaplains articulate the authority on which they do their work in terms of policies, historical precentdent, and need. They do not refer to organizational or financial models for the work or other forms of evidence, and their arguments sometimes become insular. Outside of federal and healthcare contexts, chaplains tend to see "work" in places and around issues that other professionals do not.

I reflected on the invisibility of this work as the time I spent with fire chaplains at their retreat center ended. At the bottom of my notebook, I scribbled a final note about a chaplain who meets with all new recruits to the fire department. Most of them are not interested in talking. Just recently, though, someone he met year ago when the person was new to the department went to see him with a problem. Much of what fire chaplains do is build relationships and wait until they are needed: "They [the firefighters] are brothers. . . . The kitchen table [in the fire house] is sacred, and that is where people come together. . . . There isn't a guideline . . . they call you when they need you."[89] What chaplains see as the value they add when that call comes is the focus of the next chapter.

5
The Value Added of Holding the Space

> So a chaplain, for me, is holding that space—whether it's in the hospital, the nursing home, the prison, or even with—especially in—the community itself, which is so diverse. They're gonna gather to whoever has that collar around their neck. That's where they're [people] going to and God too, because I just wanna know why this is happening, what else it's gonna take till He's [God's] here, and how can I get through this at that moment.
>
> —Darnell, Community Chaplain, Boston[1]

Nancy, the director of spiritual care at one of the large academic medical centers in Boston, believes "very strongly that there is a tenderness and a kind of noticing that chaplains do that can make a world of difference for a patient moving through the chaotic and fast-paced medical center . . . that stillness and presence of mind and soul is really . . . important in this setting." She continued telling me, "These are liminal moments for patients who are facing a crisis of some sort and family members and having a person—and if it's me, having the opportunity to be the person—who creates a bit of a holding space and can validate what a person is feeling and give them some sense of hope or stability in the midst of chaotic times . . . that is an extremely valuable contribution."

Nancy explained that there is no one way to do this work. "Part of the assessment that you have to do in like thirty seconds is to figure out what kind of presence you can bring or be. . . . Whether this person needs a lot of medical information . . . or this person can't handle much information right now and needs to be kind of held on an emotional level. . . . I have to figure that out really quickly and try to embody whatever is needed . . . and that crosses races and classes." Nancy concluded by reflecting on studies that describe the effects that so-called good deaths and bad deaths have on family members: "if someone has a 'good death,' that is a gift that stays with family members."[2]

Spiritual Care. Wendy Cadge, Oxford University Press. © Oxford University Press 2023.
DOI: 10.1093/oso/9780197647813.003.0005

I thought about Nancy's emphasis on holding space and on liminal moments several months later when I spoke with an administrator at an institution of higher education in the city. This organization was on a list of accredited institutes of higher education I was systematically reviewing to see which ones had chaplains or spiritual care providers. I could not find any information on the website and emailed a friend who works there. He told me that they do have a chaplain and directed me to Tom, an academic support professional for students.

The first thing Tom told me as we started to talk is that he is not doing chaplaincy work right now, except very sporadically. "You know, if I know someone who needs a favor . . . I still have connections from the old days but really quite sporadically." As his story emerged, I learned that he was ordained for twenty years, did chaplaincy work in various healthcare contexts alongside his work with congregations, and then left ordained ministry and moved into the student support work he does now. When I asked him whether chaplains are needed in higher education today, his response was quick and definitive: "Absolutely." He went on to say:

> As someone who now lives in a really secular world and works with students [mostly training to be health professionals] . . . religion is not part of my job. But those big questions are always at the core, and I think that's where chaplaincy is so important because people are asking big questions. So when the twenty-year-old ends up in a hospital bed and the doctor says, "you're going to be dead in six months and there's nothing we can do," how does that kid make sense of the world and make sense of life and the doc and the nurse and the social worker . . . the social worker might begin, but there is something about having to ask the big questions that a spiritual person, a truly spiritual person—and I don't mean ordained because that's not a marker of anything—but someone who is deeply connected to the big issues is going to be comfortable with.

While clear that he is not formally a chaplain for the university, Tom explained:

> I tend to be comfortable with things that even some of my colleagues who are lifetime nurses probably aren't comfortable with. I'm comfortable with the ambiguity of life and the big complicated and messy questions. I don't get all ruffled when a student starts to cry in my office because they just

lost their dad or because they just failed an exam and they don't know what it means. . . . I'm comfortable with ambiguity and with difficult questions and . . . good chaplaincy can do that—allow the space for asking those questions, being uncomfortable with the ambiguity and being present to suffering in a way that a lot of other people in our culture simply can't. I think it is more valued than it ever was.

I asked if he plays this role for students, wondering out loud about why my colleague sent me to him when I asked about a chaplain:

Well, I think that's the role I pay unofficially. And increasingly, the funny part of it is, that I tease my colleagues all the time because my office is quite Zen. I have my little fountain in the corner and—unbeknownst to them—I actually have this piece of cloth on the table where I do my counseling, and it is an old stole [from his time as an ordained clergy person] that I cut up. It is there for me more than anything. It looks lovely on the table. Increasingly, faculty find their way here and the door gets closed, and they vent about something or ask my advice about something. I think I have sort of become a bit of the institution's guru around all things spiritual and mindful.[3]

* * *

Chaplains—and perhaps those doing the work of chaplaincy under other professional titles—are engaged in different ways in the settings where they work. Many spend time with people at some of their most difficult moments—as they die; in the midst of traumatic and life-altering situations; and at transition points when the line between what was, what is, and what will be is, perhaps, at its thinnest.[4] While their daily work also involves emails, meetings, and other more routine bureaucratic tasks, it is the relational and transitional tasks most gravitated to when I asked them what in their work most matters to the people they serve. This is how and why they explained their work to be valuable.

I focus in this chapter on what chaplains see themselves most contributing to the organizations and individuals with whom they work—part of what Lyn Spillman and Sorcha Brophy call "cultural claims-making."[5] While previous chapters described how people become chaplains and what chaplains actually do, this one focuses on what, if anything, they bring that they think is unique to them as chaplains. Scholars and members of the public often ask about the value chaplains add as they try to understand what chaplains do, and why and how they do their work.[6] Executive leaders and others who make budgetary decisions also ask, trying to figure out what they are getting for their dollar and whether that so-called product is cost-effective.[7] Social scientists concerned with questions of professional boundaries also ask how chaplains are different from social workers or counselors like Tom, or others in adjacent professions, wondering implicitly and explicitly what difference, if any, the religious part of their training makes.[8]

I address these questions by first describing who the people are that chaplains are working with in greater Boston. Too much of the talk and study of chaplains focuses on supply—who the chaplains are, how and where they are trained, and how they come to their positions. I attempt here—albeit in a very preliminary way—to address questions of demand by describing the people with whom chaplains work. I then describe how chaplains describe the value they add, with some emphasizing their work with individuals and others with institutions. While I expected chaplains to talk with me about how they help people wrestle with existential questions of theodicy—why bad things happen and what role, if any, God plays—such talk was relatively rare.[9] More often chaplains like Nancy and chaplaincy-like people like Tom spoke about the space they help people create and hold in the midst of difficult moments rather than of content they intentionally contribute to that space. Some speak of tensions between being pastoral and prophetic; between caring and challenging individuals and institutions to more clearly orient toward their values. I conclude by considering the language chaplains use to articulate their value added, and the ways most move between more traditional religious languages and broader emotional languages as they do their work and make sense personally of it in the everyday.

Constituents

Chaplains generally work with two broad groups of people—*individual clients* (or patients or students) and the *staff or workers* of the organizations they serve. The balance between these two groups depends on the setting. Chaplains in community settings mostly work with clients, and those who work in the military or municipal settings (including fire and police) mostly work with staff. Chaplains in other settings like healthcare (including hospice and the Veterans Administration), prisons, universities, or ports and airports move between clients and staff.

The clients themselves vary widely from students to patients to prisoners to members of the public. They include people of all ages and backgrounds and trend toward those who are in some kind of transition or crisis—college and university students, those who are imprisoned, people dealing with bad health news, those recently or suddenly bereaved, seafarers far from their home countries. The people chaplains in greater Boston serve range from those who are unhoused to those who are homebound. Debra, a chaplain to the unhoused, spoke of the time between when the shelters close in the morning and the library opens: "There's time where essentially there is no place to be, but this [McDonald's] is a place that a lot of people congregate, so we go there. And we have little McDonald's cards. . . . Sometimes we just pack those with five dollars each, and we buy people a cup of coffee or something else on the dollar menu just like if you and I were going to talk and have a cup of tea or something."[10] On the other end of the spectrum are people unable to leave their homes or nursing homes who are visited by chaplains in those institutions, as well as hospice chaplains. "About sixty percent of my patients," one hospice chaplain estimated, "are in a nursing home setting." Another placed that number at 95%.

Many of those with whom chaplains work are in the midst of transition—physically or existentially. They are at the end of life. They are students in a transitional phase of life trying to discern next steps or grapple with daily challenges. Still Harbor, a community chaplaincy organization, has offered chaplaincy and spiritual accompaniment to those placed abroad through a global health fellowship: "When we are serving a global organization that has folks from all sorts of different backgrounds, the people in that organization that we're going to see—most tend to be people who are not 'home.' They are not in a place that they have yet identified as home."[11]

Most chaplains also support the staff or workers of their organizations generally and in the midst of their own personal transitions. Fire and police chaplains spoke at length about the support they provide officers. "The chief would call me," a fire chaplain explained, and say, for example, 'Just had a bad call. Firefighter Jones is very upset, can you come talk to him or maybe set up a time to have a cup of coffee with her?' That type of thing."[12] They also link firefighters to statewide peer support networks of clinicians, firefighter peers and chaplains who are available to them. Healthcare chaplains also spoke a lot about their work with staff. One does what he calls "resilience rounds" for nurses, "to give them time for their own issues and their own psychological recovery and spirituality."[13] Others spoke about being available particularly in units where there are a lot of deaths. Prison chaplains also pay careful attention to the guards: "A lot of the system is based on dehumanization so . . . the guards need support as well, and our job is to befriend them."[14]

Some chaplains note how often their supervisors are unaware of the support they provide staff. Two chaplains serving an understaffed academic medical center are regularly called when staff have serious illnesses or die: "Then we get called to provide emotional support and if it is needed, memorial services and things like that." This happened the day before we spoke: "This is the invisible part. We don't chart that. That's not recorded anywhere, . . . but when we say we need another chaplain, the administration pushes back at us and says, 'Why are you so busy?' and I said, 'Well, I'm not just seeing patients and families. I'm also seeing staff.' " One administrator told the chaplains that staff should go to employee assistance. "They're not going to go," the chaplain told me. "They will stop us in the stairwell . . . and say, 'My son is looking for a job, can you say a prayer?' " Interestingly, the hospital recently hired someone in human relations to organize wellness programs for staff and, the chaplains laughed, this person called them last week and asked if she could put their names on a list of emergency contacts for staff. They explained, "So here is a person whose been hired by HR to provide support, and yet we're the ones most likely to be called at eleven p.m., two a.m., three a.m. by a resident who is frantic because they've been working for eighty-five hours this week, and they're ready to jump off a bridge or something. . . . I mean I'm serious, so it's like what are we supposed to say, no? I guess we could but . . ."[15] While staff support is the work of some chaplains, how much time they should devote to it, as well as how their work connects to other organizational actors responsible for supporting staff, is often an open question.[16]

Value Added

When I speak to academic audiences, I am often asked what chaplains add or contribute to their settings. While federal policies and local practices shape their work in some settings as outlined in the last chapter, I asked all the chaplains I interviewed this question directly and watched and listened carefully for answers. The healthcare chaplains I spent time with when writing *Paging God* framed their main contributions in terms of wholeness, presence, and hope.[17] I heard these themes in conversation with chaplains outside of healthcare and heard clear distinctions between what chaplains bring to individuals versus the institutions they serve and the tensions some experience between being pastoral and prophetic.

For Individuals

When chaplains speak about what they most bring to individuals, which they do regardless of the setting in which they work, it is their presence—physically, emotionally, existentially, and/or spirituality—that most emphasize first. Chaplains describe being with people, listening to them, and helping create a space or container for whatever is happening in their lives at that moment. "Being in the hospital," a hospital chaplain explained, "brings up for most patients . . . existential issues; they can really use just having someone to listen to them even if they're not going to actually solve any of them, but just to be able to say out loud this is what I'm worried about or stressed about or whatever."[18] Chaplains speak about "accompanying" people, being "spiritual companions," "accepting people where they are," and "not trying to fix or change them." It is about "how to keep your mouth shut," one chaplain explained, "and let people go through their process."[19] Many emphasize compassion and an absence of judgment as central to this work. In their talk of presence, chaplains offer emotional stability in the midst of transition as well as someone physically or emotionally there with them in silence or in touch or small offerings.

It is the job of the chaplain, many told me, to accompany and support people in their meaning-making processes while not giving them answers or meanings along the way.[20] In the words of a hospice chaplain, "I think the thing that enables somebody to get from here to here is just knowing that they're not here alone . . . helping people to come up with their own answers. Not giving them answers."[21] A pediatric chaplain similarly described her work saying, "Our job is not to try to provide our meaning, . . . it is to appreciate that they are making meaning and to be a compassion companion in that."[22] The best chaplains, a military chaplain reflected, bring perspective. Not their own, but the perspective that "we believe people have intrinsic value. . . . And I think people feel empowered when they're listened to without being judged and when they are being listened to by someone who genuinely has their best interests in mind and not necessarily the institution's or anybody else's."[23]

As they accompany and try to create and hold a space for people's own meaning making, chaplains speak of approaching people holistically. Sometimes, a military chaplain explained, that means helping people "take a step back, take a deep breath" and try to think about things "in a constructive way. . . . I like the word reframe . . . you can reframe something in a way that maybe helps people see it from another angle."[24] Sometimes it involves helping people see and claim aspects of their identities hidden in difficult situations. A pediatric chaplain says it is "reminding parents [whose children are hospitalized] you can read your child a book for bedtime . . . asking people who they are and in so doing reminding them of what their strengths are. . . . People want to be known; they completely lose their identity once they walk into this building [the hospital] and helping them get that back. I think that is something that we do."[25] For a chaplain who works with patients with some dementia, this approach had nothing to with words but with experimenting and discovering that "even though she had some dementia and forgetfulness and couldn't take care of herself, someone put a paint brush in her hands, and we have her artwork all over this building. . . . And she was like I never knew I was artistic until I was eighty-eight."[26]

In this work, many chaplains work to help people gain or regain bigger picture perspective, what one university chaplain calls their "peripheral vision." When she is called after a patient gets a new diagnosis, a healthcare chaplain explained,

> I have that conversation [with patients and family] about what matters most to you now that you know you have this illness? And how can I support what matters most to you from a nonmedical perspective? Because sometimes the things people tell me are very different from the things they would tell the person in a white lab coat. To the person in the white lab coat, they may say what matters most to me is not being in pain or remaining in my own home at the end of life. What they may tell me is my granddaughter's getting married in eight months. I want to be at that wedding. And so I work very well with my interdisciplinary team, and we really get a full picture of what really the goals of the patient are.[27]

In a different example, a police chaplain spoke about comforting police officers who take a life. He mentioned, "If you think for one minute that they are OK, they are not." He often reads a passage from the New Testament letter by Paul to the Romans saying, "Good police officers get comfort from that." I ask what they hear, and he responded, "Some hear you are forgiven even though they haven't done anything wrong. It is OK that you took a life. Not good but OK. And that is why they are struggling. Then they don't have those nightmares and wake up in cold sweats and such."[28] Moral injuries or wounds of conscience that result from people engaging in or witnessing acts that go against their values and conscience require more than just chaplaincy care and a bigger picture perspective, and chaplains are often part of teams that support people struggling with them.[29]

It is by seeing many aspects of a situation that chaplains are sometimes able to understand the whole and be a companion to those involved. A pediatric chaplain shared her experience supporting the mother of an ill child who was also a physician, as well as the nurses caring for the child. "There are very few people in the healthcare setting," the chaplain began, "who have time to sit down and listen to how illness and hospitalization is affecting the patient and family." This chaplain was there—she was physically present—and got to know the mother who was grappling first with not realizing her child had this (rare) medical condition and second with guilt. When speaking with the mother, the chaplain recalls her saying, " 'I can't forgive myself for not having seen it, and I can't forgive myself for giving my child the genetic cause of this life-limiting illness.' " These are not the kinds of questions, the chaplain reflected, "that social workers can deal with, and when the nurses turn to me and say, 'Oh my God, I think God blinked for a minute and this terrible thing happened and this healthy boy was discovered to have this condition.' " This child had multiple surgeries that resulted in complications. "It breaks my heart every time I go into this room," the chaplain told me. "I love these parents. I love this patient, and everything went right except that there were these complications afterwards that nobody could have foreseen. . . . And so you have a nurse having a crisis of faith, or you could use the secular language—a crisis of how the world works, a crisis of justice." The chaplain did her best to support this child's parents and nurses through an extremely difficult situation by being present and seeing the situation as a whole.[30]

Chaplains use the trope of presence or accompaniment to distinguish their work from that of colleagues, which they frame as more outcome or results driven. Some are comfortable with this amorphous frame and resist efforts to evaluate their impact, while a growing number challenge it and advocate outcomes-oriented work.[31] A hospice chaplain, for example, explained how the "social worker has to deal with the fact that . . . your son hasn't signed a DNR and he needs to sign a DNR and there are expectations along the road," but the chaplain does not. The chaplain went on to say, "With patients and families, I can take them where they're at and help them figure out where they want to go and maybe nudge them along the way, but I don't have this set of apps for them."[32] Social workers triage, gather resources, and help solve problems. "Other disciplines have to ask a lot of questions," the director of chaplaincy at a hospice explained. She recalls them asking, "'Where is your pain? Do you move your bowels? Are you sleeping?' And the social workers . . . they have to ask things like family makeup and drug and alcohol abuse and safety and stuff like that. We don't have to ask anything, which means that people can talk about whatever they feel like talking about. So if they're not religious or they don't have that framework, they will still talk about whatever it is that they need and that is their spirituality." The chaplain, she continued, "is a witness and a companion to that storytelling."[33] Chaplains describe themselves meeting people as they are, on their own terms, as a human presence absent an agenda. Some chaplains also distinguish themselves from therapists, making clear that they refer to therapists and can support people along the way, but they are not there to diagnosis or treat.

A number of chaplains—particularly those who came to chaplaincy out of personal commitments to social justice and social change—further emphasize that a central contribution of chaplains is their ability to see and support people that current institutional systems overlook, dehumanize, or judge. "We affirm the inherent worth and dignity of the people we know," a prison chaplain explained, "who we encounter because they go through the day time and time again being unseen or unrecognized. Being called a last name or even a booking number or a nickname. . . . We create safe spaces for people to feel free, safe, and loved. And that is antithetical to what is the normal environment in the jail."[34] A chaplain who works with the homeless repeated this sentiment, pointing out how the people with whom she works are "often ignored by the systems and people are disempowered. Often, they're told, 'Just wait. I don't have time for you right now' . . . so to be able to have someone listen to you and not tell you what to do but just listen to your pain even if it can't be fixed is huge." It is this listening, this chaplain believes, that can help her clients find the "resilience, the courage, the strength to go on even when the system keeps putting obstacles everywhere for them or they themselves fail with meeting their goals."[35] Calling the people he serves at a large safety net hospital "casualties of war" battling systematic inequality, racism, and the challenges of immigration, one chaplain says, "you know what, this person is a survivor . . . if I can just sit here and be with them, that is what I will do."[36]

If there is any common outcome the chaplains I spent time with aim toward it is hope. Both the prisoners and the guards, a former prison chaplain argued, "need that hope and encouragement. They're not gonna get because it's a very negative place."[37] The chaplain who works with the unhoused described this by saying, "Part of my job is to help people to tap into that hope within themselves that is usually there. People cannot always find it or see it." I asked her how she does this and she explained, "Usually I find . . . letting people think about other times in their lives when they did have the tools they needed or when they did have hope even if they can't experience that right now. A lot of times, the hope more comes from helping them to realize the tools and resources they have right now even if they are very few."[38]

For Institutions

In addition to what they describe themselves bringing to individuals, chaplains across settings talk about how their work enlarges the capacity of the organizations they serve. By taking care of the staff, some believe, they enable the staff to do their work in safer or better ways in support of the mission of the organization. Several fire chaplains emphasized how they extend the eyes and ears of the chief by keeping an eye on victims and supporting firefighters as they fight fires. "In my situation," one explained, "what the chief has communicated to me is that he does not have the time or capacity or wherewithal to deal with the victims of the fire who have been displaced. So when I'm there that is my role . . . in addition to that he is hoping I will keep my eye on the firefighters. Firefighters are notorious for wanting to stay on the scene and in the buildings."[39] This is also the case for healthcare chaplains who spend time talking with and supporting staff. In describing the work he does with staff both one on one and in groups, a chaplain explained, "I think we are a very valuable resource for the staff and the organization of the hospital itself."[40]

Military chaplains specifically describe how their work with soldiers supports the mission of the military. "I always place the mission first," a military chaplain explained, "that's our motto." But there are times, he continued, when "we place the mission first and we negate everything else, and my job as a chaplain is to pull everyone back in and say, 'We are placing the mission first, absolutely, but we can't leave behind . . . we have to make sure we take care of them and their families. . . . How can we do this in a different sort of way?' "[41] Chaplains help ensure soldiers are taking care of themselves, that their families are cared for, and that there is a confidential space to discuss moral concerns they may have about the mission in which they are engaged. "I have to collect data that ends up getting reported to the Army," a chaplain supervisor explained, "about just how many times they [chaplains] are doing counseling interactions or worship services . . . how many times they're doing counseling related to marriage or family issues or to their career."[42]

Some chaplains also speak of their work as a kind of safety valve for organizations; they are the people who can absorb problems and complaints in ways that make it easier for people to work together. "I would say we mop up a lot of angst," a healthcare chaplain explained, "we ingest a lot of complaints that then get out of the way so that patients and families can work better with the medical teams. Like I go into a room after a family has spent thirty-six hours waiting in the emergency room. . . . I'm a very safe person to complain to . . . so even if we did nothing else, as we do plenty, being safe people whose ears can be chewed off. It's an important function."[43] Part of this is made possible by the flexibility most chaplains have in how they spend their time. Most can move through organizations and spend time where it is needed. One described her ability to float and said she "tends to stay longer with someone who is unbound . . . I think that's a huge gift for everybody. For patients and also for staff."[44] Community chaplains also see themselves building capacity, albeit less for organizations and more for the communities they serve. Some are aware of the problems their work can help smooth over, which they tend to talk about in terms of tensions between being pastoral and prophetic.

Tensions between the Pastoral and Prophetic

In this work and the unique contributions chaplains see themselves bringing, some struggle with tension between being pastoral and prophetic. They wonder when they are—and should be—caring for people and institutions versus challenging those people and organizations to act or be in different ways. It is the classic question about whether chaplains become "organizational men" or remain accountable to aims outside and sometimes at odds with those of their organizations.[45]

Some chaplains, like one who works in a large academic medical center, clearly name this tension directly by saying, "It turns out . . . the hospital's primary goal is not always the welfare of the patient. My primary goal is the welfare of the patient. The welfare of the hospital is not my primary goal."[46] A military chaplain echoed this, describing his "sense of call" as being around "advocacy for people who were disenfranchised or lacked power or voice." He says he feels this tension sometimes and is "not ashamed or afraid to really stand up for somebody. And the institution, I don't want to say is who I'm fighting against, but I understand the institution is often the problem."[47]

The strategies chaplains use to mitigate these tensions may be as varied as they are themselves. The ones they shared with me usually involved quiet organizational workarounds done with the intention of supporting the people more than the institutions they serve, even when they quietly break the rules. A recently retired prison chaplain, for example, met me with a bag of notes and gifts made for her by inmates as forms of thanks. She pulled out crosses made from candy wrappers, strings of underwear, and plastic ties. Making these things was not allowed in the prison. This chaplain said the prisoners should not have made them, and she should not have taken them home. She went on to show me poems and drawings done on bed sheets (also not allowed) that prisoners shared with her as part of the relationships she had with them. She told me her "whole ministry there" was to bring a sense to prisoners that you are not alone. And these small gifts and the relationships were a part of what she named as her central responsibility and mission: "to bring hope forward."[48]

Individual chaplains also shared stories of being prophetic with students or patients or staff by pushing back against the conclusions of those higher in the status hierarchy in their organizations and/or naming the broader institutional factors at play. A healthcare chaplain spoke of working with patients to push back on the prognoses' physicians offer that say, "there is no more hope." She explained, "As a former English teacher, I want the doctor to finish his or her sentence and say, 'There is no more hope for treatment that will cure your disease.' As a chaplain there is always hope as a spiritual value. The hope that I see is that it becomes a wonderful opportunity . . . for healing and relationship to oneself, with others, and with the divine."[49]

A number of chaplains emphasized that the relationships they have are themselves prophetic. "I feel in my work," one told me "that the pastoral is prophetic. At the end of the day, I go home knowing that I have taken a stand, a prophetic stand in some small way against the injustices that our patients suffer." She continued saying that this stand does not look like a speech or a protest, rather, in her words, "I show up and listen to our patients: the countless losses, how they world has fucked them over, why they started using alcohol/substances to survive, how they were sentenced to prison, how they were abused, why they joined a gang, as if many had a choice, et cetera, and we offer a prayer. . . . I'd like to believe that, at least for that moment, they have the feeling that the universe hasn't given up on them."[50] Some chaplains see in the relationships they build with the people they serve glimpses of prophetic, hope-filled exchanges. "We as a society are failing," a prison chaplain told me. He said, "When historians write about us fifty years from now it is going to be, 'What the hell are they doing?' " While society at large—and churches in particular—are failing around issues of justice and mass incarceration, this chaplain sees himself as prophetic as he comes into the jails and prisons to build relationships. "People aren't lining up from our churches to come into jails and prisons, so you know I feel the weight of that responsibility," and it is what makes the pastoral prophetic.[51]

Traditionally Religious and More Humanistic Approaches

In conversation about what they see themselves most bringing, chaplains use different languages, tropes, and frames. Some speak in explicit religious language, others in more emotional or humanistic frames. Most move between these languages depending on the situation and context. Among the chaplains I interviewed, those who work in prisons and community contexts were most likely to speak in religious frames (all of which were Christian) and those who worked in healthcare (including hospice) were most likely to use broader frames in discussions about their work. While talk of presence was consistent among chaplains, there is no common underlying theological or psychological frame they all share. Much about their approaches is influenced by the institutional settings where they do the work.

A prison chaplain who invited me to attend the Sunday morning service he leads in a local prison best exemplified the religious frame. I accompanied him throughout the morning and sat quietly on the edge of the nondescript room where the Protestant worship service took place complete with music, Bible readings, electric candles, and a video clip about becoming a man that was part of an education series he was using at the time. I asked him later what he feels he most brings and why it is important he is there. He answered this by saying, "I bring a sense of hope, a sense of connecting, an ability to connect with God on a personal level with Jesus Christ. And knowing Christ as your Savior, knowing Jesus as your friend." He went on to explain how he has been in the position these men are in and is open about his past. "Most of the guys that are locked up are men who have always wanted to control their own destiny . . . some of them have low self-esteem. Some of them are very fragile, like all of us are. . . . So I'll not just talk about having integrity but bringing integrity, bringing character."[52] A Catholic deacon who is a chaplain at another prison echoed this religious—Christian—frame when I asked him what he most brings. He answered with one word: Jesus. "There is a line in scripture," he went on to explain, "that salvation comes through sin. These guys can taste that through acceptance of what they did or ways to use this time to straighten themselves out. I will go into a unit with four guys sitting around a Bible working through Revelation or Paul's letter to the Thessalonians—they are doing their own Bible study."[53]

The religious frames used by prison chaplains mirror broader studies about the role of religious traditions—typically Christianity and Islam—in prisons, and the evangelism that often takes place there, perhaps as much by other inmates as by religious volunteers and chaplains.[54] "I hope as chaplains we orient their attitude toward repentance," one prison chaplain told me. "For me as a Christian they will find that piece through redemption which only comes through Jesus." Viewing the prison explicitly as a site to evangelize, this chaplain was direct: "Time to evangelize you know. We're all in the same boat. We all sin and need repentance and forgiveness. The point is that Jesus already took the slap. So I point to the crucifix and say that is the slap that you should have taken. . . . The time here can be time for us to be reconciled."[55] This emphasis on evangelism was not present among all prison chaplains I interviewed, like one who told me he thought he would have "more of an impact on people's larger spiritual formation" when he started the job. He now sees that as "more of a dessert. The main course is just trying to accompany people as they survive this experience of being in jail which is a traumatic experience."[56]

One of the police chaplains I interviewed also invoked this religious frame, seeing it as central to supporting officers who take a life. Rather than putting it on officers, this chaplain says that faith is already central to the lives of many officers and you must engage with it to support them. All officers who take a life, he told me, need comfort and support. From his perspective, "According to what we believe, and I say that [to officers], you don't look at it as murder. Faith comes up in everything. Thou shalt not kill means murder. When it is done to save another life or to save your own—that is something you have to come to terms with—but that is no murder." Sometimes in these moments, he reads a passage from the book of Romans 13 off of his phone, which he pulled out to read to me, emphasizing the points about everyone needing to submit themselves to the governing authorities and that those who rebel against those authorities rebel against God. Good police officers, he argued, get comfort from these passages. Some hear in them forgiveness, even though this chaplain argues they have not done anything wrong.[57]

At the other end of the spectrum are chaplains, mostly in healthcare settings, whose frames are centered on emotional or humanistic rather than religious language. A hospice chaplain told me that what he brings is his presence as he is with people as they struggle with questions of meaning. When patients and family members ask him "why" questions he says, "I don't have a good answer as to why, but I think the most important thing is that it isn't why I'm suffering but the fact that you are suffering, and you don't have to do it alone, and I would always point to us as a whole team." These questions are particularly acute when young people are dying and he says, "I don't have an answer. I really don't. And I think it is OK . . . not having an answer." This chaplain is explicit about not offering his own answers to existential "why" questions, which he thinks "may bring more harm than good." He told a story about a middle-aged man dying from a brain tumor whose mother, in her eighties, was in distress: "She asked, 'Why is he suffering when he is fifty-six and I'm eighty? I should be the one dying not him.'" In their time together she told the chaplain that "God has a plan, and everything happens for a reason." If that approach works for her, the chaplain told me, "that is enough."[58]

Many of the chaplains I interviewed move between religious and emotional or humanistic frames as they go through their days. Most common are chaplains who speak publicly, and with those they serve, in broader frames while explaining their own personal connection to the work in religious terms. A chaplain who works with the unhoused, for example, says what she most brings is presence while, in the same breath, saying she has to "trust in God," particularly in cases when it seems that her presence is not enough: "Sometimes that can be challenging, but that's part of chaplaincy."[59] A military chaplain echoed this public emphasis on presence and then spoke in a religious frame describing his personal motivations by saying, "Regularly, I think you are in situations where you realize that you're exactly where God wants you to be." Similarly, a hospice chaplain says what he brings is his time and connection to those he serves, which he personally roots in his view that the "eternal gospel" is based on "God's knowledge which really transcends religious boundaries."[60]

Most of the chaplains I interviewed were Christians, and their personal faith anchors how they understand their work, even as they describe it in other ways. A chaplain who serves in a nursing facility tries to "draw a map of what is meaningful" for each of the elders she engages. Personally, "as a Christian," she explained, "I would say one of the things that to me feels most important in my faith is the incarnation and just the presence of God among us and in the messy places. It is really easy to think of a place like this as not holy." She thinks her work is to help people "understand that this too is a place that is holy and the care that people are given is holy" even though she does not frame it that way in her conversations with them.[61]

A Christian hospice chaplain with a mystical bent describes what she most brings by saying, "I think I'm a channel for something mystical, supernatural, inexplicable . . . that is really hard to define and describe, and we are constantly trying to find descriptions and measurements." She does not talk to her clients this way, seeing her role as to "help people find their own groundingness" and be what she calls a "bridge or connector" back to that.[62] A Unitarian Universalist tells people she offers a "ministry of presence" that she explains privately saying, "I never feel like I'm bringing God because I know God is already there. But I'm facilitating and being . . . opening a possibility of connection both to me and to the holy and there is something that transcends."[63]

In religious, humanistic, and emotional terms, the chaplains I met do what Darnell described in the epigraph to this chapter, something he calls "holding the space." Most see themselves as holding the space for God or the holy and marking these moments as sacred or distinct from normal time. Rather than offering explanations or intentionally filling these moments, most chaplains simply hold them, allowing the people they are with to do or be or act as they need to within them. While I expected chaplains to have well developed everyday theodicies crafted through years of being with people in difficult times, such theodicies did not occur in our conversations and time together. Explanations and answers are not what chaplains see themselves most bringing. It is not the content, but the space that comes in the pauses chaplains help people take, mark, and name that most see as their central contribution. A hospice chaplain who also serves as a chaplain to first responders described it this way,

> The way I see it . . . people always will have a spiritual side. They're always gonna wonder what happens after I die: where am I going, what is this all about, why am I here? Why am I—why did I get cancer? . . . And it's like, OK, I don't have answers to all that, but I'm willing to reflect with you. Michelangelo, famous quote, when they were complimenting him about the Pietà, the sculpture, he said, "All I'm doing is freeing the sculpture from the stone." Love that quote. My feeling is, the answers we have to our questions are in us. We need someone sometimes from the outside to look in . . . and help us find them.[64]

Pauses, Not Answers or Conclusions

The chaplains I spent time with in Boston serve patients, students, prisoners, and other clients of the organizations where they work as well as the staff of those organizations. They see themselves making a difference to these individuals and their institutions not in any answers they share about life's difficult questions, but in the liminal spaces they name and help people hold. It is within these spaces that they believe people can come to their own answers, eventually. By helping name and create these spaces and being present with people in them, chaplains aid people to see things more holistically and know they are not alone in the struggle. They help people have peripheral vision and accompany them through processes. Some chaplains think this work enlarges the impact their organizations can have, while others concentrate primarily on their work with individuals, seeing it not just as relational or pastoral but also radical in the prophetic possibilities of relationships.

Most chaplains move between traditionally religious and more emotional or humanistic frames as they go through their day and as they talk about their work with various constituents. While some of the prison chaplains I interviewed speak almost exclusively in Christian terms and see evangelism as central to the work, most of the other chaplains I met describe their work in emotional or humanistic terms. As they do their work, they are able to also follow the language and frames of those with whom they are serving. While the motivations of individual chaplains are often rooted in their faith commitments (largely Christian in Boston), which they articulate as such, these are not the frames most share with their constituents. Much about these frames is also influenced by the different institutional settings where chaplains do their work.

Kathleen, a chaplaincy director at a local hospice, wrapped up our conversation telling me that rarely a day goes by when chaplains do not get asked "why me" questions. She said, "That's the most frequent question—'why me?' And 'have I been good enough to go to heaven?'" Chaplains respond to these theodicy questions, she said, "by helping people to not only identify what their own faith tradition teaches them in terms of grace or in terms of forgiveness or in terms of mercy but also what their own experiences are of giving grace and mercy." In these conversations, Kathleen said she and her colleagues try to shift the question from "why me" to "why not you." She told a story about meeting a fifteen-year-old girl with a horrible disease in a hospital during her chaplaincy training: "The next guy I went to see was in his eighties, and he was crying, and he said, 'Why me?' And I just remember looking at him and thinking—and I know I'm going to be thinking the same thing when it is my turn—but you've lived eighty-five years with nothing really bad happening to you. That's pretty good because nobody doesn't suffer."[65]

When I started this project, I expected the chaplains I met would do a lot of on-the-ground theodicy. Following the old question about whether there are atheists in foxholes, I expected to hear from chaplains about the foxholes they find themselves in regularly and to learn how they help people find and create meaning in those moments. Most chaplains, as this chapter demonstrates, think their main contribution comes from being in the foxhole with people, not from anything they say in it. So rather than seeing how chaplains work with people to create on-the-ground theodicies, the story for most is about how they work with people to create and hold the space in which they can be as they are, where they are, in the way they most need to be, often oriented toward hope. Many of these struggles take place during transitions and are around death, the only topic or experience that all the chaplains I interviewed share as part of their daily work. I consider the work all the chaplains do around death in the next chapter.

6
Brokering Deaths
Chaplains as Midwives and Escorts

"It was a Monday," Heather, a Jewish chaplain at a geriatric facility remembered. "I had Luna, my therapy dog, and I was walking the halls with her. I got called to the short-term unit. The regular chaplain was not there, and we just had a death. Three sisters of the woman who died were completely hysterical. . . . I put Luna out in the hall. I told her down and stay quiet, and I went into the room."

"'I'm sorry,'" Heather remembered saying to the three sisters, "I wasn't your sister's chaplain, and I didn't get to know her. Can you tell me about her?" The body of the women who died was still in bed with two sisters on one side and one sister on the other. "They all started talking at the same time," Heather remembered, "this was a much older sister who raised all of them. And oh, how she loved dogs." The stories poured out about how she took in stray dogs, "helped lost dogs get home."

"You can't make this up," Heather reflected. "I gave a low whistle, and Luna came patting in and sat down next to me, and they erupted. This is a sign from her, she's letting us know she is OK," the sisters exclaimed. One grabbed Luna, put her in bed with the woman, and put the woman's hand on Luna's head. She just laid there, Heather remembered, quietly offering comfort and reassurance in the midst of immediate death.

As Heather told me this story, we sat in her small office with Luna in the kennel under her desk. She spoke about the many ways she works around death and dying. The oldest of the old are cared for in the facility where she works, and a collage of photographs of residents who died covers one wall of her office. "One of the things I say at new staff orientation," Heather told me, "is in order to do our jobs well, you have to open your hearts to these people, . . . your heart will get broken, and how you deal with that informs whether or not you're going to burn out. I have staff in my office crying a lot because they lost someone that they loved; it brings up their own losses."[1]

Spiritual Care. Wendy Cadge, Oxford University Press. © Oxford University Press 2023.
DOI: 10.1093/oso/9780197647813.003.0006

Heather's office door is always unlocked for any staff member to use. "I have staff from all over the building coming in to just sit in that chair," she told me, "and look up [at the collage] and remember, 'like, oh yeah, remember when she said . . .' and I think having the knowledge that you touched someone's life makes it easier to go, and the residents know they'll be remembered, and I think that's really important."

In her work with residents nearing the end of life, Heather helps them name worries and fears if relevant and/or reflect on the lives they have lived. One woman, she remembered, "She said I'm afraid I won't be here, and we talked about the ways she actually would be here in a daughter that she was a fantastic mother to and in grandchildren that she adored." They talked about the ways "she gave her daughter and grandchildren an unbelievable legacy." Heather went to this resident's funeral, which she does not usually do, to meet and provide support for her daughter.[2]

She also helps staff say goodbye when a resident is dying: "We do plan the session so that as many staff as possible can be there, including our cleaning staff and our kitchen staff, because everybody gets connected, so everybody gets to gather around the bed and say goodbye and say in all the worlds of possibility, our paths crossed, that's a miracle and you touched my life, and sometimes staff will just stand there and cry, sometimes staff will just say goodbye, and other times we have staff kneel by the bed and say, 'I will never forget your smile, I will never forget your advice,' and that's really powerful. So I like to do that, as hard as it is. It gives me a sense of where staff are, and it gives the resident the reality that even at the end of their lives, they have touched people. They made a difference."[3]

While Heather works with elderly residents in a setting where death is rarely sudden, other chaplains in greater Boston are present when death is unexpected. Michelle, a minister and a former prison chaplain, is one of those. She buries many of the people—mostly men, mostly African American—in her neighborhood and across the city who are killed by gun violence. Remembering one of her first such funerals, more than ten years ago, she told me, "All funerals are different, but homicide funerals are much more emotional, much more painful, much more intense. You know you really have to keep things in control and show your authority when you're scared to death. . . . I had about fourteen or fifteen gangs in here [her church building] that day . . . I said, 'This is the house of God. Good morning gentlemen. I have some housekeeping rules today. . . . I need all gentlemen to take off their hats and respect the house. I need you to turn your phones on vibrate or turn them off. And I need you to keep your guns in your pocket.' "

She met one of the men who complained about having to remove his hat later in the jail where she did chaplaincy work at the time: "Three weeks later, I'm going through the new man unit. . . . He said, 'Can I speak to you?' I said, 'Yes, what's the matter?' He said, 'Remember me? I was the one who wouldn't take off my hat.' I said, 'Well you took it off now. . . . Why are you here?' He said, 'gun charges.' I can't go anywhere where those boys don't know me."

"Two weeks ago," she continued, "my car is parked on the side [of the church] and this black car pulls up. They rolled the window down and I said, 'Oh what is this?' 'Hey Sister.' I was like, 'Oh hey.' It was four guys in the car, but when they opened the window the weed was coming out the window. . . . So OK, 'what's up guys?'. . . 'We need a blessing,' and they wanted me to pray. I said, 'A blessing? You've got all that weed coming out of there what am I going to bless you for?' And they said, 'What are you doing coming out late?' So anyway, I prayed for them. I said, 'When are you coming to church?' 'I ain't promising I'm coming Sunday but I'm coming.' I said, 'OK, all right love you guys,' and they said, 'love you too.' "[4]

* * *

Death, in all its forms, and in all the relationships it touches, is a part of the work all chaplains do. While working around death is not all that chaplains do, it was the only thing—other than trying to help people see bigger perspectives—that every chaplain I interviewed spoke about and is a central part of many of their jobs. From helping people prepare to die, to being present as people die, to caring for loved ones after a death, to helping institutions manage death, chaplains are nothing if not what sociologist Karla Erickson calls "escorts" through the dying process.[5] Some scholars conceive of death work as dirty work, mostly done by low-status workers around the edges of institutions.[6] This is not how the chaplains I interviewed experience this work. As they broker and help ease tensions around death; help loved ones better understand death; and create rituals for those who are dying, their loved ones, and their institutions—these chaplains push against an American culture many see as death-phobic.[7] They act as what sociologist Stefan Timmermans calls "death brokers" who "render individual deaths culturally meaningful."[8] They are one of few groups of professionals that willingly place themselves in death's path over and over and over again. In addition to experiencing the dirty and difficult aspects of the work, they describe liminal and transitional aspects, many of which they believe to have longer term consequences.[9]

While chaplains and religious leaders have long been perceived as death experts, and even more so during the COVID-19 pandemic, this chapter shows how they do this work in the broad array of institutions in and through which people die.[10] As people are more geographically mobile and more die in institutionalized settings, chaplains may be taking on these responsibilities even more as fewer have local religious leaders to call, particularly for funerals and memorial services. Chaplains care for those who are religiously like and religiously different from them. They work in settings diverse in mission and purpose and comprised of staff and family members who are pluralistic in spirituality and religion as well as race, ethnicity, age, and other factors. The brokering and escorting work chaplains do is different from that of congregational clergy in that it often bridges many axes of difference while aiming to attend to the person who is dying and their loved ones. While some chaplains get to know those they attend in death, many more do not, adding another level of relational improvisation to these exchanges.

I describe first how chaplains engage when a death is sudden and then how they engage when a death is more expected. All of this is what sociologist Arlie Hochschild calls emotional labor.[11] I pay particular attention to how they broker death through relationships—mostly improvised ritual and reflective listening—as they attend to both individuals and to institutions. I point to commonalities and differences in how chaplains work around sudden deaths and more expected deaths and explore how that work is shaped by the institutions where they work. Reports in the media and public opinion are accurate in equating chaplains with death and dying, but they often do not go far enough in naming the breadth of work chaplains do at the end of life to broker and serve as midwives to death, as well as help create chains of memory that are part of how loved ones and institutions remember.[12] The pandemic brought this work into the public eye in hundreds of media pieces showing chaplains with victims of COVID-19, facilitating goodbyes with loved ones through Facetime and Zoom, and supporting healthcare staff steeped in death.[13] While the specifics were new with the pandemic, the underlying work, as I describe in this chapter, was not.

Always Called

The daily work of chaplains varies, as described in previous chapters, and there is no single event that leads chaplains across institutions or within similar types of institutions to always be called. Death is the closest such event, the time at which chaplains are most likely to be called or are always called in some institutions. In prisons and the military, chaplains either provide death notices or accompany those who do. In prisons, this happens when a family member of a prisoner dies. "The unfortunate part," one of the prison chaplains explained, "was delivering the death notices . . . for the chaplain to have the power to give that person the space. 'Take as much time as you need to process this,' you know? . . . Regardless of what the individual is there for, that loss superseded everything else."[14] In the words of another prison chaplain, "usually the family would call in and say, 'you know, our family member died' . . . how I dealt with it [with the person incarcerated] depended on the individual and how I knew them."[15]

In the military, chaplains accompany the officers who formally deliver the death notice. Several military chaplains referred to this as their most sacred work. "When there is a soldier who has died, whether it is combat related or non-combat . . . the Massachusetts National Guard gets called."[16] They handle the notification if the soldier was from Massachusetts or there is a notification in Massachusetts. The National Guard sometimes lets the local police department know, and then they make the visit in their dress uniforms with someone of equal or greater rank to deliver the news to the next of kin. "I'm standing quietly with that presence," a chaplain explained, "here is where I think, where it is holy ground. . . . I've seen everything from someone punch a wall to cry to give the chaplain a hug and the staff a hug. The other part I think is important for the chaplain is I'm also there for the notifier . . . especially if it is their first time doing it."[17] Another chaplain described this saying, "Our job is supposed to be the spiritual component for the family . . . and for the soldier that has to utter those words . . . I take great pride in being there for that particular solider too."[18] In the words of another, "I've gone over more than two hundred thresholds of people to tell them the news. . . . Could be war, could be suicide, could be an accident. . . . I'm proud of the army on that [how well they care for families around death]."[19]

Some municipal chaplains also do death notifications or accompany those who do. If someone dies while on a commercial flight in route to Boston's Logan airport, an airport chaplain works with the state police to notify next of kin. Similarly, if someone dies while a close loved one is on a flight coming into the airport, an airport chaplain meets the flight and notifies the loved one. Some fire and police chaplains play similar roles. An airport chaplain also works with local officials when the remains of a member of the military are returned to their family through Logan airport. More common in cities with larger military presences, the military sometimes transports dead bodies on commercial airlines. Passengers are typically told when the flight lands and are asked to remain seated while the family is brought out to the tarmac and the fire and state police do an honor guard ceremony as the body is removed from the plane.[20]

In addition to prisons and the military, chaplains are called to deaths in a few other settings. Some, not all, of the chaplains in higher education are called for student deaths. The president of one university asked to speak with the newly hired chaplain. He welcomed him, the chaplain remembered, "and also said that he would be very grateful if I could take off the president's desk the main work or at least the directing of logistical support and in-person presence for memorials as they need to happen."[21] When a student at this university died (the student was out of state at the time), the chaplain was notified almost immediately. He worked with senior leadership and colleagues in student affairs on an email and support plan that went out to the university community very soon after they received the news. In hospices and healthcare organizations, chaplains are usually not called to every death because death is so common.[22] Some do call for the death of a child. A hospice chaplain explained, "We might not even go into the home . . . it might be that the family doesn't want anyone else. But we'll be down at the corner at Dunkin Donuts waiting for the nurse so they can debrief because nobody should have to do that alone. It is just too sad."[23]

Unexpected Deaths

Chaplains who work with first responders, as well as those working in the military, ports, and community contexts, are often present or called when someone dies suddenly or unexpectedly. They improvise rituals in the moment and provide emotional and practical support, both for family members and for the caregivers afterward. A fire chaplain who also works as a firefighter in a town outside of Boston arrived at a home where a young man had committed suicide and was found by his mother. He was called as a medic and, after assessing the situation, asked the other firefighters whether he could metaphorically take off his medic hat and put on his chaplain hat. They agreed, and he remembers, "I went in and started comforting mom, and it is all about being an advocate now. . . . It is something as simple as getting mom a box of tissues, a bottle of water, asking her what she needs. Does she have family to call? What do you want me to do?" He was first "a shoulder to cry on." He then made sure she got to the hospital safely and eventually connected with a priest from her church and a funeral home.[24]

Historically comprised of many Catholics, the chaplains that support the Boston Fire Department almost always improvise a ritual and support officers and family members—from the time of the incident through the funeral—when a colleague is killed on the job. One chaplain remembered a large fire in which two firefighters were trapped inside a burning building and died:

> I was involved in the horrific fire at Kennedy and Walsh on Beacon Street back two or three years ago. At the time, we knew both of them were Catholic, so there were two Catholic chaplains that went to the scene of the fire. Those two men were trapped inside and died inside. They got one of the men out and the other chaplain went with him to the hospital. I stayed at the fire . . . eventually when it was safe enough to get the second man out, they brought him out the back of the building. . . . It was a very moving emotional time for the firefighters, for myself. . . . I remember the fire was still roaring at the top of the building, but they knew they could get in at the bottom and get him out fast enough. . . . I was right there . . . so we brought him over a fence and down onto the ground and then into the waiting ambulance, and that's when I anointed him inside the ambulance. At that time, the entire ambulance was surrounded by hundreds of firefighters. It was moving . . . they took their hats off.[25]

This ritual continued after the ambulance arrived at the hospital, where the chaplain met and stayed with the family late into the night and again the following day. Because the fire was of unknown origin and was a crime scene, there was a delay during which the family could not see the firefighter who died, making the situation more difficult. Eventually, the chaplain remembered, "his whole unit came in and surrounded us . . . and we said some more prayers with the family there, similar to what happened in the back of the ambulance." He then helped organize and lead the funeral mass: "I sat down with the family and planned the readings and music and so forth" for the funeral service to make sure "the mass is beautiful for them." Similar stories were shared by police and fire department chaplains who provided support and ritual in the moment and then officiated at the funerals of those who died in the line of duty.

In and through these rituals, chaplains offer emotional and practical support particularly for people living at a distance from loved ones and/or not closely connected to other religious leaders. A police chaplain spoke of the funerals he leads and the ways they enable him to support officers and help them to support one another: "This is one place they [police officers] see their faith and are able to see how much we have in common. . . . In grief there is real common ground."[26] A chaplain who works in an organization that serves the unhoused provided spiritual care to the staff and friends of a resident who died suddenly and supported various members of the community when another resident died of a drug overdose shortly after leaving the center. "That was really a traumatic situation and they called me," she remembered.[27] Suicides are among the most difficult unexpected deaths for chaplains: "You try to be available . . . you try to be present," one chaplain reflected—it is difficult and painful.[28]

Chaplains talk with people, hold their hands, offer them water or food, and are otherwise present alongside them. A chaplain who works with family members of trauma victims explained, "just holding people when they cry, not being afraid to touch people and be physical with them, just let them experience what they need to experience. . . . I went to a workshop once where they talked about using water . . . bringing water, it sounds like a small thing . . . water is a great thing to use to help a person calm down."[29] Municipal chaplains also sometimes provide information to families. A fire chaplain, for example, said he sometimes acts as a buffer explaining to families why the firefighters are cutting a hole in their roof in the midst of a house fire or keeping family members at a safe distance from the fire. In some settings, chaplains also provide counsel to patients and family members and/or to institutions called to make ethically complicated decisions about end-of-life issues.[30]

Expected Deaths

In their early work on death, Glaser and Strauss described the trajectories or social processes that take place in hospitals around people as they die.[31]

Chaplains work with people in various places in these trajectories when death is expected—supporting them and their loved ones in different ways at different points in the process. They are a kind of escort or midwife to these processes.[32] Chaplains are, in the words of one, typically at the bottom of the organizational food chain and have to push early to get access to people who are dying so that they can build the relationships they find most valuable. "We try to explain to them [the administrators]," a hospice chaplain explained, "that it would be much better if we could get in there early and build a relationship with them so that when there is a crisis at the end of life, if there is one, there's a relationship with the patient and the family."[33] In the words of another hospice chaplain, "as a society, we are very poor at preparing for death."[34]

Many chaplains—especially in hospice and palliative care—do life reviews with patients who are dying, helping patients and family members reflect on the life of someone nearing death in a way that many find cathartic. Sometimes this begins when the person nearing death is very much able to participate, and other times it is closer to the end and mostly engages loved ones. Hospice and palliative chaplains are eager to connect with patients and families as early as possible to build relationships of support over time that facilitate these life reviews and other kinds of engagement. While this engagement is welcomed by some families, it is feared by others. "Many times people don't want to see the chaplain until they're ready to die," a hospice chaplain explained, "they don't want to think of death. They want to think of life."[35] In a case where a hospice chaplain was welcomed, she—Susan—developed a relationship with a client who had multiple sclerosis and supported him through what she called a "slow, painful, arduous death." They spent time together talking, reflecting, and telling stories. "He gave me this enormous gift," she said, "he was basically an agnostic born a Lutheran . . . at the end of his life he spoke about the nothingness of death . . . he was very scientific . . . he was explaining to me that there was nothingness." They engaged in this idea of nothingness with Susan asking him what it was like and him eventually, in her words, "finding peace in the unknown."[36]

Chaplains argue that life reviews, and the relationships they describe developing with some clients over time, are gifts to both parties. In the words of one chaplain, "people tell their stories and share their truths at the end of life."[37] In the words of another, "I've had some really incredible conversations with people around end-of-life things that I thought it's so important that somebody like me is able to be there to have the conversations about regret and need for forgiveness. . . . Some really deep, deep things that we can open . . . there can be a place to talk about it."[38] Chaplains reflected on stories that clients and family members shared about big, meaningful moments in their lives in addition to the small everyday pleasures of life with pets, family members, and/or being outdoors.

Chaplains help people whose deaths are expected reflect on their stories, reframe hopes in ways that lead to acceptance or comfort or closure, and/or create bridges along the trajectory of dying. Sometimes these are bridges to God or the sacred. "We were a bridge," said one chaplain about a case they reflected on, "or connector back to where is God in this or notions of the holy."[39] Other times, God or notions of the sacred are not mentioned. Several hospice chaplains spoke of doing puzzles with patients, playing cards, and otherwise being with them in ways not obviously connected to anything spiritual or religious. One described a patient she played cards with saying, "She taught me her game, and sometimes we play and sometimes we don't, but that is her way of connecting."[40] Families often struggle, another hospice chaplain explained, because they want to do something at the end of life: "Their mother or father is lying in a bed, and they're unable to respond." He reminds loved ones, "all you have to do is tell them you love them. For men—I see sons in their fifties and sixties—and they're seeing their parent there and they want to do something. And I say, 'Here, take a little hand lotion, rub your mom's hand. You can play some music, tell her a story, tell her what is going on, tell her the best or worst part of your day.' To be able to give people a skill set that they can use in probably what is one of the most horrible experiences of their lives and make it meaningful."[41]

While some relationships build over time, several chaplains in hospices and healthcare organizations described types of life reviews they facilitate in single short visits. A chaplain in a healthcare organization described a family, tired after their husband/father's long illness, who she met just once after they decided to stop aggressive treatments and enter hospice. She said, "I went in to meet with them and, you know, all things were taken off—no more wires, no more tubes." She asked them about what he was like before he got sick, "And the two of them started sharing stories about this guy . . . they were laughing . . . and they painted a picture of this man that was so full of color and this wife and daughter just came alive in front of me, and it was like a little memorial service in his room. Other family members started coming in and finally a nurse came down and said you have to keep it down."[42] Such impromptu life reviews, usually very close to a patient's death, are another way chaplains act as midwives to the process.

The work chaplains do as midwives is not easy and sometimes is messy and downright painful. As they listen, assist people and their loved ones prepare for death, and help educate everyone involved, they see death in all its forms. "It's not all the Hollywood death where you're on the pillow, and you just expire in your beautiful gown," one chaplain explained, "There are fluids and aspiration pneumonia and family dysfunction and fights and scenes."[43] Family members often experience a lot of anticipatory grief as a loved one is dying and see their loved one doing things they have not done before: "For example, if she [a family member], sees her mother begin to aspirate with the labored breathing. That's going to trigger a lot of emotion within her because that's her anticipatory grief."[44] This chaplain talks with family members about these feelings, saying that much of what he does is normalize the situation and let family members know that what they are observing and feeling is normal: "Even though this is a very difficult time, we want you to know that we're here to support you every step of the way."[45] Studies of bereaved family members suggest they find this support from chaplains helpful.[46]

This is particularly the case in diverse medical settings where the grieving practices of some cultures and communities may be seen as disruptive or threatening to other patients or healthcare staff. A chaplaincy director explained, "vociferous or really demonstrative grieving is a challenge for the staff. . . . When members of a family are kind of throwing themselves on the floor, it is a lot to manage." Here and elsewhere, chaplains work with social workers to answer questions about "where can we help this family be so they can grieve. And how can we reassure the other patients and family members who maybe . . . don't know what to make of this? And how can we help the nurses who are trying to take care of their two patients in the ICU and this family keeps on making noise?"[47]

There is also a ritual dimension to the work chaplains do for some patients at the end of their lives. Some Catholic patients in Boston want to see a priest, and chaplains arrange that if they do not have a local priest. A chaplain at a local health center explained one such situation saying, "I'm not a Catholic priest. I can't do last rites. So I made some connections with the local priest. Quite frankly that took a little bit of work because local priests are just overwhelmed with what they've got to do in their parish. . . The priest did make it before the person died, and it was so important particularly for the family member that that took place. It was just very, very meaningful."[48]

Several chaplains also worked with families to plan funerals and memorials and connect them to religious leaders who can lead them as needed.

A few chaplains described rituals they have created and amended over the years for patients who are dying. Heather, whose story started this chapter, was moved by the comfort rituals seem to offer Catholics and built a ritual based on a Jewish end-of-life prayer she has engaged in with many at the end of their lives. She explained, "Basically, it has three parts. It has a part of acknowledging everything is in God's hands, and it has a part forgiving anyone who has done you wrong and asking for forgiveness . . . and the last part is about asking God to watch over your family." She improvises using it now, working with people who are dying around the parts that are most important to them: "It gives the dying person a feeling of action—they're doing something."[49]

Connecting the Living and the Dead

Once someone dies, whether suddenly or in a more expected way, chaplains work in the thin space between life and death. Like the fire chaplains described earlier, many lead funerals or memorial services. A police chaplain remembered a major incident in which officers were killed and he supported their families and offered the eulogy: "It just so happened that one of the fire persons who was killed lived right across the street from the church. His mother knew about the church, and friends, but was not a member. They asked me to do the eulogy. It was a really big event at another church, but I eulogized."[50] In another conversation, a chaplain described a hospice patient who did not have any church connections, and whose family asked the chaplain to do the service when he died, which the chaplain did. A rabbi who visits several nursing homes sometimes does funerals where she is the only person—in addition to the person who died and the funeral director—who is present. Several chaplains also spoke about leading or attending funeral services for co-workers; "this was not required," a prison chaplain said, but she felt it was important.

A number of chaplains also lead memorial and funeral services for people at the institutions where they lived or worked, an important marker of the changing relationships residents have with local religious leaders outside of these facilities. The chaplain at a residential facility that cares for people with physical disabilities said that in addition to the funerals or memorial services many families have when residents die, they have a memorial service at the facility for each person that dies where "all of the residents are invited to speak into the microphone."[51] This also happens in other social service organizations, especially when clients have strong relationships with other clients or staff. Many of these services are necessarily inter- or multifaith. As a university chaplain explained, "We'll have professors who die. We'll have students who die in car accidents and students who die from diseases. We will hold memorial services, and that's a huge interfaith center project because the person who passed away may be Roman Catholic but the attendants in the campus community will not be Roman Catholic. . . . You need to provide a memorial in a place where students grieve in a truly interfaith fashion."[52]

Many institutions also hold annual memorial services in recognition of everyone who died in the setting that year. A part-time chaplain at a community health center, for example, explained, "Some years ago they wanted to start doing memorial services for the participants and the staff when they would have people who died, to just have a way to—as a community—allow people to deal with and address that."[53] One of the hospice organizations also has an annual service: "We take part in the annual memorial service that's for all of the patients that have died and their families over the past year. They're all invited, and it is a very, very meaningful service to us."[54] The form of these services varies from more traditional, sit-down gatherings to what a chaplain with people who are unhoused explained as, "people come up to say a story about somebody at a memorial service and put a beautiful colorful stone into a glass bowl that has water in it. And we walk the labyrinth."[55] Usually these services recognize people who died in or were connected to the organization; though, at one healthcare organization, chaplains help organize services to name people who died across the country and around the world from domestic violence, AIDS, and as a result of being transgendered on awareness days of remembrance.

In addition to services, chaplains also spoke a lot about checking in with staff to acknowledge losses and emotional compartmentalization. After a week in which four residents died in three days, the chaplain at a nursing home told me, "I think the clinical staff—in order to keep doing what they do—they really compartmentalize a lot. They keep closed doors around those places. But it was good in that week to be able to find people in the hallway and just lean up against someone—be like—'how are you doing with all this?'" I asked if people talked to her, and she said yes. They would "lean against the med cart for two minutes and then say, 'This is rough, I really loved that person.'"[56]

Some chaplains, particularly those who work in hospice and palliative care, also offer bereavement care to loved ones. Some hospices have the chaplain do this, while others have a formal bereavement counselor as a separate role. "Medicare mandates that bereavement counseling be provided to any family members or loved ones who need that support," a chaplain in this role explained.[57] This typically involves one or more visits with the primary caregiver following a death and helping that person get connected to broader networks of resources. One chaplain described this by saying, "I had a bereavement visit the other day. . . . People establish this trust with you, and they're able to open their hearts . . . I think because of the spiritual component. People know that we will honor confidences."[58] Several chaplains acknowledged that this is difficult: "It is helping them through their process of grief but also helping them come to a measure of peace," especially when the relationship with the person who died was difficult.[59]

While chaplains stand in front of groups when they lead funerals and memorial services, much of the work they do around death takes place quietly and out of public view. Some of this quiet reflects the personal, often intimate, nature of the work. Other aspects of the quiet reflect broader societal silences around death and the discomfort many feel with it. In healthcare, most chaplains have the experience of a physician delivering bad news and then quickly exiting the room, leaving the chaplain to be with the patient and family in all their emotions.[60] A chaplain with the Mass Corps of Fire Chaplains had a similar experience when called to an incident where someone died: "When there is a dead body that they [the firefighters] are not going to bring back, they are done. They want out. So as soon as I get there, 'Oh chaplain, you are here, thanks so for much for coming, bye,' and they leave, and I am alone with the family." When the deputy reported over the radio that "all fire personnel have cleared the house," the chaplain thought no, "the chaplain is still with the grieving family in the house." He looked up at me as he told this story to conclude, "it is a challenge to change the culture."[61]

These silences and invisibilities around death and mourning were present in a story another chaplain shared about the relationship two elderly people developed at the nursing facility where they lived. "We live in a death-denying culture," this chaplain reflected, but at this facility "it is much closer—in the front-view window." He went on to talk about the two people who fell in love and wanted to get married, which would have put their Medicaid funds in question. Instead, the staff organized a service in the chapel to celebrate their love complete with flowers, new clothes, and all the excitement of a wedding. About a year later, one of them died. The chaplain explained, "They shared the same room. They can't share the same bed, but they were married. . . . Everyone knew they had a special relationship." The facility needed to fill the bed for financial reasons, and the chaplain was working, as he told me this story, to help the remaining spouse. He continued, "Now she is going to get a new roommate, and it isn't going to be her husband. . . . She lost her husband and her roommate. . . . We just listen and give her time."[62] He was also supporting the staff who were much more comfortable with the wedding than the memorial service and helping them name and make space for the grief of transition.

Conclusions

Death work is essential work for chaplains in Boston and nationally. Every chaplain I interviewed spoke about death and the many ways caring for the dying and their loved ones figures into their work. While there is no single time chaplains are called across all the settings where they work, someone's expected or unexpected death is when chaplains are most likely to be present. As they talk with people nearing the end of their lives, support shocked loved ones when someone has died unexpectedly, and/or deliver news of these deaths to the next of kin, chaplains are midwives to death, escorting them and those they leave behind through the process.[63]

Some of the work chaplains do around death is similar regardless of the circumstances and institutions that shape it. Chaplains are present with people dying and their loved ones; they improvise rituals in the moment and often collaborate on funerals or memorial services later. They listen reflectively, help educate loved ones about what dying looks like, and assist the institutions where people die to name and honor those deaths in annual memorial services. They regularly speak of the death-phobic or death-denying culture in which they work and try to normalize experiences of death for loved ones. In the words of one chaplain, "We just don't understand death in our culture. We don't face it. We don't discuss it . . . we don't like it. I don't know why we should, but we fear it."[64] They may be the only people in the lives of those dying and their loved ones with these orientations as people are more geographically mobile and less likely to have close connections to local religious leaders.

Some of this work varies based on situation and institution. In cases of sudden death, chaplains do more improvisation than in cases when death was expected, where they were able to get to know the person dying and/or their loved ones. When death is expected, chaplains do more educational work with loved ones and are witnesses to more of the conflicts and difficulties sometimes present as families wait for someone to die. Some institutions—most notable the military and prisons—have stronger standard practices around death, including death notifications, which more strongly shape what happens after someone dies than do other more flexible institutions.

Regardless of the situations in which death occurs, as mentioned, chaplains may be doing more of this kind of work individually with loved ones and collectively around memorial services and funerals because fewer people are affiliated with religious organizations and do not have local clergy to call for support. Like the chaplain whose story of a homicide funeral was presented in this chapter, other chaplains spoke of doing private services for people they meet in their work and/or of getting calls from funeral homes to do services for whom no one else is available. In all of this work—for people they have come to know and those they just met—chaplains are midwives or escorts to people who are dying and to their loved ones. and they help, in the moment and in what follows, to care for the living and the dead. For some people it is the spiritual or religious role of chaplains and their actual or imagined connection to God that helps them link the living and the dead. For others it is the memories that chaplains help create as midwives to the process. In all of this, chaplains work from the hope that they can facilitate so-called good deaths and in some way begin to alleviate the grief of those left behind.[65]

7

Engaging Religious and Spiritual Differences

Organizational and Individual Approaches

A municipal chaplain in Boston struggles when asked to pray at public events. "What does a true ecumenical and/or interfaith prayer sound like?" he asked me. "How do we truly consider having the interfaith language inflected and spoken and honored?" When he accepted this chaplaincy position years ago, more senior chaplains told him not to talk about Jesus. "I do talk about God—for the Christian, God and Jesus are one," he explained. He struggles each time he is asked to pray, not really knowing what to say and how to be inclusive and respectful while also authentic to his Protestant experience.[1]

These struggles are mirrored around the city—and across the country—as broader questions and tensions around religious differences are played out in debates about public prayer.[2] "I mean in the military now," a local chaplain with the Masons told me, "there's a big skirmish about how the chaplain can pray and what kinds of words they can use and stuff. . . . We [the Masons] recognize that there are people from all kinds of faiths and traditions . . . we tend to use generic kinds of God language so whoever is out there can feel comfortable."[3]

A local university chaplain previously used God language in the opening prayers at commencement, followed by words about the joyousness of the occasion and the importance of treating all people with respect and honesty. She was recently told to omit the God language. "There were so many lawsuits against colleges and universities for praise . . . in the name of God and this is not a Christian country. So the legal department, and the president and the trustees said, 'Well you can still pray, but you have to pray generically.' " This felt "kind of like a punch in the heart . . . it is very difficult . . . to use words like 'graceful,' 'appreciate' and 'come together.' I can do it but . . ."[4]

While not all chaplains pray regularly or in public, most engage daily with people from a range of spiritual and religious backgrounds, including none

Spiritual Care. Wendy Cadge, Oxford University Press. © Oxford University Press 2023.
DOI: 10.1093/oso/9780197647813.003.0007

at all. How they do this and what their formal and informal responsibilities are around spiritual and religious differences have changed over time in Boston and nationally as the people with whom they work (including other chaplains) have become more diverse along multiple axes. When pushed, all three of the chaplains quoted above want to pray and engage diverse others in thoughtful, respectful ways while simultaneously being true to who they are and what they understand their roles require.[5] How to do so, however, is far from obvious and often shifting with changing political contexts, national and local leadership, demographic changes, a lack of clear policy guidance, and other social factors.

This chapter considers how chaplains and the organizations they serve have responded to spiritual and religious diversity in and through the work of chaplains over time. I begin with three extended case studies to show how three Boston organizations—the New England Seafarer's Mission (NESM), the Boston Fire Department, and Massachusetts General Hospital—occupy three different places on an organizational typology that describes their responses to growing spiritual and religious diversity between 1965 and the present. The military and federal prisons occupy a fourth set of organizations in this typology I do not consider in this chapter.[6] One set of organizations in the typology are religious organizations that do what they today call the work of chaplaincy. Evident in the NESM—which was founded as a Protestant organization and remains as such—Protestant chaplains and largely Protestant volunteers see in their actions a way to engage as Christians with their largely non-Protestant clients. Another set of organizations are federal, state, and local municipal organizations, like the Boston Fire Department (BFD), that decide whether to have chaplains and from what religious backgrounds. Chaplains in the BFD reflected the city's historic demographics—Catholic, Protestant, then Jewish—but have not included chaplains from other traditions. And a third set of organizations are private nonprofits, like Massachusetts General Hospital (MGH), that decide whether and how to hire chaplains as they wish. MGH started with Protestant chaplains and quickly grew to include Catholics. As the staff, patients, and families became more diverse, MGH later included chaplains from a range of spiritual and religious backgrounds, marking themselves as an organization that strives to accommodate diversity in all its forms.

In a recent edited volume focused on prayer in healthcare organizations, Sheryl Reimer-Kirkham and Lori Beaman explore how generic models of spiritual care have emerged alongside historical approaches to pastoral care and more contemporary multifaith models. Generic or universal models emphasize a shared spirituality assumed common to all people. Historical pastoral care approaches privileged people from the religious tradition of the institution when it was founded (usually Christian) and also provided care to all patients. And multifaith approaches tend to have people from a range of religious backgrounds supporting those with whom they share a background. While none of these frames map exactly onto the three case studies here, the NESM is best described by the historical pastoral care approach, the BFD by the multifaith approach, and MGH by the generic or universal model. Each approach elevates the spiritual and religious experiences of some while silencing others as evident in Reimer-Kirkham and Beaman's chapter and the cases in Boston that follow here.[7]

In the second half of the chapter, I consider how individual chaplains act around spiritual and religious diversity as shaped by the organizations where they work and the history, training, and guidance of the profession. In Boston, chaplains in the military and prisons have the clearest guidance around spiritual and religious diversity. Outside of these institutions, most chaplains neutralize religious differences, code switch, and/or move between different religious and spiritual languages and registers depending on who they are engaging with and to what end.[8] They learn to do this in their training and daily work—including with chaplains who are spiritually and religiously different from them—and negotiate personal boundaries around authenticity in the process. While the majority make space for everyone they serve—even if their personal beliefs and practices challenge their own—a few do not, pointing to continued variation among chaplains as a group and the space these roles allow for individual improvisation.

Organizational Approaches

Chaplains in Boston work in organizations that are religious and secular and serve people from a broad range of backgrounds as described in chapter 2. These organizations respond to diversity—spiritual, religious, and otherwise—in multiple ways, including in who they hire as chaplains, what they call these individuals, and how they train and supervise them. I consider three organizations—one religious, one municipal, and one a private nonprofit—to show how their approaches to religious diversity among chaplains changed over time and what they suggest for who the chaplains are, how they do their work, and how they think and act around spiritual and religious differences. I offer these extended case studies to show how the city's changing demographics and broader local, national, and global forces shaped organizational responses in deeply local ways that inform the chaplains' work. These examples also reveal, again, the diversity of people who consider themselves chaplains and the assumptions about historical pastoral care, multifaith, and/or more generic or universalistic approaches to religion that underlie the work of chaplains.[9]

New England Seafarer's Mission

Founded as the Scandinavian Seamen's Mission in 1881, what is today called the New England Seafarer's Mission is a Christian organization that serves the staff of cruise vessels, container ships, and tankers from a four-story building in the cruise port terminal in South Boston. The paid staff chaplain (who is an ordained minister) and volunteers from local Protestant congregations visit seafarers, operate a MoneyGram terminal where seafarers can send paychecks home, staff a package delivery service where seafarers can pick up personal items ordered online, and run a small convenience store designed to provide seafarers with essentials and some of the comforts of home. The organization took many forms over time, responding to changes in who seafarers were, what they needed, and what the organization's leadership felt their unique call or mission was in the midst.

Several Protestant organizations ministered to seafarers in nineteenth-century Boston, evangelizing and offering social services in what they perceived to be morally corrupt and dangerous conditions.[10] They visited seafarers and operated boarding houses drawing from key tenants of the Social Gospel. The Scandinavian Seamen's Mission was founded by a Swedish immigrant specifically to serve seamen from Scandinavia in their local languages. It grew quickly while seamen from Scandinavia came through the port, though by 1924 had switched to English-language service provision to seafarers from all countries of origin. The group continued their work during and after both world wars, serving an even more diverse group of seafarers with support from volunteers from local congregations of the Evangelical Covenant Church in greater Boston.[11] Increasingly, they collaborated with other Protestant organizations to offer regular church services in the port, give seafarers religious and secular magazines and other reading materials to take on board, and host seafarers in their inns when ships were in the port overnight.[12]

The work of port chaplaincy organizations in Boston, and nationally, changed dramatically in the 1970s as containers revolutionized the shipping industry and made the entire process more efficient.[13] Such changes led to automation and declining numbers of workers onboard ships. In the same generation, the legal innovation of "flagging out" ships began, allowing owners to register ships in countries outside the company's domicile as a legal way to avoid labor and tax regulations. In Boston, this led inns to close (as overnight stays were no longer needed), and the demographics of the seafarers in the port shifted over time from Europeans to workers from the Philippines, India, China, and other parts of the Global South.[14] In Boston, chaplains at the now-renamed New England Seafarer's Mission responded by focusing more on social services and less on evangelism as currents in American religious life shifted and the people arriving in port were more often foreign born and in need of practical assistance.

In 1986, port chaplaincy organizations in Boston also responded to the decision to welcome cruise ships to the city.[15] Leaders of NESM pivoted, recognizing that the staff of cruise ships had vastly different needs than the staff of the container and cargo ships they had served historically. They set up banks of telephones, found ways to help seafarers send paychecks home and, over time, developed ways to get seafarers internet access and transportation in the port so they could connect with families and have a few hours off the ship during their stay.

Steve Cushing, ordained minister in the Evangelical Covenant Church, port chaplain, and executive director of the New England Seafarer's Mission, sees himself as continuing the historical work of this organization but in a slightly different manner. He provides services to all seafarers, in English, and focuses on acts of service rather than evangelism. With support from members of Evangelical Covenant congregations in the region, he visits with seafarers; welcomes the staff of cruise ships to their building for package delivery, MoneyGram, and other services; and supports and advocates for seafarers through personal challenges such as nonpayment for work or the death of a loved one in their home country.

While Steve Cushing wears street clothes and rarely talks about explicitly religious topics, he sees himself through his actions as "bring[ing] the church to where people are." His "witness," he says, is being present and supporting seafarers mostly from the Global South who work long hours. He sees no

Photo 7.1 Rev. Stephen Cushing, executive director and port chaplain for the New England Seafarers Mission visiting with seafarers on board a ship in the Boston Harbor. Photo credit: Stephen Cushing.

tensions or issues around questions of religious diversity in his daily work. Volunteers are not allowed to try to convince seafarers of their beliefs, and he only speaks about his own when specifically asked by a seafarer. Before he allowed me to volunteer at the center and write about it, he made this commitment clear while simultaneously telling me about two people who were Jehovah's Witnesses who had come to the center two months earlier wanting to hand out literature. He told them no.

Still Protestant, this organization transitioned from serving Scandinavians to all seafarers to seafarers mostly from the Global South because they are the people staffing ships passing through the port of Boston. They shifted from Swedish to English for the language of service provision, and from social service and evangelism to just social service provision as the people in the port had growing practical needs. The port chaplains and volunteers from local Evangelical Covenant churches that did this work responded to religious diversity by modeling through their practical actions what they believe as Christians it means to welcome the stranger among them. As a stand-alone organization, they were never paid by the port or local shipping companies for their work, so they had latitude in how to do it. This influenced how they negotiated the relationships that gave them access to the port and to seafarers over time and allowed them—as Christians—to continue to serve people from a range of backgrounds as the population of seafarers diversified over time as described by Sheryl Reimer-Kirkham and Lori Beaman in what they described as the historical approach to pastoral care.[16]

Boston Fire Department

The BFD's approach to chaplains and to religious diversity is different from that of the NESM. This is in part because it is a municipal rather than religious organization and because they have had chaplains from Catholic, Protestant, and Jewish backgrounds primarily serving people from those backgrounds, what Reimer-Kirkham and Beaman call a multifaith model. While not required to have chaplains, the fire department did. Over time and with changing demographics, these chaplains came to include Protestant and Jewish religious leaders in addition to the Catholic priests present from the early 1900s. The first mention of chaplains in the department's history is a request made in January 1902 that "the Fire Commissioner through His Honor the Mayor, be requested to take such action as may be necessary for the appointment of two chaplains, one a Catholic and the other a Protestant, whose duty it shall be to attend all fires in this city and to minister to the spiritual wants of members of the Fire Department who may meet with accident or sickness while in the discharge of their duties." The request, made by Mr. Young of Ward 16, was motivated by the fact that there were such chaplains in New York and that "at the last disaster, in Park Avenue, New York, the Chaplains of the Fire Department were of great service." He believed the people of Boston should have the same service and that chaplains should be appointed at the same rate and compensation as captains.[17]

A Leo Club (named after Pope Leo XIII) was set up in Boston in 1906—with Catholic priests and firemen as officers—to support the "spiritual welfare of the Catholic members of the [fire] department." They were allowed to swap their meal hours on Sunday so they could attend early morning Masses at St. James Church on Harrison Avenue and planned to regularly visit members who were sick.[18] Catholic priests who led local congregations served as chaplains to the BFD and did not seem to have been paid extra to do so. Fire department records suggest that the first Protestant chaplain, Howard Pomeroy, was appointed alongside Catholic chaplains in 1945, and the first Jewish chaplain, Samuel Korff, in 1950.[19] In the 1960s, the BFD included a Protestant, Catholic, and Jewish chaplain, reflecting the demographics in

Boston and nationally at the time. This pattern has continued to the present. Since the first appointment in 1906, 60% of the official chaplains have been Catholic priests ($N = 12$). Just under a third (30%) have been Protestants ($N = 6$), all appointed since 1945. Two rabbis, or 10%, were appointed since 1950.[20] There was only ever one Protestant, one Catholic, and one Jewish religious leader as a chaplain at a time. There were also often unpaid assistants to the Catholic chaplain given that the majority of firefighters have been Catholic over time.[21]

Chaplains provided individual support to fire fighters and were present at ceremonies and events across the city. They also accompanied officers to notify next of kin when firefighters died. Most held multiple responsibilities in different settings. For example, Monsignor James Keating, who was appointed as Catholic chaplain to the BFD in 1969, was also chaplain to the Newton Fire Department and director of the St. Sebastian's Country Day School when appointed.[22] Their contributions are particularly noted at the city's biggest fires: the fire in 1942 at Coconut Grove, a popular night spot in which 490 people were killed and 166 injured,[23] and the Hotel Vendome fire in 1972, in which nine firefighters died.[24] They officiated at funerals for many of these firefighters and others killed in the line of duty, and their relationships with next of kin often remained strong thereafter.[25]

Monsignor James Keating—chief chaplain from 1969 until his retirement in 1991—was particularly close to Catholic firefighters and remained close when he took on the role of chaplain, despite being paid one dollar per year following his official retirement. He described his answer to the often-asked question, "Father, what do you do during a fire?" in his unpublished book manuscript. He wrote, "1.) station oneself at a central point, informing the Officer-in-Charge of the same; 2.) roaming the fireground, keeping an eye on the Troops, helping, advising in terms of safety, obtaining assistance and granting of the same, to the wounded warriors; 3.) Repeatedly returning to the central point . . . so that he can be reached immediately when needed."[26]

In June 17, 1972, the Hotel Vendome fire took the lives of nine firefighters and injured nine more, making it one of the worst fires in Boston's history.[27] Father Keating was present and was deposed in subsequent legal action. In an article written at the time, Father Keating was reportedly "dropped by crane into gaping holes of building construction during that tragedy at enormous risk to his person to administer the last rites of the Catholic Church to the dead and dying firefighters."[28] In his unpublished manuscript, Keating said the fire precipitated the appointment of two assistant chaplains to the

Photo 7.2 Monsignor James Keating working with the Boston Fire Department in the late 1980s. Reprinted with permission of the archives of the Boston Archdiocese. Photo credit: Bill Noonan.

department.[29] At the funeral service of the firefighters lost to the fire, Father Keating remarked, "You are my fellow firefighters; you are my family; I am most grateful to be one of you. We all know what you the firefighter—means to us all—God Bless You." He also reflected, "Never in my 31 years of priesthood have I been more of a priest than last Saturday night [when the fire occurred]."[30]

In 1999, the Massachusetts Corps of Fire Chaplains was organized to support the training of fire chaplains, provide general support for fire chaplains across the state, and offer aid during large fires. Most are trained in critical incident stress debriefing, an approach to helping firefighters and other first responders deal with traumatic situations. The Corps supported colleagues during a range of natural and man-made disasters in recent years, including tornadoes in the western part of the state and large fires in Rhode Island.[31] The Corps was awarded the State Fire Marshal's Award for Critical Incident Stress Management in 2015.[32]

Little in the historical record about the fire department addresses questions of religious diversity in Boston or across the state, perhaps in part because there was so little diversity on the force and that chaplains in Boston were primarily Catholic priests. Perhaps the non-Catholic chaplains were appointed more for symbolic than practical reasons. As mentioned, today, there are three chaplains appointed to the BFD: one Catholic, one Protestant, and one Jewish.[33] The case of chaplaincy in the department points to the role that local religious demographics have in who becomes a chaplain and what the work includes.

Massachusetts General Hospital

MGH differs from the NESM and the BFD in its status as a private non-profit organization. John Bartlett, chaplain of Boston's Almhouse in the early 1800s, dreamed of the hospital. Fundraising was encouraged by Boston physicians James Jackson and John Collins Warren, and the hospital was incorporated by the Massachusetts Legislature in 1811. The first patient was admitted in 1821.[34] MGH welcomed religious leaders, community clergy, and local chaplains who were joined by Protestant hospital chaplains in the 1920s as healthcare chaplaincy began to emerge as a distinct profession at the hospital.[35] Over time, Protestants trained to be professional chaplains were joined by Catholics with this training and then others as the hospital aimed to include people with diverse religious backgrounds on their chaplaincy staff.

As a distinct profession, hospital chaplaincy emerged in the 1920s from efforts by theological educators to more thoroughly engage students with psychology in the classroom and in new field education programs. The initial goal—to jolt theological education and ultimately transform Protestant churches—led to the development of clinical pastoral education (CPE) and eventually to the development of healthcare-specific chaplaincy. Richard Cabot, a prominent Harvard physician who established medical social work at the hospital, played a key role in this, arguing in 1925 that theological students should spend a year doing clinical training. In collaboration with Anton T. Boisen, a pastor with training in pastoral counseling and psychology, Cabot invested in CPE education at MGH where students first worked with patients who had physical illnesses. With Cabot's financial support, the hospital appointed their first CPE-trained chaplain in 1930, Austin P. Guiles, who was followed by Russell Dicks in 1933. Students enrolled in CPE visited patients and worked as orderlies under the guidance of Cabot and Dicks who wrote *The Art of Ministering to the Sick* in 1936, which shifted attention from the education of theological students to the care of patients.[36]

Chaplains at MGH were primarily Protestant and male through the early 1950s. Catholic Cardinal Richard Cushing appointed the first full-time Catholic chaplain-priest at MGH in 1951. While the Board of Trustees affirmed its support for hospital chaplains, they maintained an unwillingness to have the hospital pay them directly.[37] Chaplains and chaplaincy educators were paid by the Episcopal City, the Catholic Archdiocese, the Synagogue Council of Massachusetts, and other local religious organizations until the mid-1970s. Several Jewish leaders and religious leaders from local Greek Orthodox churches were appointed in the early 1970s to visit hospitalized patients.[38]

The number of chaplains and their religious backgrounds expanded in subsequent years as the hospital slowly shifted from what Sheryl Reimer-Kirkham and Lori Beaman call a historical pastoral care approach to a more generic or universal one. Until recently, the department directors have remained largely Protestant. By the 1990s, chaplains included individuals from Buddhist and Muslim backgrounds as well individuals who spoke Hebrew, Spanish, Arabic, and Igbo. The chapel was relocated in the early 1990s, and a Muslim prayer room opened in 1999.[39] Gatherings or services from a range of religious traditions were broadcast to patients through the hospital's internal television station beginning in the early 2000s.

Chaplains at MGH today include people from a range of spiritual and religious backgrounds who work along interfaith lines and are trained to care for all patients regardless of differences between their own religious background and that of the patient, family member, or staff member. A chaplain who was hired years ago to see patients in his religious tradition described the change in his position saying, "starting within two or three years, as a function of how the chaplaincy itself was changing, everyone became more interfaith chaplains, and so all the chaplains were taking on floors, taking on call, so we were now seeing members of different faith communities other than our

Photo 7.3 The Muslim prayer room at Massachusetts General Hospital opened in 1999. The mihrab that indicates the direction of Mecca was added in 2005. Photo credit: Randall Armor.

own and that was the direction we were moving in."[40] That continues to be how chaplains work at MGH where the department, now the Department of Spiritual Care, is directed by a chaplain trained in the Buddhist tradition and adopts a more generic or universalist approach.[41]

These three organizations illustrate different ways the places chaplains work in Boston have responded organizationally to changing religious demographics. The Seafarer's Mission was and remains Protestant and found ways its Protestant staff and volunteers could serve people from all religious backgrounds, which today includes large numbers of people born abroad. The BFD diversified slowly and currently has chaplains who are Protestant, Catholic, and Jewish—with the largest number being Catholic. And MGH diversified their chaplaincy staff earlier and more broadly to include people from a range of religious backgrounds, supporting their commitment to being a diverse and inclusive healthcare organization. While chaplains in each setting aim to accommodate and serve others regardless of their backgrounds, these organizational contexts shape who they hire as chaplains and how those people are trained and act around religious differences. They also, as Sheryl Reimer-Kirkham and Lori Beaman note, privilege some voices and perspectives while silencing others along the way.

Individual Approaches

Learning

In addition to the ways organizations respond to and negotiate religious diversity, individual chaplains do as well, informed by the kinds of institutions where they work. Most all the chaplains I interviewed in Boston work regularly, if not daily, across axes of religious difference. These differences are with the constituents with whom they work, as well as with other chaplains in their organizations. Most speak about learning from chaplaincy colleagues on the job and in the training that prepared them for the work. A Jewish chaplain in a local hospital, for example, explained, "One of the things I find most rewarding, aside from saying every time someone comes into an elevator when I'm there with the priest—'so a rabbi and a priest get into an elevator . . .' which is just endlessly entertaining for me, but more seriously we have real discussions about the similarities and differences in our traditions, and we have them informally and formally, and it is just very rewarding."[42] Most all the chaplains who work with other chaplains also mentioned these kinds of opportunities for learning and engagement.

Learning to engage across religious differences was central to how many chaplains were trained as they learned experientially from others they trained alongside. Military chaplains typically go to an intensive chaplaincy school for a few weeks with people from a range of religious backgrounds who are also preparing to be military chaplains. One remembered not a formal part of the training but an informal learning as meals were shared with chaplains from Protestant, Catholic, Mormon, Christian Scientist, Jewish, and Jehovah's Witness backgrounds. People asked one another frank questions as they got to know each other, he remembered, about terms, stereotypes, beliefs, and practices. Most people enjoy the training another military chaplain explained: "They [chaplains in training] encounter in a very powerful way this diversity of religious expression, and so typically the Catholics will get challenged by some Assemblies of God clergy saying 'you guys are the anti-Christ' or whatever, and they figure out how they are going to live there together."[43]

Those who complete units in clinical pastoral education (CPE) in their training—which includes almost all chaplains in healthcare—also described this experiential work across religious traditions as part of the point of CPE. "What you are there for in CPE," a hospice chaplain explained, "is to kind of transform those rough edges and grow a bit." If there were tensions around religious difference, she remembered, "that is what you are there to do, to learn that . . . that is what the program is about."[44] A few chaplains in healthcare and the military also mentioned academic classes as ways they learned about religious difference. "I took Hinduism as an undergraduate. I took a lot of Judaic studies classes," a chaplain who works in both healthcare and prisons explained.[45] And a military chaplain pointed to graduate-level religion courses he took as part of his training that helped round out his knowledge about other traditions.

Most chaplains are also clear that they learn a lot about how to work across religious differences—including with people who are not religiously affiliated—from those they serve on the job. A community chaplain explained, "We are working with folks who span all sorts of religions and no religion at all. . . . Our training is really to discover the person's own language and sort of unpack that. . . . We are really doing a lot more of the dialogue reflective discernment kinds of work."[46] And a healthcare chaplain spoke at length about how she learned over the course of her career to provide support to those who are not religious as more of them were present in the hospital where she works. She said, "You need to use secular language and to be inclusive . . . instead of asking what religious preference someone is and having that be part of one of their interview goals, you might start with narrative and explore what someone is going through. For example, 'listening to you talk about the events of this last week, it sounds like it has been really, really challenging, and you're doing an amazing job supporting your loved one . . . and I'm wondering what is getting you through? Where are you finding strength in a time like this?' "[47]

Organizational Guidelines

Some organizations have policies formally structuring how chaplains should engage across religious differences. Federal and state facilities like the military and prisons are the most specific. A chaplain with the National Guard said that when candidates go to chaplaincy school, "they have to sign documents saying that they understand this diversity."[48] Military chaplains are expected to "perform or provide," meaning they serve the need of a military service person or find someone who can. "If you're a Roman Catholic priest," one explained, "your commander can't order you to do a same-sex wedding . . . but you're expected to either perform or provide the support . . . so if you can't do it, you have to find somebody who can."[49] Several of the military chaplains I interviewed, however, were clear that this policy is not always followed on the ground: "The role of the chaplain is to perform and provide for the religious aspects . . . it is something I take incredibly seriously. There are some of my colleagues who don't and who see it as a time for them to evangelize and push Jesus."[50] Some of this is changing he continued, saying it was worse in the past than the present.

The military chaplains I interviewed described the different ways they work across these religious differences. Most focus on facilitating practical arrangements and educating others about different religious traditions. One chaplain was very clear about the three things chaplains are supposed to do: "care for the living, honor the dead, and nurture the wounded," while "protecting people's first amendment rights to practice their faith."[51] While deployed, he told me, a Wiccan soldier came to him asking for accommodation. He explained, "I had no idea what a Wiccan was up until that point, and I said, 'What do you need?' He said, 'I need a candle and a room,'" which the chaplain was able to arrange for him. In addition to practical arrangements, this chaplain explained, "The other thing I had to do was to make sure . . . he was not harassed [by others when they learned he was Wiccan]." I asked what such an intervention looked like, and he explained that it is like "pulling a person aside and saying listen, you know, this is his belief and how would you like it if somebody made fun of your belief." If that does not work, this chaplain said he then speaks to the person's supervisor so that person can address the issue.[52]

In addition to their work with individual members of the military, some chaplains also advise leadership about religious affairs, ethics, and religious accommodation. This may relate to decisions about individuals in the military and ethical breaches, as well local issues in the cultural and religious contexts where members of the military are deployed. They are also consulted when individuals change religious traditions in ways that influence military regulations around dress, diet, or other factors. "My job is to interview the person and just to assess the sincerity of their faith . . . so that as it goes up the chain for approval they say OK, this is someone that didn't just decide yesterday, but it is a part of who they are," one chaplain explained. I asked how this works in practice, and he explained that he asks people about their backgrounds, involvement with communities, maybe about some of the basic tenants of their faith, and so forth.[53]

Like in the military, prisons tend to prioritize first amendment protection of religion in shaping the work of chaplains.[54] While individual prisons have different rules, several of the chaplains I interviewed spoke about fairly rigid guidelines that required them to serve only inmates from their own religious backgrounds. A Protestant chaplain, for example, spoke of a Muslim inmate asking for a Qur'an and being told by a supervisor that only the Muslim chaplain (who would not be in for three days) could deliver a Qur'an. "I'm a chaplain," he reflected, "I'm here to serve whoever," adding, "I not gonna sit there and try to google a Qur'an with anybody, but I know the basics to try to sit down with you and provide for you and what else do you need."[55] In this facility, the efforts—this chaplain argued—to keep religious traditions distinct and only allow particular chaplains to serve inmates in those constituencies restricted what he was able to do and the care he felt he could provide.

The Joint Commission, which sets policies that healthcare organizations must follow to receive federal funds, has policies not about chaplains, but about the importance of respecting patients' religious backgrounds and meeting their spiritual and religious needs. Specific guidelines have focused on paying attention to spirituality and religion as related to patient education, end-of-life care, food, rehabilitation services, mental and behavioral disorders, and staff. Despite years of lobbying by professional associations of chaplains, these guidelines do not say that chaplains are required in the institutions. Some institutions meet the guidelines by having social workers do this work.[56] Medicare guidelines are similar, stating that a "spiritual assessment must be completed and updated on every patient and family" but not specifying that it is a chaplain who must do so.[57]

Neutralizing and Code Switching

With the exception of chaplains in the military and prisons who tended to "perform or provide," the majority of chaplains I interviewed neutralize and code switch or move between different religious and spiritual languages and registers depending on who they are engaging with and to what end.[58] Some carry texts or religious symbols or objects from different traditions in their pockets, depending on the demographics of their constituents, while others speak of letting the people they are with lead and figure out the register or frame to use during this interaction. A community chaplain who works with the unhoused keeps pocket editions of various texts on hand and also materials written by the Catholic monk Thomas Merton: "I carry them in my bag, and I can flip through one of those in a conversation that we're having at McDonald's or anywhere." In addition to Christian and Hebrew scriptures, which she says often come up in conversation, she carries poems including by "Mary Oliver and all of that . . . I try to bring all of that in . . . that is usually welcoming," which leads to conversations about "hope, talking about trust, talking about shame, what to have faith in, lots of things. Those are all holy conversations."[59]

Most chaplains neutralize or emphasize the similarities they have with those they serve. The language of journey is common. "I always present it as someone to journey with you without judgment" one explained.[60] And in the words of another, "I start with everyone the same way. I say, 'You and I are on a journey. We share this journey.' "[61] By emphasizing a shared journey, chaplains aim to build rapport and initial connections. Many chaplains find their clients feel judged by religious people or institutions and spend time in the first few minutes trying to put that at bay: "Even if the clergy person isn't meaning to judge and has no judgment, people tend to feel judged. I haven't been to church in X number of years. I haven't been to synagogue. I'm not that religious. . . . I'm just journeying with them, and I don't care if you've been to synagogue."[62]

Chaplains further neutralize by asking open-ended questions not about religion or spirituality, but rather about sources of coping and strength that people answer through a number of registers. "You get some really interesting answers," a hospice chaplain recounted. "I have a woman who I was talking with about this last week . . . she said I think I get it from music. Well, I thought that's an interesting way of answering it. So we had this whole conversation about music and finding out it is a very important part for her to get inspiration. . . . She finds things that inspire her."[63] Several hospice chaplains spoke about life and death being common across all people. In the words of one, "I'm a human being just like you are. I'm another person for you to talk with, another person who can walk with you. I say, 'If you want to get spiritual, I'll get spiritual with you . . . I'm here to help you with this common experience you and I share, and that is life and death.' "[64] While some chaplains use the language of journey and commonality, others use terms like "human flourishing" and "self-actualization." In the words of a prison chaplain, "My goal is to invite their own human flourishing, their own self-actualization.... I think the space for religion or religious background kind of collapses, and it doesn't really matter what you've claimed or what you know or don't know."[65]

Some also emphasize their deep interest and training across faith traditions. "My predisposition is an openness to people of other faiths," a healthcare chaplain explained. "I identify first as a multifaith chaplain. I'm grounded in my own faith, but I don't walk into a room as a minister or an ordained professional.... And I'm just so genuinely interested in the other person ... I think people know that about me ... sense that about me."[66] A hospice chaplain tells people he is an interfaith chaplain "trained to be able to minister to anybody regardless of what their belief system is.... We have absolutely no agenda at all ... we actually have the same goal for every single patient ... spiritual companionship."[67] A third chaplain explained, "We tell them [hospice patients and their families] right up front that we don't come in and try to preach or to proselytize ... we come as a good listener."[68]

Some chaplains also spoke of code switching—moving between the languages and assumptions of different religious traditions in their efforts to best serve. A hospice chaplain was raised in and practiced both Protestantism and Catholicism: "I'm kind of a hybrid ... I was raised Catholic, but I went to Bible college and seminary as a Protestant." He is especially adept at code switching: "If someone's Catholic, I pray for them in the Roman Catholic tradition. If someone is Protestant," he explained that he uses Protestant concepts and prayers.[69] Another Christian chaplain with strong Jewish connections in her family has a similar approach. While she always calls a rabbi when asked by Jewish patients, she will pray with them in Hebrew depending on the degree of observance and if it seems appropriate.[70]

Through their presence, chaplains say they attract and draw out people who are religiously different from themselves. Several military chaplains spoke of colleagues outside of their religious traditions, seeking them out for conversation. One said, "I really do believe because I was a Jewish chaplain and was able to just hear the person where they were. I knew enough of Christian thought that I could reframe."[71] A prison chaplain spoke of a Jewish inmate she got to know who sat in the back of her Christian services. She connected him with a rabbi. Chaplains in higher education described many examples of individual students and groups seeking them out to request support not yet provided by the institution.

Personal Negotiations

The majority of chaplains are thoughtful about personal boundaries of belief and practice. In the words of a military chaplain: "One of the challenges of being a chaplain is, 'Can you speak universally and be true to your denomination or your specific faith group?' I think that's really important."[72] A hospital chaplain offered an example of these tensions when she was called to perform a baptism for a child who was dying and was the only chaplain in the building. She said, "I needed to pay attention to two things. One, I did not personally, as a rabbi, feel comfortable and certainly not competent to do that, and two, this kid needed to be baptized." She went on to explain, "I felt that my role as a chaplain was to make sure that happened. . . . And so I encouraged and supported and gave the parents the wherewithal to do the baptism themselves, which turned out to be a very lovely experience for them."[73] This chaplain entered the place where the parents were and found a way—a workaround perhaps—to maintain her authenticity while enabling the parents to get what they needed in the situation.

There are exceptions, however, of chaplains who are unable or unwilling to put their personal religious commitments to the side when engaging with those who are religiously different from themselves. Although definitely more the exception than the norm, this reality points—again—to the fact that there are no common credentials for chaplains across the settings where they work or mechanisms in place to recognize chaplains who are not neutralizing or code switching. A chaplain who worked in a prison fit this profile. A strong and committed Christian, he was vocal about his beliefs. He spoke about his work with atheists in prisons saying, "I talk to atheists. . . . They said you're cool you know . . . I said I love you anyway . . . I'm not going to change who I am, but in the meantime we are going to have communication." He continued describing his interactions with others, including explaining his religious objections to homosexuality: "There was one particular guy, he was in holding, and he said, 'I need you. Everybody says you're pretty cool.'" This man asked for a prayer for him and his partner. The chaplain told me, "I looked at him. I smiled and I said, 'let me say this to you—I'm going to pray for you. And I'll pray for your partner, but not as a unit, because this is where according to my faith . . . the scripture says it is not pleasing under God.'"[74] The chaplain continued telling me how much this individual appreciated his honesty and that he did not judge him. While this may have been the case, I think that other chaplains I interviewed would argue that he let his religious beliefs limit his ability to be present and support someone in need. Regardless of interpretation, this example illustrates that not all chaplains neutralize or code switch when confronted with religious differences in their work.

Conclusions

The majority of chaplains I interviewed in Boston were Christian, and underlying Christian hegemony was evident in many of my conversations with them about religious diversity. Almost all the examples they offered about religious difference were of non-Christian others, and in most examples included in this chapter (and in my interviews and fieldnotes), Christianity was the default position. Interestingly, given the strong Catholic history of Boston, it was a general Christianity rather than a Catholic-specific version, except in the fire department, likely representing the Protestant history of chaplains as a professional group and the overrepresentation of Protestants among those I interviewed. While some people might want a chaplain from their own religious tradition and feel uncomfortable with others, growing numbers of people in the United States are religiously unaffiliated and growing numbers combine religious traditions, shifting the demographic space in which chaplains do their work.

In thinking about how individual chaplains negotiate across religious differences, it is essential to not lose sight of the very different ways that these chaplains' organizations responded to changing religious demographics over time. It is also important to recognize how their shifts in mission and staffing shape the demographics of the very chaplains that are on the ground, as well as the people they work with from different backgrounds during training and preparation. The extended case studies in the first half of the chapter show how MGH made decisions to hire non-Christian chaplains earlier and in larger numbers than the BFD did. This shifted the awareness that individual chaplains had about non-Christian religious traditions and symbolically represented their commitment to greater spiritual and religious inclusivity.

It is within these organizational constraints that chaplains learn about people from a range of religious backgrounds—including other chaplains—and engage with those they serve. Those who have completed some clinical pastoral education learn how to work across such differences in their training. Those who have not completed this training may be most likely—like the prison chaplain described above—to not serve others in the ways or on the terms the others expect because of religious differences. The rabbi who helped parents baptize their dying child when she was not able to because of her personal beliefs offers a counter-example of how chaplains can remain true to their own beliefs while also serving those in need.

This variation in how chaplains engage religious differences individually and as shaped by their institutional settings came back to me, again, when I listened to a volunteer police chaplain talk about the walks he helps organize through local communities in the summer. While the police chaplain whose story opened this chapter (who also leads a congregation in the city) struggles with knowing how to pray in an inclusive way, this volunteer chaplain (who has a day job in another sector) seemed unaware of the challenge. Seeming not to recognize the religious diversity of potential participants, he explained, "At the beginning [of a walk], we'll get everyone together . . . and say a nice prayer. Pray for our city, for safety, for the people to understand that the police are their friends and that the community is here to help them all and just for God to prevent some of the stuff that happens in our city." The group, including city commissioners, then walks for an hour and concludes, again, with a prayer: "And then the next night is another neighborhood, and we just go all summer long. It gets hot out there."[75] To engage across religious differences, chaplains first need to recognize them, which some, but not all, chaplains in the city do.

8

Conclusions Can Be Beginnings

I was almost finished writing this book when the COVID-19 pandemic hit. As hospitals in New York City started seeing COVID-19 cases and hospitals across the country prepared, I started to get calls from reporters asking about the roles chaplains were playing. Bari Weiss published an opinion piece in the *New York Times* early in the pandemic, with the headline, "The Men and Women Who Run Toward the Dying: Meeting the New York City Chaplains Praying for Coronavirus Patients." Chaplains were featured over the next year in the *Boston Globe*, the *Los Angeles Times*, the *Atlanta Journal Constitution*, and on a long list of radio and news programs. While some hospitals sent chaplains home to work remotely, others saw them as essential and asked them to care not just for patients but also for increasingly traumatized staff. Reporters described chaplains alongside dying patients, facilitating zoom calls and goodbyes between patients and families, and with staff at the bedside in full personal protective equipment (PPE).[1] An international survey of 1,600 chaplains found chaplains doing this work around the globe even as their roles and clarity about their work were mixed.[2]

Media reports showed the public—many for the first time—the intimate, usually quiet, work chaplains do with people in some of their darkest moments. While this was new to reporters and many in the public, it was not new to chaplains. When reporters called, I reminded them first that I have never seen a chaplain run. Most walk, calmly and sometimes urgently, but running is not part of being a calm and supportive presence. Second—and much more importantly—chaplains are not new. The pandemic led the media to shine a light on them, but their positions, work, and the relationships with those they serve were not new or a result of the pandemic, as I show in this book. They were in position before COVID-19 and responded to it in new and creative ways because that is what their work is: serving people where they are, as they are, in hospitals, nursing facilities, prisons, and other settings across the country.

This book tells a broader and deeper story about the history and work of people calling themselves chaplains than was possible for reporters in the

Spiritual Care. Wendy Cadge, Oxford University Press. © Oxford University Press 2023.
DOI: 10.1093/oso/9780197647813.003.0008

midst of a pandemic with short deadlines and limited word counts. I conclude here by briefly summarizing the findings and then outlining how these findings should inform the work of theological educators, religious leaders, and chaplains, and how their work matters for scholars and the general public. Chaplains and spiritual care providers are central to the future of spiritual and religious life in the United States. I look forward in this chapter, reflecting on how we came to this place and what I think is to come.

A Brief Summary

Who Chaplains Are

Chaplains today, like their predecessors in years past, are a disparate group. They are congregational clergy, part-timers, and people—especially in healthcare and the military—for whom chaplaincy is a full-time job and their life's work. Some of those I met in Boston sought out the work and others ended up there through personal connections, commitments to social justice, or the simple need for a job. Some came to the work because their gender, sexuality, family situation, or sense of vocation did not fit to the jobs people with their credentials usually obtain. Over time, chaplains in Boston shifted from being white, Protestant men to include women, people from more diverse racial and ethnic backgrounds, and people from a range of religious traditions. Despite national debates about specific certification and credentials for chaplains, less than a third of the people I interviewed were officially certified or credentialed as chaplains.

The breadth of people calling themselves chaplains and the varieties of training they bring to the work remains one of the defining features of the field. The title "chaplain" has specific meanings and credentialing requirements in the military and prisons, but the volunteer police chaplain who prays before walks in Boston uses the term despite having no formal theological education. This fluidity—combined with the oft used and rarely defined talk of presence among chaplains—leads to a slippery, hard to define profession, particularly in the U.S. context of free exercise and limited regulation of things termed "religion." Legally, Winnifred Sullivan argues, this leads to a new kind of spiritual establishment: "Through this ambiguous but insistent practice of the ministry of presence, chaplains honor the right of their flock to exercise their rights to religious freedom and claim there is no imposition or coercion even while they witness to their own religious commitments, structure that of others through their practice, and legitimate the purposes of their employers."[3] Broadening the field beyond state-sponsored chaplaincies, as I have in this book, as well as listening to what chaplains do every day, challenges the piece of this argument about witnessing to their own religious commitments while still acknowledging how the law structures and makes possible the work. I also show how chaplains in almost all settings see and enter liminal—in-between—spaces that do not have neat institutional definitions and are, therefore, frequently not just overlooked but also not even seen by other professionals.

Part of what this book shows are the ways religious entrepreneurs are using the term "chaplain" and the space it allows outside of state-supported institutions to frame and legitimize their work. While some chaplains remain connected to historical institutions like the Catholic Church or prisons or the military, others see in the cultural fog around the concept the opportunity to use and claim it as their own. Mostly women in my interviews, these entrepreneurs use the category of chaplain to describe work with groups not historically connected to the term. "I'm thinking of one chaplain," an entrepreneur described, who is soon to retire and aiming to be a chaplain for lawyers. "The stress level of attorneys and the types of cases that they're navigating, the intensity of the legal environment, and there's often no outlet that is a confidential, safe space for these attorneys to get in touch with themselves."[4]

Possible, perhaps even encouraged, by the ways religion is pluralistic, structurally adaptable, and empowering in the United States, this kind of entrepreneurism by people using the term "chaplain" is possible outside of state institutions and is contentious and challenged within them.[5] Historical commitments to Christian assumptions about religion and about chaplains continue to curtail efforts by humanists and others to serve as chaplains in the military and prisons, for example.[6] Long-standing inequities around gender and race are also glaring, as only 5% of chaplains in the federal prison system are women, and few chaplains in the Veterans Administration are people of color.[7] These disparities are more alarming when considered alongside the demographics of the people these chaplains serve and the growing cultural misalignment between them and, especially, younger people. "I think the need is still there," a fire chaplain explained, but it is different from how it was in the past when "there were more people going to church including police and firemen. Today there are not so many, and so the value of a chaplain, just like the value of going to church, has decreased."[8] Requiring chaplains in state settings to have the same kinds of traditional religious education as in the past challenges their relevance and limits their impact when they are serving growing numbers of people who have never been religiously affiliated.

A lack of national demographics about chaplains make generalization from Boston as a case study difficult, and the situation is likely different in Atlanta, Houston, Los Angeles, and other places across the United States. We know from data collected by the Bureau of Labor Statistics that growing numbers of clergy have been working outside of congregations since the 1970s. We do not know how many of them are chaplains. The largest fraction of clergy working outside of congregations in the Bureau's data and in my interviews, work in healthcare. National trends towards bi-vocational work among religious leaders are also reflected in these interviews, as many combine multiple chaplaincy positions and/or work as chaplains alongside their work in local congregations.[9] Many chaplains were bi-vocational before the term existed, though often were not paid for their work in hospitals, prisons, and other settings. Nationally, growing numbers of chaplains are women and people of color than in the past. Alongside the entrepreneurs, non-Christians in the United States are using and adapting the term and category of "chaplaincy" to obtain education and degrees that make them employable and grant standing—especially in religious traditions like Buddhism and Hinduism—often without the kind of structured training and leadership easily recognized in the American institutional context. Demographics and geography matter in who becomes chaplains, what institutions chaplains are found in, and how and with whom they do their work.

What Chaplains Do

Chaplains work with individual clients (or patients or students) and the staff or workers of the organizations they serve. They work with people where they are, as they are, often in the midst of transitions. Almost all the chaplains I met do two things. First, they engage with people wholistically and help remind them of bigger picture questions and concerns. Second, they work around death—willingly and repeatedly placing themselves in the path of death as brokers and midwives for those who are dying, their loved ones and caregivers, and the institutions to which they are connected. As the pandemic clearly demonstrated, chaplains are uniquely prepared to support people at the end of their lives—whether expected or sudden—and gently connect the living and the dead.

While people who are aware of chaplains think of them supporting patients, their work with staff—in healthcare organizations and beyond—is just as important and often overlooked. In interviews with healthcare executives, it was their work with staff—even before the pandemic—that many saw as a defining feature of their work.[10] This was, perhaps, nowhere clearer than in the (dreaded) rollout of a new electronic medical charting system at a large Boston hospital. To ease the transition, chaplains changed the words of the Village People's "YMCA" song into the acronym for the electronic medical record. "The chaplaincy helped give voice to the anxiety and bring it out in the open—that yes, we're all scared about this, and we're going to get through it, and it is OK. . . . That was the way in which we ministered to the whole organization," a chaplain explained.[11] They sang their new song, recorded it, and also held a service in the chapel to support people through the transition. Some chaplains identify the ways their work with staff enlarges the capacity of organizations and makes them what the military calls "force multipliers."

All chaplains talk of being present, serving everyone, and creating and holding space for people. They hold people in transitional places like in-between life and death, what is and what might be, and what is and what they hoped would be. They see work in these in-between places where others do not and, in many cases, end up providing a kind of invisible support, an organizational extra in settings where there are not policies requiring them to be there. They mostly speak about the space they help people create and hold in difficult moments, not anything they contribute to that space. A chaplain who has worked in healthcare and higher education emphasized the "embodied presence" of his work, describing how his work as a bartender, in part, led him to chaplaincy. He said, "I worked at a bar as a host talking to thousands of tourists . . . and for whatever reason, I enjoy it. I think people feel good with me, comfortable at least. I arrive [as a chaplain] in a way that can allow them to bring the conversation where they want it to be whether in one visit in a hospital ward to over months for a teenage suicidal patient who is in the inpatient unit."[12] In emphasizing their presence, chaplains mostly value *being* rather than any outcomes that might result. This simultaneously continues what Lawrence Holt years ago called the "tension or enigma" that shapes their work and is what remains confusing to some of those they serve and with whom they work.[13]

Organizational Connections

The ways chaplains do their work depends largely on the organizations where they are. It is those organizations—more than religious, demographic, or other factors about the chaplains themselves—that most shape that work. The work most chaplains do begins and ends with relationships and is often improvisational. They describe themselves coming alongside others, acting as a kind of companion profession. In settings with a chain of command, they are outside of it and can maintain confidentiality. Not surprisingly, chaplains who are more embedded in their institutions do a broader range of tasks with a wide range of people than those who are more peripheral. In my interviews, it was chaplains in healthcare and the military who were most embedded, while those in higher education, prison, and municipal settings less so. Those who are the least embedded mostly do rituals and ceremonies, while those who are more embedded also do individual support in addition to mediating and bridging communities. More than personal factors, organizational structures and culture inform where chaplains fall along this continuum. Chaplains in settings where they are not required are sometimes aware of that and sensitive to maintaining good relationships with organizational gatekeepers.

In addition to the organizations they serve, some chaplains are local clergy and fit into local religious ecologies in various ways. Chaplains in one setting, like prisons, are rarely if ever connected to chaplains in other settings, like healthcare organizations. It was only a few African Americans who work as chaplains in Boston who knew chaplains in other settings through networks of Black clergy in the city. Chaplains who are local clergy are aware of and negotiate dual roles. "Sometimes as a chaplain," one African American chaplain explained, "you have to be conscious of how you present things. You are also a local clergy and to do what you do you have to have a relationship with the community. Especially in the Black community, you don't want to be a 'sell out' or your words will fall on deaf ears."[14] From their positions historically on the edges of religious organizations and the organizations they serve, chaplains are connected to and are a part of local religious ecologies more through individual than institutional relationships. Few local congregations, in other words, have formal connections with chaplaincy departments in prisons or healthcare organizations in the city. Some local clergy know chaplains in those settings, often because they went to school with them.

Despite their long histories in Boston, scholars and the media have not viewed chaplains as central to the religious ecology or makeup of the city or others across the country. In some ways this is not surprising; chaplains exist in-between religious and more public mostly secular organizations. They serve people who are often themselves in-between or in transition. In other ways, this oversight is surprising as a fair number of chaplains are (and have long been) city, state, and federal employees. Most trained in theological schools alongside colleagues who went into local religious leadership in congregations. And they are almost always present in urgent and emergency situations ranging from the Charlestown State Prison riot in 1952 to the Boston Marathon bombing in 2013 to the COVID-19 pandemic in 2020. This oversight may not be the same in other cities across the United States that have different religious histories and are today more religious than Boston.

Regardless of where they are, chaplains today are cultivating connections with people around existential, spiritual, and/or religious questions that would not happen without them. Near the end of our conversation, a hospice chaplain reflected on how "being in Boston, people don't talk about faith—especially Protestants and Catholics. They think it will lead to anger and people will get hurt." He talked about how that makes it even more important for him to approach these topics in nonthreatening ways and validate the stories and experiences people share with him. He sees society moving away from religious involvement and almost never sees another religious leader or chaplain as he visits patients at home and in nursing facilities.[15] What that means for the future of his work and that of his colleagues is, he acknowledges, an open question. It is clear that it leaves chaplains—much like the people they serve—in in-between places in professional religious life and local religious ecologies.

Looking Ahead

Looking forward, I see social factors that may lead chaplaincy and spiritual care to expand in scope and presence, as well as factors that may lead to decline. The media tends to turn to chaplains during and after armed conflicts, pandemics, and more generally when people have or need an emerging hope. Writing in the midst of the pandemic which has been one of those periods, it is easy to tell a simple story about chaplaincy—increasingly called spiritual care—on the rise. I think the future is likely to be more complicated as markers of growth are present among a secularizing American public where religious affiliation and organizations are on a slow decline. "We're tied to the free exercise of religion—not the free exercise of spirituality," a military chaplain reflected on what the future will hold. "We can't become social workers, and we're not behavioral health people—we have behavioral health people, and they are trained."[16] With secularization and generational change, I suspect that the title or category of chaplain will continue to sound more and more old-fashioned, especially to growing numbers of people who were never religiously affiliated. The existential topics chaplains work around, however, are ageless, and with the challenges of recent years, even more acute. Whether people who call themselves chaplains or spiritual care providers will be the ones to do this work (maybe in a new guise) and whether new financial models will emerge to support that work are questions for the future.

I suspect the continued decline of people who are religiously affiliated will challenge chaplains working in state institutions, particularly if the state remains resistant to recognizing a more diverse group of people as chaplains. The long history of chaplaincy in the military will likely protect positions there, and I worry that without significant structural change and openness to a broader range of religious traditions, those chaplains will be more and more challenged to serve their constituents who will be demographically more different from them, especially around religion. Father Bagetta who long worked as a chaplain for the Department of Youth Services as described in chapter 3 retired while I was writing this book. He was not replaced.

I expect chaplaincy to continue in healthcare, particularly in hospice and other settings where the work chaplains do around death is specific, unique, and helpful to the organizations that employ and pay them. "You look at the national surveys in the past decade," a hospice chaplain told me. "More people are identifying as spiritual than they are religious. Some of my colleagues think that's a bad thing. I don't. I think that's a good thing. And somebody said, 'Well it's going to put you chaplains out of work,' but no. The way I see it, this is why chaplaincy is so good . . . people will always have a spiritual side."[17] To the extent that organizations work in their own self-interests, I think that healthcare organizations in particular will continue to support chaplains, so long as they make things easier for patients and other staff and fit within budgetary frameworks.

I also expect growing numbers of religious entrepreneurs to continue to utilize the notion of chaplaincy and use it in new ways. The work of the Faith Matters Network around social movement chaplaincy combined with smaller efforts to support the staff of veterinary clinics, first responders, and other groups that—even outside of pandemics—will likely continue to emerge. Whether there are financial models that enable them to remain and the people doing the work to make a living wage remain to be seen.

Much of what happens going forward will depend on how quickly and in what ways religious organizations—from congregations to national religious bodies to theological institutions—are willing to adapt and change. If history is a guide, these changes will be spurred not by chaplains, but by continued declines in the students and tuition dollars needed for these institutions to survive and thrive. People's geographic mobility and institutional living—especially among elders—are likely to maintain the demand for the work of chaplains but whether and how institutions respond is a separate question.

Data from the National Congregations Study shows congregations continuing to decline in number and in members.[18] Chaplaincy is firmly a part of the movement to bi-vocational leadership in some religious organizations, even as national religious bodies and many theological schools only slowly shift their curriculum to train people for it. The 2019–2020 National Survey of Religious Leaders reported that 14% of the ministerial staff of local congregations also work as chaplains. The largest fraction of primary religious leaders who also work as chaplains are white evangelical Protestants (31%) followed by Black Protestant (26%), white liberal Protestants (17%), Catholics (15%), and non-Christian (11%). The largest numbers work in other settings (42%), hospitals (24%), police or fire departments (18%), prisons or jails (15%), nursing homes (13%) and colleges or universities (5%).[19]

What this means practically is, like in years past, many local religious leaders are also serving as chaplains. Their congregations help pay their salaries, and, in turn, help make the work of chaplaincy possible. As religious institutions, particularly mainline Protestant and Catholic ones continue to decline, financial support for chaplains is likely to become shakier both at the national and local levels. Nationally, religious organizations have tended to under-support full-time chaplains both educationally and financially, seeing them as secondary to congregational clergy. At the local level, fewer and/or smaller congregations may be less able to help support part-time chaplains in their communities because they do not have the financial or staff resources to spare. In some cases—like with a hospice chaplain I interviewed—this is changing. This chaplain is a full-time employee with benefits at a hospice organization. It is his chaplaincy work (specifically the benefits) that are subsidizing his ability to work for a local (small) congregation that otherwise cannot pay a full-time minister.[20] Whether this is an unusual case or an example of changes to come is an open question.

All these changes are taking place in the context of shifting public trust in religious leaders. While responses during the pandemic may have suggested otherwise, survey data over time clearly demonstrate that people in the United States have less confidence in religious leaders than they did in the past. Mark Chaves reports that between 1973 and 2014, the number of people reporting a great deal of confidence in religious leaders declined from 35% to 20%. Similar declines were seen in other areas of leadership though confidence in religious leaders has declined faster than confidence in leaders in other spheres.[21]

Theological Educators and Religious Leaders

Theological educators and religious leaders who are not chaplains have important—key—roles to play in supporting and furthering the work of chaplaincy and spiritual care. These groups historically paid little attention to chaplains. Today, they need to ask bolder questions about the shape of religious leadership—not just for the future of chaplaincy but also for the future of their religious leadership more broadly. While traditional congregations are declining, the irony is that chaplains work every day—by design—with people not in their congregations. Codes of ethics forbid most from proselyting, and they are the religious leaders with the most up-to-date front-line knowledge about what people are seeking and why many of them are not involved in existing religious organizations. Religious leaders need to ask chaplains (regularly) what they are hearing, use that information to think about the limits of their current delivery models, and experiment with bold new approaches. Current approaches to religious leadership and growth are limited, often, by their reliance on religious leaders not regularly in conversation with the very people (currently outside of religious organizations) many seek to serve.

Theological and rabbinical schools need to take the lead. They should do this not by tweaking the training historically provided for leaders of congregations, but by asking bigger questions about what chaplains and spiritual care providers need to know and how they are uniquely prepared to train in those ways. These efforts need to start not from what *they* think chaplains need to know, but from what *the people* who work with chaplains say they need and most benefit from. They need to start from demand—both as articulated by individuals and by institutions that employ large numbers of chaplains. It is only by building curriculum and training models from the demand side that theological and rabbinical schools will start to train chaplains not for the work of yesterday but for tomorrow. These changes are structural—not to individual classes but to whole degree programs—and need to be made in a way that is sensitive to the time it takes students to train and the debt many incur in the process. Educators frequently argue that the process of formation takes time—which it does—in ways that make it challenging to shorten degree programs. That may be, and with more people coming to chaplaincy after first careers in other fields, educators need to think deeply about how and when the life formation that has already taken place prepares them for the work.

One-quarter of theological schools already have degree programs with chaplaincy or spiritual care in the title. Most degree programs were developed by tweaking, not from stepping back to ask big picture strategic questions or working from demand.[22] That said, schools with existing degree programs in chaplaincy and spiritual care have a headstart in existing courses and—perhaps mostly importantly—groups of alumni who have worked as chaplains that should be asked for vital feedback about how their training did and did not prepare them for the work. Nationally, each of the existing degree programs has its own educational and learning objectives, often not in alignment with the clinical training individuals receive or with the needs of their employers. Educators affiliated with the Chaplaincy Innovation Lab recently published a textbook focused on three sets of competencies related to meaning making, interpersonal work, and organizational awareness that we think all chaplains need to know, and that we hope will help streamline learning goals and objectives across degrees and theological schools.[23] The structural changes theological schools need to make are important not just for chaplains but also for the future of religious leadership. As enrollments in theological schools continue to fall, chaplaincy degree programs are one of the few areas that may grow because the skills they emphasize are important for all religious leaders.

Outside of theological schools, it is important to recognize what some are calling "third spaces," including the Daring Compassion Movement Chaplaincy Project at the Faith Matters Network that is preparing people for the work of chaplaincy who do not necessarily have theological education. Such spaces name and respond to inequities rooted in race, class, and other social disparities that have limited who can train for and obtain positions of religious leadership. They also tend to be more flexible, less expensive, and more accessible. A leader in one such effort described it as a pathway for those who do not come to chaplaincy along the traditional route: "And if there was a pizza shop that came to us and said, 'You know, this might be unconventional, but we have students that gather between these hours, would you chaplains be willing to hang out in the store?' Sure. These [the chaplains] are people who don't necessarily get those opportunities because they don't fall into our traditional realm of chaplaincy."[24] The challenges, of course, are what the minimum competencies are for this work, that anyone can call themselves a chaplain, and that codes of ethics for chaplains are not enforceable outside of particular employment settings or optional membership in professional associations.

Attention to third-space efforts often lead to questions about whether chaplains trained outside of theological schools are doing more harm than good. These questions are misplaced and need to be asked at the broadest level about all chaplains. As evident throughout this book, the training of people who call themselves chaplains is uneven, as are many of the certification and credentialing processes in place. These bureaucratic, multilayered training and certification processes are archaic and discriminatory for those without the financial means or patience to make their ways through them and thus need to be reformed. They are left over from the past where they were developed in different social and religious contexts; they are not a vision for the future. The inequities these bureaucracies lead to are real and—for chaplaincy and spiritual care to have a strong future—such structural inequalities must be named and addressed across the institutions that train chaplains and those that employ them.[25] The challenges of chaplains trained outside of theological schools are also real, as many are rooted in single religious traditions, do not have or enforce codes or ethics, and, in many cases, prepare people who call themselves chaplains and have not agreed to not proselyte. Reforms to questions of training are not easy and must be grappled with based on data about demand and the experiences of the people chaplains serve.

Local religious leaders also have a role to play here by being more aware of chaplains in their communities and asking themselves how they might network with and support them. We might imagine how chaplains in healthcare organizations, rehabilitation centers, nursing facilities, and local congregations could work together to support those who are elderly or chronically ill and move often between care facilities. With a massive investment of resources in staff and organization, we can imagine care plans and sign offs from one spiritual care provider to another in ways that seek to support the emotional and spiritual health of an individual alongside their physical health. Knowing where chaplains in Boston are now, I see invisible networks across the city that—if resourced and knit together—would more consistently and coherently support some of the city's most vulnerable and isolated members. Such efforts are less about chaplains and more about problems like social isolation that chaplains are in positions to collaborate on and address.

Chaplains

During the research for this book, I shadowed and sat with chaplains doing gentle supportive work and with those doing the opposite. In one particularly painful incident, I was with a port chaplain who made his way onto a cargo ship, greeted a few crew members, and spent most of the next two hours eating the lunch the crew served while offering little in return. While I advocate chaplains doing gentle and supportive work, that is not all of them, and I share thoughts for chaplains with that in mind.

Looking forward, I encourage chaplains doing the gentle and supportive work to claim their places at the table and how they respond to our struggling world. While chaplains have often been there, they are frequently overlooked, and need to (loudly) name their presence in the in-between and see it as a strength rather than a weakness. From military engagements to pandemics to disaster responses, chaplains are—and have been—on the front lines doing the quiet and intense work of care. That work—not in its confidential detail but in the fact that it is central to wholistic care and resilience—needs to be named, owned, and asserted by the people doing it.

I encourage chaplains to raise their voices through op-eds, interviews, first-person accounts, social media, and more. I encourage them to code switch and to approach their work from the perspective of demand. It is too easy for chaplains to talk to other chaplains, religious leaders, and the people they are already serving in religious-specific terms. They need, instead, to broaden their frames so everyone can understand how they address universal human problems of loneliness, grief, loss, and transition. I encourage them to engage flexibly with people around these challenges, no matter who or where they are.

Historically lone rangers, I believe that those doing the work of chaplaincy and spiritual care are stronger as a group than as individuals. I encourage them, as we are trying to do through the Chaplaincy Innovation Lab, to listen and learn from one another, even when working in vastly different settings. Too often, chaplains are trapped in internal bureaucratic struggles and/or are talking only within their own echo chambers. I encourage chaplains to continue to refine their value proposition; to support and train leaders who can work across all their differences; to build pipelines to radically diversify the profession; and to simplify, simplify, simplify as much of the multilayered bureaucracy of training and certification as possible.

I also encourage chaplains to not be afraid of outcomes and to learn from research about their work.[26] While chaplains love to talk about being present, this trope is confusing to clients and employers who take it literally—of course you are present, otherwise are you absent? Showing up is not enough, in my view, to justify the time and expense of chaplains. While improvisation will always be a part of the work, chaplains need to continually learn from research about their work so they are improvising—like the best jazz musicians—from a set of skills based on solid training and understanding. "It is really hard to measure your efficacy as a chaplain," one Protestant chaplain joked: "Is it if they get to heaven? Is it if they feel a little better after they've spoke to me? I really don't know."[27] Chaplains can best understand and measure efficacy—which is daunting but not insurmountable—in partnership with colleagues who have skills in research and are trained to do so. Outcomes for chaplains must include organizational awareness, a continued sense of how the work of chaplaincy best serves the organizations where it takes place, and a curiosity about financial models that might support chaplaincy entrepreneurs of the future.

Finally—and most importantly—I encourage chaplains, like everyone in helping professions, to take care of themselves. "It can get overwhelming," one told me, "especially in hospice. . . . Sometimes we've had ten deaths in two weeks and that can be really heavy. That's the most challenging part, sustaining some sort of resilience."[28] Many of the chaplains I met in Boston echoed this, a rallying cry that became even louder during the pandemic.

Strong training programs in chaplaincy and spiritual care emphasize practices of self-care.[29] Chaplains cannot do their work—during a pandemic and beyond—from places of depletion or exhaustion which we have tried to name and respond to through pilot retreats for chaplains offered through the Chaplaincy Innovation Lab.

Beginnings

I hope this book will lead scholars and members of the public to see the in-between places chaplains identify and where chaplains dwell. I hope this book encourages scholars of religion to look for the chaplains around the edges and consider who the people are that use the term and concept. The flexibility of the title, the improvisational nature of the work, and the ways both have changed yet been continuous since the earliest years of the republic reminds scholars of the cultural space for religion (and things marked as such) in the United States. For sociologists thinking beyond religion, following the work of chaplains can show us where the liminal or in-between spaces are in organizations, how different people in organizations see and define work, and how boundaries are drawn between professionals. A colleague asked me early on in this project whether chaplains were like vacuum cleaners—sucking up all the work that remained that no one else wanted or was able to do. Sometimes yes, and sometimes no—and the metaphor helps. The liminal nature of the work chaplains sometimes do challenges the neat institutional definitions we use to divide work in today's institutions.

In talks with academics and broader audiences, I frequently remind listeners that they can call a chaplain, or they can say no if offered one in any setting. While writing this book, I partnered with a hospital chaplain to get information about how my partner was doing after a minor medical procedure. I tried to call an airport chaplain (there was no answer) when on a layover my daughter developed a fever and there was no children's Tylenol for sale where we were past the security screening. When a family member died unexpectedly in an emergency room, I called the hospital's chaplain, not to ask for information about him but to ask how to navigate the system. I quietly refer chaplains at area hospitals to friends and their loved ones who are admitted when it seems they would welcome a little extra support. Well-trained chaplains know how to move between the raindrops and help people in between. As we begin (slowly) to recover from the pandemic, they are working around COVID-19 memorials rapidly becoming a part of the landscape.[30]

Chaplains in almost all settings see and enter liminal—in-between—spaces that do not have neat institutional definitions and are, therefore, frequently not just overlooked but also not even seen by other professionals. Trace Haythorn, the executive director of the ACPE, names the paradoxical nature of chaplaincy writing:

> It is centuries old and yet is only beginning to grow into its potential. It is historically tied to religious communities, traditions and/or practices, but best practices today are embodied by those who serve people regardless of faith tradition or source of meaning. Much of this work is done in private moments of pain and grief, yet its public role is rarely understood. It has often been an area that administrators struggle to fund, and yet in the wake of pandemics it has never seemed more essential.[31]

In the conclusion to the 1973 volume *Toward a Creative Chaplaincy*, written by Carroll A. Wise, he comes to a similar conclusion: "The course of future developments in society and in this profession [chaplaincy] lie hidden from view. This should be seen as a challenge."[32] This challenge remains today. By making visible the too-frequently invisible work of chaplains and inductively demonstrating how the category is being used in daily life, I hope this book provides new tools and perspectives.

APPENDIX

Initial Glimpses and Focused Attention: A Methodological Approach at Mid-Life

When I started to learn about chaplains and spiritual care providers in large academic medical centers almost two decades ago, a senior physician told me to stop. "Don't waste your time," he said, describing how chaplains are at the bottom of the status hierarchy and make little difference. In the next breath, he described being a medical student doing chest compressions on a patient. A chaplain was there, and this senior physician—then a medical student—asked the chaplain to pray for him in addition to the prayers offered for the patient. Hmmm, I remember thinking as I heard these seemingly contradictory pieces of information. Don't waste your time on chaplains yet ask them to pray for *you* in an emergency. I had a hunch there was a story here to tell.

I learned more and told part of the story about how spirituality and religion are present in large academic medical centers in my book published in 2012, *Paging God: Religion in the Halls of Medicine*. The research for that book took me to chapels and meditation and prayer rooms in these hospitals; intensive care units with nurses, physicians, and other staff; and all over the hospital as I shadowed a team of chaplains—from patient support groups to staff meetings to the morgue—at a hospital I call Overbrook. While doing this fieldwork, I was aware that chaplains work in many settings in addition to hospitals. I wondered how their work compared, if they knew one another, and who and how they served people from a range of spiritual and religious backgrounds, including those with none. Deeply curious by nature, I also thought about what sociologist Erving Goffman calls "the backstage"—the behind-the-scenes pieces of Overbrook Hospital I had seen with chaplains out of the public eye and without an audience. I selfishly wondered about the other backstage places I might be able to see and people I might meet while shadowing chaplains in other locations.

As I completed *Paging God* in 2011, my first child was born. When the haze of sleeplessness started to lift a year later, I returned to these questions. Where, in addition to hospitals, do chaplains and spiritual care providers work? What is the work? Who do they serve? How do those they work with think about them? What difference, if any, does their work make to others in their settings? As a sociologist of religion, I wondered about their role in local religious ecologies; their connections to diverse people, including those with no religious affiliation or backgrounds; how they work across religious differences; and how they occupy religious roles in nonreligious settings. As someone who reads in the sociology of work and occupations, I had questions about chaplains' professional jurisdictions, their relationships with others in their workplaces, and how different workplaces structure their work.

Trained as an ethnographer, I tend to be motivated more by puzzles and seeming empirical contradictions I see in the world than by the theoretical questions that animate some other sociologists. In this spirit, I started a list of institutions in greater Boston that had chaplains and set out to learn about them. Initially, I wanted to do a project about military chaplains focused on how chaplains fill a required, federally paid religious role in a diverse nation that is formally committed to the separation of church and state. Boston is not home to many military installations, however, and with time I came to realize I was not going to be able to do an ethnographic project outside of Boston with a young child at home. In the summer of 2012, I traveled around greater Boston having informal background conversations with chaplains in as broad a range of institutions as possible. I was looking for a secular site where I could write a book, like *Paging God*, focused on how religion and spirituality were present in a seemingly nonreligious setting, including through the work of chaplains.

Initial Glimpses

I learned a lot in these initial conversations and was most intrigued by chaplains that attend to crew on ships in the port of Boston. These chaplains go onboard container ships, tankers, and cruise ships and I was curious to learn more. I knew nothing about the work of seafarers, the extent to which their invisible work literally around the globe makes our lifestyles possible, and how they are (or are not) cared for by chaplains in that work. While the U.S. Coast Guard and customs pay attention to the vessels and their goods, the chaplains I shadowed told me that no one cares for the crew unless they are present. For crew who are detained or do not have the paperwork required to leave the vessel, this means chaplains bring local newspapers on board, in addition to supporting Wi-Fi and cell phones, and whatever else is needed to enable seafarers to connect with their loved ones at home in China, Indonesia, the Philippines, Russia, Ukraine, and other countries around the world.

Wearing a hard hat and yellow safety vest, I carried knitted hats and toiletries in my backpack along with jigsaw puzzles and cookbooks when boarding vessels with chaplains in the port of Boston. I drove with chaplains in vans, taking seafarers permitted to leave vessels to the Cambridge side Galleria and other shopping malls. I also volunteered at the New England Seafarers Mission, serving the staff of cruise ships—who disembark for very short periods—as they pick up packages, send money home, shop in the small store onsite, and stretch their legs. I stopped this work in 2013 when pregnant enough with my second child that it was difficult to climb ladders and get onboard vessels without attracting attention.[1] Along the way, I wrote a series of articles about port chaplains in Boston and nationally and started an international collaboration through which we look at these issues globally.[2]

Increasingly aware that chaplains who work in different settings have limited contact with one another and simply curious about why, for example, airports have chaplains and chapels, I pursued other case studies that would enable me to compare chaplains across settings. Boston was the first city in the United States to have an airport chapel, and learning about it led me to interview chaplains at the largest airports across the country.[3] With now two small children and teaching and administrative work at Brandeis, smaller projects with data I could gather by phone were more feasible (especially with collaborators) than a longer book project, as much as I wanted to write one. I also published an article with colleagues about chaplains in the U.S. Senate and House of Representatives and developed brainstorming tables naming the factors I thought might explain variation in the work of chaplains in different settings and sectors.[4] I had an eye to the bigger story but not yet the unstructured time needed to really think through and develop it.[5]

Many chaplains are responsible for sacred spaces in their settings, and as I saw some of them across Boston and in airports across the country, I wanted to tell their stories in pictures as well as words. Photographer Randall Armor and I started photographing such spaces in Boston in the summer of 2016, which developed into a project on Hidden Sacred Spaces in the city.[6] The idea came from earlier work with the late architect Karla Johnson and architectural historian Alice Friedman.[7] Asking permission to see and photograph such spaces also introduced me to more chaplains across the city in a relatively unthreatening way as we gave everyone we met free copies of the photographs, which also were (and remain) available online for free download and later in a print exhibit that traveled across the city. Like the projects about port and airport chaplains, this project enabled me to continue learning from and thinking about chaplains in the limited (and precious) chunks of time I had for research.

Focused Attention

During the 2016–2017 academic year, when my first child was five and second child two, I had research leave from Brandeis University—a gift that gave me unstructured time to think, focus, and gather the data that became the core of this book. Wanting to think among colleagues who study work, I was a visiting scholar in Work & Organization Studies at the MIT Sloan School of Management where conversations with Erin Kelly, Mary Rowe, and others helped me develop the focus that became this book.

With the exception of Winnifred Sullivan's wonderful book *A Ministry of Presence: Chaplaincy, Spiritual Care, and the Law*, scholars of religion rarely study chaplaincy and spiritual care and almost never situate the work in broader scholarly conversations. The few who do, for example, Ronit Stahl in *Enlisting Faith: How the Military Chaplaincy Shaped Religion and the State in Modern America*, focus on single sectors like the military, healthcare, or higher education.[8]

In this book, I learn from and challenge these sectoral approaches by focusing geographically on the chaplains I could locate in a wide range of places in greater Boston. This approach allows me to compare across settings and put the work of chaplains in new places—like social service programs for the unhoused—in dialogue with those in traditional places like prisons. It also enables me to see all the people calling themselves chaplains or spiritual care providers as a single occupational group and to think about them as such. By focusing geographically, I am also able to situate chaplains historically in greater Boston, developing a case study of one city with its historical and cultural components that can be considered in relation to other cities in the future.

During the fall of 2016 and spring of 2017, I located people who considered themselves chaplains or spiritual care providers in as broad a range of organizations in greater Boston as possible. I focused primarily on chaplains who work inside Boston's city limits, including hospice chaplains who serve patients within these limits but are staffed through offices outside of them. I aimed to maximize the number of different organizations where chaplains work—rather than the number of chaplains working for the same organization—to develop as a varied sample as possible. I worked through existing professional and personal networks, local rabbinical and theological schools, and public records—primarily the *Boston Globe*—to locate these chaplains and organizations. I also asked every chaplain I interviewed to introduce me to others, continuing until I was rarely introduced to a chaplain in an organization where I had not already interviewed someone.

I met and interviewed over one hundred chaplains who work in greater Boston and primarily include in the analysis here the sixty-six who work in the city.

I approached each chaplain by phone or email explaining the project and asking for time to talk. I interviewed three-quarters of the sixty-six in-person and took time to look around their workplaces whenever possible. Sitting with chaplains in the settings where they work and watching them engage with others in the hallway or cafeterias where we spoke gave me glimpses of their work not otherwise available. I knew from my time shadowing chaplains in healthcare that much of what chaplains speak with people about is private and a third-person researcher is disruptive. I suspect, for example, that chaplains talk more about meaning and questions of theodicy with those they serve than is reflected in their interviews with me. In places—like the port or in higher education—where I could quietly shadow, I did. Most of what I describe in this book, however, came from interviews. In one-quarter of cases, chaplains asked to speak by phone rather than in person, so I conducted phone interviews. At MIT, I was privileged to work with Katherine Wong, then a student at Wellesley College, through the UROP program, and she conducted three of the interviews with chaplains in higher education and hospice. The demographics of the sixty-six chaplains we interviewed are included in tables A.1 through A.3.

To situate the chaplains I met in historical context and make sure I was locating chaplains in all the organizations in Boston where they work, Katherine Wong and I reviewed the *Boston Globe*. We first identified every mention of the word "chaplain" every ten years between 1945 and 2015 (i.e., in 1945, 1955, 1965, 1975, 1985, 1995, 2005, 2015). Our initial search yielded 2,028 articles; we disregarded obituaries. We also ignored articles that focused exclusively on chaplains who were physically outside the greater Boston. This reduced our sample size to 548. We began to review these articles and eliminated 214 because they mentioned a chaplain in passing but contained no other information about the person or their work. We analyzed the remaining 334 articles in detail and published an article.[9] I also draw on these newspaper reports extensively in chapter 2 of this book. This process also helped me identify and interview several chaplains I otherwise did not know.

In addition, I gathered archival material from a range of Boston organizations and worked with a team of undergraduates at Brandeis University to analyze it. We constructed timelines about chaplains at Boston City Hospital (now Boston Medical Center), Beth Israel Deaconess Medical Center, Logan airport, the Boston Police and Fire Departments, the Massachusetts State Police, Spaulding Rehabilitation Hospital, Massachusetts General Hospital, the Department of Youth Services, Long Island Hospital (now defunct), and Brigham and Women's Hospital. We also tracked statutes and rulings about chaplains in city and state governments and gathered the information we could about chaplains in these bodies. Sources included institutional archives, the state archives, archives of the Catholic Archdiocese and other major religious organizations, and personal papers including those of a fire chaplain located in the basement of a former chief's house. I was not able to locate any historical records about chaplains in city or state correctional settings. I use all these sources, in dialogue with the articles in the *Boston Globe*, to construct the best historical narrative I can (as a non-historian) in chapter 2.

Finally, to situate Boston as a case study in national conversations about chaplains, I interviewed the leaders of professional chaplaincy organizations in as many sectors as I could identify across the country during the 2016–2017 academic year. This included national chaplaincy leaders focused on corrections, aviation, disaster, military, fire, immigration, for-profit workplaces, colleges and universities, and training and endorsing

Table A.1 Demographics of Chaplains Interviewed in Boston, $N = 66$[a]

Characteristic	No. (%)
Gender	
Male	36 (55)
Female	30 (45)
Age	
< 40	7 (11)
41–50	9 (14)
51–60	24 (36)
61–70	17 (26)
> 70	7 (11)
Unknown	2 (3)
Race	
White	55 (83)
African American	9 (14)
Asian American	2 (3)
Religion	
Protestant	38 (58)
Catholic	10 (15)
Jewish	9 (14)
Buddhist	2 (3)
Unitarian	3 (3)
Muslim	1 (1.5)
Orthodox Christian	1 (1.5)
Quaker	1 (1.5)

[a] Data gathered during interviews with chaplains.

organizations. These eighteen interviews quickly enabled me to see how little connection there was among chaplains in different settings nationally and how deep and distinct the silos are. Findings from these interviews are published elsewhere.[10]

Parallel Interventions

Alongside the data collection for this book, I was involved in a series of collaborative initiatives designed to improve the training and work of chaplains. These include the Transforming Chaplaincy Project—a project funded by the John Templeton Foundation between 2015 and 2019—that aimed to expand and better communicate the research base on which chaplains work and make their work more evidence-based. In addition to enabling seventeen board-certified chaplains in healthcare to complete master's degrees in epidemiology, biostatistics, public health and other fields, these funds allowed one-third of chaplaincy residency programs in the United States to make research literacy education a permanent part of their curriculum. Close to one hundred chaplains also completed a free online course about becoming research literate.[11] Strategic thinking webinars, research networks, a management certificate program for administrative leaders in

Table A.2 Educational Backgrounds of Chaplains in Boston, $N = 66$[a]

Education	No. (%)
Highest degree earned	
Bachelors or less	2 (3)
Masters, including MDiv	48 (73)
PhD/ThD	10 (15)
Unknown	6 (9)
Completed some CPE	
Yes	35 (53)
No	27 (41)
Unknown	4 (6)
Ordained[b]	
Yes	54 (83)
No	7 (11)
Unknown	3 (5)
Certified as a chaplain	
Yes	20 (30)
No	43 (65)
Unknown	3 (5)
Of those certified (*N*=20), certification body	
International Fellowship of Chaplains	3 (15)
Association for Professional Chaplains/ National Association of Catholic Chaplains/ Neshama, Association of Jewish Chaplains	12 (60)
Military	5 (25)

[a] Data gathered during interviews with chaplains.

[b] Ordained includes deacons. There are two deacons in the sample.

healthcare chaplaincy and other educational and networking efforts also emerged from this project.[12]

Continuing to think about how chaplains can learn from one another and improve the care they provide across the settings where they work, I launched the Chaplaincy Innovation Lab in the fall of 2018 with colleagues to bring chaplains, educators, and social scientists into a common conversation. Since then, the Lab has developed as an applied research effort committed to sparking practical innovation in chaplaincy and spiritual care to improve the care chaplains provide on the ground. We see the Lab as a site of dialogue and experimentation based on research, seeking not to offer ready-made answers, but rather to encourage an ongoing conversation about the present state and future of spiritual care. We collaborate with sixty-plus advisors on a range of research, educational, and networking projects to strengthen and professionalize the field and improve the care chaplains provide.[13]

I engaged in all these parallel interventions in collaboration with chaplains, chaplaincy researchers, clinical and theological educators, and other social scientists. Grant-funded projects focused on how theological and clinical educators are training chaplains; ways to strengthen the relationships among theological and clinical educators and build curriculum for training; training materials about spiritual care for non-chaplaincy staff in healthcare; a study of how healthcare executives think about

Table A.3 Experience and Organizational Location of Chaplains in Boston, $N = 66$[a]

Experience/Organizational Location	No. (%)
Primary sector of work	
Healthcare (not hospice)	16 (24)
Hospice	9 (14)
Community	8 (12)
College/University	8 (12)
Prison	6 (9)
Military	5 (8)
Other	5 (8)
Police	3 (5)
Fire	2 (3)
Veterans Administration	2 (3)
Port/Airport	2 (3)
Currently works across sectors	
Yes	16 (24)
No	50 (76)
Average time working in chaplaincy[b]	13 years
Average time working in this organization[b]	9 years
Status	
Full-time	30 (45)
Part-time	36 (55)
Paid for work as a chaplain	
Yes	58 (88)
No	8 (12)
Is or was a city or state employee in work as a chaplain	
Yes	20 (30)
No	46 (70)
Connected to a congregation in work as a chaplain	
Yes	21 (32)
No	45 (68)

[a] Data gathered during interviews with chaplains.

[b] Time ranges from 6 months to more than 30 years.

spiritual care; an effort to link the work of chaplains in higher education to outcomes for students; an analysis of port chaplain-congregation relationships; a national mapping of Jewish chaplaincy; conversation circles and resource for chaplains of color; convenings that brought chaplains across settings into physical conversation with one another; and more.

With COVID-19, the Lab quickly pivoted. We offered webinars attended by more than 1,000 people about transitioning to tele-chaplaincy, held weekly townhall gatherings to support chaplains for the first few months of the pandemic, gathered and developed resource guides about grief and other topics, and—with the support of the Henry Luce Foundation and in partnership with the Danielson Institute at Boston University—offered free support groups for chaplains working during the pandemic. The Henry Luce Foundation also enabled us to re-grant $440,000 to sixteen chaplain-administrator teams to expand support for front-line staff during the pandemic and offer a series of educational sessions for chaplains focused on trauma, resilience, and coping.[14] In these and all our efforts, the Lab addresses short-term problems while collaborating and pushing for change in underlying structural issues.

Gifts from foundations and individual donors make the work of the Lab possible. Foundation partners include the Blue Cross Blue Shield Foundation of Massachusetts, BTS Center, Centerbridge Foundation, Charles H. Revson Foundation, E. Rhodes and Leona B. Carpenter Foundation, David and Lura Lovell Foundation, Fetzer Institute, Funding Individual Spiritual Health (FISH), Henry Luce Foundation, John Templeton Foundation, Josiah Macy Jr. Foundation, Louisville Institute, Ruderman Family Foundation, Russell Berrie Foundation, Templeton Religion Trust, and the Wabash Center.[15]

Analysis and Writing

This book is based primarily on the interviews I conducted with sixty-six chaplains in Boston and all the historical materials I gathered. All the interviews were transcribed and analyzed in ATLAS.ti. I read the interviews several times and then coded inductively first by question and then by themes and subthemes. Themes emerged through the analysis and were clustered into chapters over time. While I was aware of conversations in the sociology of religion, religious studies, and chaplaincy as I read and coded, I did not come to these data with specific theoretical frameworks. Insights emerged inductively in the analysis and writing. I wrote the empirical chapters based on the Boston interview data first, and I then revised and revised in the context of the historical materials in chapter 2.

I was aware of—and concerned about—my positionality from the beginning of this project to the end. A white woman married to a white woman and raised in a Protestant context outside of Philadelphia, I had access to and saw aspects of these topics different from someone with a different background and upbringing. While getting access to write *Paging God* when I was a postdoctoral fellow and new to the topic took almost a year and multiple starts and stops, most chaplains were quite willing to talk with me in this project and many had read or heard of *Paging God*. In addition to being older and now a faculty member with a title that denoted status, I was aware of how my experience as someone who had published a book and various public opinion pieces about chaplains in healthcare opened doors. While I strove to be reflexive in the data collection and analysis, I also tried—as in *Paging God*—to be constructive in the practical suggestions I make to chaplains, religious leaders, and educators in the book's conclusions. Some people conclude that makes me an advocate for chaplains. I prefer to think of myself as a supporter of spiritual care and chaplaincy when provided in ethically and culturally appropriate ways (which is not always).

I aim in this book to move between two perspectives I try to gently hold simultaneously. One is as a scholar of American religious life and culture steeped in historical and sociological questions about the field. The second is as an institution builder—the hat I wore with the Transforming Chaplaincy Project, continue to wear in my work with the Chaplaincy Innovation Lab, and wear daily in administrative work I did as the Senior Associate Dean for Strategic Initiatives for the School of Arts & Sciences and now the Dean of the Graduate School of Arts & Sciences at Brandeis University. Put simply, I aim to understand what is happening empirically, understand why and how it came to be that way, and work to improve it—be that on Brandeis' campus or in the care chaplains provide to reduce suffering among those with whom they work. I try in this book to name when these perspectives come into conflict and to identify, always, the empirical evidence on which my practical suggestions are made.

This book is just the first step, in what I hope will be a long and deep conversation among scholars, educators, religious leaders, chaplains and spiritual care providers, and the leaders of the institutions they serve about what chaplains do and how it can be strengthened (and in some cases reframed) across settings. Chaplains and spiritual care providers have been largely overlooked by social scientists, which will lead some readers to want to generalize from my findings beyond Boston because there is little other information out there. Please do so with care. Local factors shape much about how and where chaplains work, and more research is needed to tell the national story.

This book is shaped (and limited) by my unique scholarly perspective and access; my age (I started the project when I was thirty-six and am concluding it at forty-five), my white/Caucasian race/ethnic markers, and other identity markers; my focus on Boston as a single city; my training as a sociologist that leads me to focus more on the present than in what I could learn in the archives; and by the time period in which it was written. The research and writing process also took time—my first child celebrated his tenth birthday when the manuscript was completed and my second was six. As with the best sociology, I hope the material offered here—limitations and all—becomes grist for scholarly and applied conversations today and for historians in the future.

Interview Guide

Thank you for participating in this study. I'm hoping to learn a bit about your work, how you came to this work, and how you see religion and spirituality in your daily work with this organization. I'm particularly interested in learning—as well—about how you work with people in crisis. Do you have any questions for me before we begin?

Background

1. To start, how did you come to this work?
   a. Education
   b. Previous positions
   c. Formal certification or licensure
   d. Which organizations were involved in training? In endorsing?
   e. Did you feel called to this work in some sense?
   f. What has kept you doing this work over time?
   g. Who is your boss?
   h. Where is God for you in this?
2. Can you tell me about a usual day?
   a. Walk through a day
   b. Are there other things you do in a usual week? Month? Ask about attending formal ceremonies, giving prayers, etc.
   c. Are there times or situations in this organization in which you are always called?
   d. Tell me about the people you work with—their demographics including religious demographics

   e. Who do you work most closely with in this organization?
   f. Are there people here that you don't work with much at all?
   g. When your work is in house, where are you located physically?
   h. When you are working away from your office, what are the usual places you go?
   i. Do you have a formal relationship with a local congregation?
   j. To what extent do you work as an educator? What are you educating about?
3. How often are you called to be with people in crisis?
   a. Can you offer some examples?
   b. How do you respond to people in these situations?
   c. What do you bring that is unique to your work as a chaplain?
   d. How do you think personally about these crisis situations?
   e. How do you respond when people ask why me or why now questions?
   f. Can you say something about your underlying theology or beliefs about why bad things happen?
4. What do you most bring to this organization as a chaplain?
5. What do you most bring to people in crisis?
6. What is the best part of this work for you?
   a. Can you tell me about an especially memorable situation?
   b. How about a situation in which you felt like you really made a difference
7. What is the most difficult part of this work for you?
   a. What makes it challenging?
   b. How often and in what ways do you deal with death or end-of-life situations?
   c. How often and in what ways do you deal with conflicts?
8. How do you work with people who are religiously different from you?
   a. Can you give me an example of a situation that went well? Not so well?
   b. Does your organization have a formal policy about religious diversity?
9. For the leaders of professional organizations:
   a. Can you give me a sense of the history of this profession?
   b. Can you tell me about the history of this organization?
   c. What are some of the challenges you are facing or problems you are trying to solve?
   d. How do you see chaplains in this organization work around crisis and suffering?
   e. What do you hope this profession will look like in 20 years?
   f. What would this work like with unlimited time and resources?
10. What questions am I not asking that I should be to better understand your work?
    a. Do you know other chaplains in the greater Boston area?

Demographics

11. Gender
12. Religion
13. Formal certifications
14. Age range
15. Time in chaplaincy/religious work
16. Time at this organization
17. What professional organizations do you belong to?

Notes

Chapter 1

1. *Daily Boston Globe* (*DBG* hereafter),"Chaplain Braves Guns of Convicts to Aid Hostages."
2. *DBG*, "Chaplain Braves Guns of Convicts to Aid Hostages"; Menzies, "Prisoner Welfare Continued Story for Fr. Hartigan."
3. *DBG*, "Latent Violence, Courtesy Weird Riot Bedfellows"; *DBG*, "Rioters' Grievances Told Priest, Doctor"; Healy, " 'Wait Rioters Out . . . for Now,' Says Warden"; Hammond, "Riot-Ending Drive Hinted."
4. *DBG*, "Sketches of Those Who Settled Revolt"; *DBG*, "Citizens Committee Settles Charlestown Prison Riot"; Hammond, "85-Hour Revolt Ends."
5. Menzies, "Prisoner Welfare Continued Story for Fr. Hartigan."
6. Interview, 6/6/17. I identify all the interviews I did for this book as "Interview" followed by the date of the interview. On days when I interviewed more than one person, the dates are followed by a, b, or c. In a few cases, I use the real names of chaplains I interviewed because they were already in the public eye, impossible to disguise, and gave me permission in writing to do so. I note each of these real names in the text and footnote the first time I introduce them.
7. Interview, 5/4/15.
8. HuffPost, "Chaplains In Great Demand in Aftermath of Boston Marathon Bombing."
9. wbur, "For Hospital Chaplains, Delicate Work after Marathon Bombings."
10. MIT News, " 'He Was Truly One of Us.' "
11. Bucheri, "Chaplain at Newtown and Boston Knew She Wasn't Alone"; PBS, "Religious Responses to Boston Bombings." Religious leaders have long been involved in responding to natural and human disasters, see Roberts and Ashley, *Disaster Spiritual Care*; Bradfield, Wylie, and Echterling, "After the Flood."
12. Boston University, "Aftermath of Marathon Bombings: Anxiety, Fear Persist for Some."
13. A history of chaplains that synthesizes their work across settings is yet to be written. Key texts that lay out the history in particular settings including how it is and has been shaped by relevant national, state, and local policies include Swift, *Hospital Chaplaincy in the Twenty-First Century*; Stahl, *Enlisting Faith*; Dubler, *Down in the Chapel*; Hansen, *Military Chaplains & Religious Diversity*; Cadge, *Paging God*; Cadge, Freese, and Christakis, "Hospital Chaplaincy in the United States"; Schmalzbauer and Mahoney, *The Resilience of Religion in Higher Education*; Sullivan, *A Ministry of Presence*; Cadge and Skaggs, "Chaplaincy? Spiritual Care? Innovation? A Case Statement."

14. Brudnick, "House and Senate Chaplains;" Cadge, Clendenen, and Olson, "Idiosyncratic Prophets"; Mueller, "Civil Religion in the Congressional Chaplaincy."
15. Stanley, "Standing Rock Chaplains Attended to Needs after Joyful News." Jenkins, " 'Protest Chaplains' Shepherd at Protests." The Faith Matters Network is training and supporting many of these chaplains through their Movement Chaplaincy Project: https://www.faithmattersnetwork.org/daringcompassion.
16. Cadge, Winfield, and Skaggs, "The Social Significance of Chaplains." How people understand who chaplains are and what they do is just becoming clear through additional studies including Stavig et al., "Patients,' Staff, and Providers' Factual Knowledge about Hospital Chaplains and Association with Desire for Chaplain Services."
17. E.g., Weiss, "The Men and Women Who Run toward the Dying"; Ridderbusch, "For Hospital Chaplains, Coronavirus Has Shifted Spiritual Care"; Walker, "Hospital Chaplains Are Bridging the Gap between Patients and Grieving Families Who Can't Stay by Their Bedside during the Coronavirus Pandemic."
18. As quoted, in this piece: https://www.wbur.org/inside/staff/bridget-power. https://www.wbur.org/cognoscenti/2020/06/19/covid-19-chaplain-dying-alone-bridget-power
19. As quoted in these pieces and others: Greene, " 'Mourning in Isolation' "; Greene, "Hospital Chaplain Who Fought in Desert Storm Faithfully Serves on the Front Lines of Coronavirus Battle"; Sells, "Hospital Chaplains Report Uptick in Questions about Eternity."
20. See a special issue of *the Journal of Pastoral Care & Counseling* published in 2021 that includes the following overview: Snowden, "What Did Chaplains Do during the Covid Pandemic? An International Survey."
21. These frames were identified in collaboration with Carolina Siegler: Seigler and Cadge, "How Leaders Negotiate Religious Differences: Frameworks of Mandate and Interpersonal Care."
22. See, e.g., guidelines for doing chaplaincy in the community and social movements: Cress, Reece, and Hobgood, *The Complete Community Chaplains Handbook*; "Daring Compassion"; Ernst and Krinks, "A Guide for Movement Chaplains." Gouse, "An Investigation of an Expanded Police Chaplaincy Model."
23. As described in the appendix to this case statement Cadge and Skaggs, "Chaplaincy? Spiritual Care? Innovation? A Case Statement." The history of this term and requirements in the military is described in Stahl, *Enlisting Faith*. For an overview of the situation in Canada see McCarroll and Schmidt, "The Present and Future of Spiritual Care and Chaplaincy in Canada."
24. See https://www.truckstopministries.org/; Sims, "Truck Stop Chapels Provide Place of Worship for Truckers."
25. E.g.: https://www.postandcourier.com/news/chaplain-experienced-in-crisis-counseling-now-tends-to-restaurant-workers/article_4e1a91a6-7627-11e8-976d-abdd51e40a32.html; Raskins, "Chaplain experienced in crisis counseling now tends to restaurant workers' mental health."

http://www.kfvs12.com/story/11965661/chaplain-lays-out-plans-for-homeless-shelter-in-cape-girardeau/; Sweeney, "Chaplain lays out plan for homeless shelter in Cape Girardeau."

https://www.apnews.com/71b1c263b5ed4dfd83a7fe7e8540a5c5; "Kansas campus minister to go to Antarctica"

http://www.wtsp.com/article/sports/olympics/local-chaplain-serves-team-usa-in-pyeongchang/67-520098179; Lewis, "Local chaplain serves Team USA in Pyeongchang"

https://religionnews.com/rns-circus-chaplain-e/ "RNS Circus Chaplain"

See also Grouse, *Ministry of Presence*; Swain, "The T. Mort. Chaplaincy at Ground Zero."

26. Cadge, *Paging God*.
27. See chapter 2 of Sullivan's text for more on the historical development and use of the term: Sullivan, *A Ministry of Presence*.
28. As described here: Cadge, Winfield, and Skaggs, "The Social Significance of Chaplains: Evidence from a National Survey."
29. Interview 3/30/17.
30. Excluded from consideration, by design, are people doing the work of chaplaincy and spiritual care but who do not identify as chaplains (with the exception of Tom whose story begins chapter 5 and whom I stumbled on by accident). Some local clergy do this work for people outside of their congregations as do some social service providers trained as religious professionals working in jobs with other titles. The number and scope of people doing the work of chaplaincy and spiritual care and not identifying as chaplains is not known.
31. Cadge, Wang, and Rowe, "Perspectives from the Edge." We hope someone will conduct a similar analysis of the *Boston Herald* for a more working-class perspective.
32. Boston City Council, January 16, 1902, Minutes.
33. *Boston Globe*, "Firemen's Spiritual Welfare."
34. Archival documents, Chaplain of the Massachusetts Senate, Harvard Divinity School Library, House and Senate; archival documents about the chaplain and chapel at Boston's Logan airport from the Library of the Boston archdiocese are posted with permission: https://brandeis.maps.arcgis.com/apps/MapJournal/index.html?appid=25e1a799ebd640d3a0506689aff8fde0.
35. This included approximately 4,500 chaplains in the military (including in the reserves and National Guard), 900 in the Veterans Administration (including 150 full-time CPE residents), and 250 in federal prisons as of January 2021. Personal communications with Col. Thomas S. Helms U.S. Army; Chaplaincy Administrator Heidi Kugler, Federal Bureau of Prisons; National Director of Veterans Administration Chaplaincy Service Juliana M. Lesher; H. Maj. Cesar Santiago-Santini U.S. Army; Capt. Charles E. Varsogea U.S. Navy. It is also not clear how many chaplains work in higher education. John Schmalzbauer estimates that if you only count people who work for the institutions, it is probably under 1,000. If you add campus ministers, Hillel directors, and so forth, it could be several times that figure (personal communication, 5/3/21).

36. Cadge, *Paging God:* Fitchett, White, and Lyndes, *Evidence-Based Healthcare Chaplaincy.*
37. Schleifer and Cadge, "Clergy Working Outside of Congregations, 1976–2016."
38. Cadge et al., "Training Healthcare Chaplains"; Cadge et al., "Training Chaplains and Spiritual Caregivers?"
39. For more on the role of local factors in shaping airport and port chaplaincy in Boston see Cadge, " 'God on the Fly?"; Cadge, "The Evolution of American Airport Chapels"; Cadge and Skaggs, "Humanizing Agents of Modern Capitalism?"; Cadge and Skaggs, "Serving Seafarers in the Boston Harbor."
40. Sullivan, *A Ministry of Presence*, x.
41. Holst, "The Hospital Chaplain between Worlds," 12.
42. PRRI, American Values Atlas.
43. Cooperman, "America's Changing Religious Landscape"; Smith and et al., "U.S. Decline of Christianity Continues at Rapid Pace."
44. Brauer, "How Many Congregations Are There?"; Pew Research Center, "Why Americans Go (and Don't Go) to Religious Services"; Chaves, *American Religion*; Brauer, "The Surprising Predictable Decline of Religion in the United States."
45. Thurston and Kuile, "How We Gather."
46. Wilcox et al., "No Money, No Honey, No Church."
47. Johnson, *The New Bostonians.*
48. See Pew Research Center, "Adults in the Boston Metro Area."
49. PRRI, American Values Atlas.
50. See, e.g., Chander and Mosher, *Hindu Approaches to Spiritual Care*; Shipman, "Hinduism and Chaplaincy"; Sanford, "The Practice of Dharma Reflection Among Buddhist Chaplains." Friedman, *Jewish Pastoral Care.* Gauthier, "Formation and Supervision in Buddhist Chaplaincy"; Fisher, *Benefit Beings!*; Giles and Miller, *The Arts of Contemplative Care:* . Fawcett, "Muslim Women Chaplains in America"; Long and Ansari, "Islamic Pastoral Care and the Development of Muslim Chaplaincy"; Kowalski and Becker, "A Developing Profession: Muslim Chaplains in American Public Life."

Chapter 2

1. See, e.g., Eck, *A New Religious America: How a "Christian Country" Has Now Become the World's Most Religiously Diverse Nation*; Johnson, " 'The Quiet Revival:' New Immigrants and the Transformation of Christianity in Greater Boston"; Johnson, *The New Bostonians: How Immigrants Have Transformed the Metro Area since the 1960s.* McRoberts, *Streets of Glory: Church and Community in a Black Urban Neighborhood*; O'Connor, *Boston Catholics: A History of the Church and Its People*; Sarna and Smith, *The Jews of Boston*; Gamm, *Urban Exodus: Why the Jews Left Boston and the Catholics Stayed*; Bendroth, *The Last Puritans: Mainline Protestants and the Power of the Past*; Bendroth, *A School of the Church: Andover Newton Across Two Centuries.*

2. Religious professionals doing the work of chaplaincy and not identifying as such are not included in this chapter by design.
3. O'Connor, *Building a New Boston: Politics and Urban Renewal 1950 to 1970.*
4. O'Connor, *Boston Catholics.*
5. Eck, *A New Religious America.*
6. Sarna and Smith, *The Jews of Boston.*
7. Trickey, "Has Boston Given Up on God?"
8. See the appendix for more information about the methods. One of the specific historical challenges is trying to trace the use of a formal term (chaplain) as well as a kind of labor (spiritual/religious work done largely outside of religious institutions). Using newspaper sources leads to more information about the use of the formal term than the kind of labor—a key limitation of this chapter. I hope a historian will take up this effort (and correct my mistakes) in the future. For good sources about the history of Boston generally see Vrabel, *The People's History of the New Boston*; O'Connor, *Boston Catholics*; Sarna and Smith, *The Jews of Boston*; Johnson, *The New Bostonians*. The role of Boston-area seminaries and theological schools in this history also remains to be written. Margaret Bendroth describes the role of Andover Newton in the emergence of clinical pastoral education in chapter 7 of her *A School of the Church.*
9. Sullivan, *A Ministry of Presence: Chaplaincy, Spiritual Care and the Law*, 4.
10. Sullivan, *A Ministry of Presence*, 6.
11. E.g., Eiesland, *A Particular Place: Urban Restructuring and Religious Ecology in a Southern Exurb*; Cimino, "Neighborhoods, Niches, and Networks: The Religious Ecology of Gentrification"; Howell et al., "When Faith, Race, and Hate Collide: Religious Ecology, Local Hate Cultures, and Church Burnings"; Marshall and Olson, "Local Religious Subcultures and Generalized Social Trust in the United States."
12. E.g., Hicks, "Role Fusion: The Occupational Socialization of Prison Chaplains"; Hicks, "Learning to Watch Out: Prison Chaplains as Risk Managers"; Otis, "An Overview of the U.S. Military Chaplaincy"; Paget and McCormack, *The Work of the Chaplain*; Beckford and Gilliat, *Religion in Prison*; Beckford and Cairns, "Muslim Prison Chaplains in Canada and Britain"; Holifield, *God's Ambassadors: A History of the Christian Clergy in America*; Berlinger, "From Julius Varwig to Julie Dupree: Professionalizing Hospital Chaplains"; Sundt and Cullen, "The Role of Contemporary Prison Chaplain"; Bergen, *The Sword of the Lord: Military Chaplains from the First to the Twenty-First Century*; Loveland, *American Evangelicals and the U.S. Military: 1942–1993*; Stahl, *Enlisting Faith*; Dubler, *Down in the Chapel: Religious Life in an American Prison*; Cadge, *Paging God*; Schmalzbauer and Mahoney, *The Resilience of Religion in Higher Education*; Hansen, *Military Chaplains & Religious Diversity*; Conrad, DeBerg, and Porterfield, *Religion on Campus*; Forster-Smith, *College & University Chaplaincy in the 21st Century: A Multifaith Look at the Practice of Ministry on Campuses across America.*
13. The few outcome-oriented studies of healthcare chaplaincy are described in Fitchett, White, and Lyndes, *Evidence-Based Healthcare*. See also Purvis et al., "Patient Appreciation of Student Chaplain Visits during Their Hospitalization." Miller,

Wambura Ngunjiri, and Lorusso, "'The Suit Cares about Us:' Employee Perceptions of Workplace Chaplains."

14. The American tradition of legislative prayer also dates to the Revolutionary War as described in Cadge, Clendenen, and Olson, "Idiosyncratic Prophets: Personal Style in the Prayers of Congressional Chaplains, 1990–2010." For details on how chaplains were present during the civil war see Faust, *The Republic of Suffering: Death and the American Civil War.*
15. Roberts, *History of the Military Company of Massachusetts Now Called the Ancient and Honorable Artillery Company of Massachusetts, 1637–1888.*
16. See Loveland, *American Evangelicals and the U.S. Military: 1942–1993*; Loveland, *Change and Conflict in the U.S. Army Chaplain Corps since 1945*; Stahl, *Enlisting Faith*; Bergen, *The Sword of the Lord.*
17. For good overviews of military chaplaincy see Stahl, *Enlisting Faith*; Bergen, *The Sword of the Lord*; Loveland, *American Evangelicals and the U.S. Military*; Loveland, *Change and Conflict in the U.S. Army Chaplain Corps since 1945.* Kim Hansen specifically addresses the diversification of the United States military in Hansen, *Military Chaplains & Religious Diversity.* And the notion of chaplains as "multipliers" is explored in Waggoner, "Taking Religion Seriously in the U.S. Military: The Chaplaincy as a National Strategic Asset." Whitt, *Bringing God to Men: American Military Chaplains and the Vietnam War.* Slomovitz, *The Fighting Rabbis: Jewish Military Chaplains and American History.* Memoirs written by military chaplains include Autry, *Gun-Totin' Chaplain*; Benimoff and Conant, *Faith under Fire: An Army Chaplain's Memoir;* Cash, *A Table in the Presence.* See also more recent conceptions of spiritual fitness: Gutierrez et al., "Victors: A Conceptual Framework for Implementing and Measuring Military Spiritual Fitness"; Hufford, Fritts, and Rhodes, "Spiritual Fitness"; Sweeney, Rhodes, and Boling, "Spiritual Fitness: A Key Component of Total Force Fitness."
18. All according to Kim Hansen as summarized in Sullivan's volume; Hansen, *Military Chaplains & Religious Diversity*; Sullivan, *A Ministry of Presence.*
19. Sullivan, *A Ministry of Presence*, 65–76; Stahl, *Enlisting Faith*; Brinsfield, "The U.S. Military Chaplaincy, Then and Now"; Waggoner, "Taking Religion Seriously in the U.S. Military."
20. Personal communications with Col. Thomas S. Helms U.S. Army; H. Maj. Cesar Santiago-Santini U.S. Army; Capt. Charles E. Varsogea U.S. Navy.
21. And summarized in Sullivan, *A Ministry of Presence*, 76–84.
22. Sundt and Cullen, "The Role of Contemporary Prison Chaplain"; Denney, "Prison Chaplains"; Hicks, "Role Fusion"; Shaw, *Chaplains to the Imprisoned*; Sundt and FraCullen, "The Correctional Ideology of Prison Chaplains: A National Survey"; Pew Forum on Religion and Public Life "Religion in Prisons: A 50 State Survey of Prison Chaplains"; Sundt, HarDammer, and Cullen, "The Role of the Prison Chaplain in Rehabilitation"; Dubler, *Down in the Chapel*, 2013.
23. Pew Forum on Religion and Public Life, "Religion in Prisons." The report also finds that the majority of state prison chaplains are male (85%), middle aged (mean

57 years), white (70%), Christian (85%), and highly educated (625 have a graduate degree).

24. Hicks, "Role Fusion"; Hicks, "Learning to Watch Out."
25. Sullivan, *A Ministry of Presence*; Sullivan, *Prison Religion: Faith-Based Reform and the Constitution*; Dubler, *Down in the Chapel.*
26. Schmalzbauer and Mahoney, *The Resilience of Religion in Higher Education.*
27. Chander, "A Room With a View: Accommodating Hindu Religious Practice on a College Campus"; Kowalski, "A New Profession: Muslim Chaplains in American Public Life"; John Schmalzbauer, "Campus Religious Life in America"; Shipman, "Hindu Chaplaincy in US Higher Education: Summary and Guidelines."
28. Schmalzbauer, "Campus Prophets, Spiritual Guides, or Interfaith Traffic Directors? The Many Lives of College and University Chaplains."
29. E.g., Cadge, *Paging God*; Rosenberg, *The Care of Strangers: The Rise of America's Hospital System*; Starr, *The Social Transformation of American Medicine*; Risse, *Mending Bodies, Saving Souls: A History of Hospitals*; Kauffman, *Ministry and Meaning: A Religious History of Catholic Health Care in the United*; Kraut, "'No Matter How Poor and Small the Building:': Health Care Institutions and the Jewish Immigrant Community"; and Tabak, "Hospitals," in *Encyclopaedia Judaica.*
30. Cabot came from the most elite class in Boston. See Baltzell, *Puritan Boston and Quaker Philadelphia.* See also a poem often recited:

    And this is good old Boston,
    The home of the bean and the cod,
    Where the Lowells talk only to the Cabots,
    And the Cabots talk only to God.

    (reprinted here and many other places: A. M. Juster, "Cabots, Lowells, and a Quatrain You Don't Really Know," *Light*, n.d., https://lightpoetrymagazine.com/historical-and-hysterical-winterspring-2015/).
31. Research about hospital chaplaincy before 1925 is still very much needed. For glimpses see McCauley, *Who Shall Take Care of Our Sick?: Roman Catholic Sisters and the Development of Catholic Hospitals in New York City*; Monfalcone, "General Hospital Chaplain," in *Dictionary of Pastoral Care and Counseling*; Tabak, "The Emergence of Jewish Health-Care Chaplaincy." Key texts in understanding the development of chaplaincy in hospitals between the 1940s and the present in pastoral care and the social sciences include Cadge, *Paging God*; Myers-Shirk, *Helping the Good Shepherd: Pastoral Counselors in a Psychotherapeutic Culture 1925–1975*; Holifield, *A History of Pastoral Care in America*; Gerkin, *An Introduction to Pastoral Care*; Hall, *Head and Heart: The Story of the Clinical Pastoral Education Movement.*
32. Cadge, "Healthcare Chaplaincy as a Companion Profession: Historical Developments."
33. Cadge, *Paging God*; Berlinger, "From Julius Varwig to Julie Dupree"; Puchalski et al., "Improving the Spiritual Dimension of Whole Person Care: Reaching National and International Consensus."
34. Cadge and Rambo, *An Introduction to Chaplaincy and Spiritual Care.*

35. Lonsway, "Profiles of Ministry: History and Present Research." The role of Boston-area theological schools in chaplaincy innovations in the city needs additional study.
36. Tabak, "The Emergence of Jewish Health-Care Chaplaincy."
37. Cadge, "Training Healthcare Chaplains: Yesterday, Today and Tomorrow"; Clevenger, "Education for Professional Chaplaincy in the US: Mapping Current Practice in Clinical Pastoral Education (CPE)"; Cadge et al., "Training Chaplains and Spiritual Caregivers? The Emergence and Growth of Chaplaincy Programs in Theological Education."
38. For a summary see Chaplaincy Innovation Lab, "Beginner's Guide to Spiritual Care."
39. Tanner, "Four Trends That May Portend the Future for ATS Enrollment"; Vaters, "The New Normal: Realities and Trends in Bivocational Ministry"; Wheeler, "Higher Calling, Lower Wages: The Vanishing of the Middle-Class Clergy"
40. E.g., the International Fellowship of Chaplains (https://ifoc.org/), the International Federation of Christian Chaplains (http://www.chaplainfederation.com/), and others. Many of these are organized by evangelical Christian individuals and institutions.
41. Faith Matters Network, "Movement Chaplaincy."
42. This is my sense based on articles about chaplains in the *Boston Globe* as well as a review of relevant documents in the archives of Boston's Catholic Archdiocese, the Episcopal Diocese of Boston, congregational church archives, and the archival materials I could locate about a range of healthcare organizations, colleges and universities, prisons, and other major institutions in greater Boston. I intend this overview as a start and hope a trained historian will continue this investigation broadening, deepening, and correcting my sense of the landscape. This history likely understates the role of congregationalists and Unitarians given what I could find in existing records.
43. Report of the Hospital Chaplain, Episcopal Convention Journal, 1920.
44. Report of the Rev. J. Edward Hand, Episcopal Convention Journal, 1925.
45. Report of G. DeWitt Dowling, Episcopal Convention Journal, 1930.
46. See Boston Archdiocese, Catholic Directories 1915 through 1945.
47. Cadge and Skaggs, "Serving Seafarers in the Boston Harbor: Local Adaptation to Global Economic Change, 1820–2015."
48. As constructed from the records of Paul Christian, retired commissioner, Boston Fire Department, March 2017. The Irish Catholic domination of civil service positions but not the Boston elite is described in O'Connor, *The Boston Irish: A Political History*.
49. Report of Henry E. Edenborg, Episcopal Convention Journal, 1935.
50. Report of Henry E. Edenborg, Episcopal Convention Journal, 1935.
51. Howard, Kellett, Report on Prison Work, Episcopal Convention Journal, 1940.
52. See *Daily Boston Globe* (hereafter *DBG*), "13 Chaplains to Get Diplomas at Devens"; *Boston Globe* (hereafter *BG*), "Nine N. E. Chaplains Among 88 Graduated at Fort Devens School."
53. Report of Henry E. Edenborg, Episcopal Convention Journal, 1940.
54. Report of Frank Stedman, Episcopal Convention Journal, 1940.
55. Also in Boston before 1945, Mayor James Michael Curley seems to have established an Office of the Chaplain for the City of Boston in the early 1900s as an honorary

position specifically for the Zvhil-Mezbuz Rebbe, Grand Rabbi Yaakov Yisroel Korff. An article from the *Boston Globe* describes big crowds gathered at Boston's South Station to see him reunited with his wife and children after six years: *BG*, "Grand Rabbi Korff Escorted with Band." The office remains today. Zvhil-Mezbuz Rebbe, Grand Rabbi Yitzhak Akaron Korff is the current chaplain succeeding his uncle Rabbi Baruch Korff, and his grandfather Zvhil-Mezbuz Rebbe, Grand Rabbi Yaakov Yisroel Korff. He was first appointed as chaplain for the Boston Police and Fire Departments in 1975: *BG*, "Rabbi Ira Korff, 25, Has Been Appointed Chaplain of the Boston Fire Dept."

56. See Stahl, *Enlisting Faith*; Kurzman, *No Greater Glory: The Four Immortal Chaplains and the Sinking of the Dorchester in World War II*. Bendroth, *A School of the Church*.
57. See De Lue, "Life under the Japs: From Bataan's Fall to Miraculous Rescue at Cabanatuan by Yanks." He was assigned to be the Catholic chaplain at Cushing General Hospital in Framingham, MA, on his return: *DBG*, "Maj Dugan Assigned as Cushing Chaplain." Former Boston City Hospital chaplain, Maj. John J. Dugan, returns from Philippines where he had been a prisoner of war of the Japanese (released Jan. 30th): *DBG*, "Five Greater Boston Men Back from Jap Prison."
58. E.g., *DBG*, "74 Bay State Nurses Graduate at Fort Devens"; *DBG*, "Crosscup Post to Install Officers Friday Night"; *DBG*, "Kosher Kitchen at Devens Brings General a Citation"; *DBG*, "Harvard to Note Founding of Navy Chaplain Corps."
59. See *DBG*, "Money Not 'Be-All, End-All,' Abp. Cushing Tells Guild"; Harris, "5-Hour Walkout Ties Up Ten of City's Docks."
60. O'Connor, *Boston Catholics*. Biographies of Cushing include Cutler, *Cardinal Cushing of Boston*; Devine, *The World's Cardinal*; Fenton, *Salt of the Earth: An Informal Profile of Richard Cardinal Cushing*.
61. Senate No. 335. Chaplains were to be furnished with "subsistence and quarters if requested." In 1948, the state also ruled that chaplains in the state Senate and House should receive a salary (House No. 896).
62. House No. 532.
63. Jewish chaplains were certainly present in greater Boston before 1955 though were not organized as such until the Jewish Chaplaincy Council emerged focused primarily on elders and healthcare organizations (http://jewishchaplaincyma.48in48sites.org/). In 1945, the first service for Jewish people was held at the Chelsea Naval Hospital: *DBG*, "1st Jewish Rites Held in Chelsea Naval Chapel." A Jewish chaplain helped establish a kosher kitchen at Fort Devens in 1955: *DBG*, "Kosher Kitchen at Devens Brings General a Citation." Additional historical materials are in the Chaplain Services folders in the Synagogue Council of Massachusetts archival materials.
64. Hall, *Head and Heart*.
65. Regan, "Marine Sheds Uniform for Tights to Perform in Shrine Circus Here."
66. Denvir, "Boston Bows Its Head in Grief for F.D.R."
67. In Wakefield, a Memorial Day event commemorated the four World War II chaplains; Shapiro, "Wakefield to Honor Four Chaplains." For a full account of the sinking see Kurzman, *No Greater Glory*.
68. Shapiro, "Feasts in Homes, Rites Usher in Passover Tonight."

69. E.g., *DBG*, "Religion Bolsters Freedom, M.I.T. Seniors Are Told"; *BG*, "Mrs. Roosevelt Will Address Seniors."
70. Griffin was the chaplain here, in part, because he was a pastor at St. James Church in Chinatown, an easy walk from both locations. The chapel at South Station, Our Lady of the Railways, was opened in 1955 in a space previously used as a movie theater. Father Christopher P. Griffin was the first chaplain and offered regular Mass there. An article in the *Globe* in 1955 claimed that 5,000 people visited the chaplain daily: "Folks of all faiths come into meditate, or just relax." Father Griffin also served as chaplain to the Massachusetts Senate and the Knights of Columbus and was quoted in a 1955 *Globe* article saying, "You might as well say that I have a black suit, and will travel." For details see Callahan, "South Station Chapel to Be Opened Monday"; *DBG*, "Sitting in with Ted Ashby: Only One America." The prayer was published: McMorrow, "What People Talk about: Chaplain's Prayer in House Calls for Love of Neighbor." More information about the role of Massachusetts Senate and House chaplains is in archival documents at the Harvard Divinity School Library. Materials from the mid-1950s report the chaplain asking other religious leaders to offer opening prayers and trying, in that selection process, to be inclusive of all religions. It is not clear when the position was retired.
71. E.g., the Catholic Archdiocese began to serve Puerto Rican agricultural workers in Spanish in outlying communities. Johnson, "'The Quiet Revival.'"
72. Center for Spiritual Life, "Sacred Places."
73. This is described in archival materials from the Synagogue Council of Massachusetts, Chaplain Services, 1949–1954.
74. The new campus and religious center was called "one of the most extraordinary religious buildings of our times" in *DBG*: "$2 Million Campus, Religious Center to Be Dedicated at M.I.T. Today." The Hindu tradition was also represented at MIT since the 1920s through the Vedanta Society. A Hindu chaplain was formally appointed in the 1980s: Long, "Hindu Chaplaincy as Karma Yoga in the Tradition of Sri Ramakrishna and Swami Vivekananda An Interview with Swami Tyagananda."
75. Documents about the history of the chapels at what is today Beth Israel Deaconess Hospital are available in the hospital's archives. See also *BG*, "Ground Broken for Dooley Chapel at Deaconess." For more on the history of deaconesses see Legath, *Sanctified Sisters: A History of Protestant Deaconesses*.
76. Report of the Episcopal City Mission, Episcopal Convention Journal, 1960.
77. Report of the Department of College Work, Episcopal Convention Journal, 1965.
78. Eisenstadt, *Against the Hounds of Hell: A Life of Howard Thurman*; Harvey, *Howard Thurman and the Disinherited*. See also Hadden, *The Gathering Storm in the Churches*.
79. For an example of local preaching see *BG*, "Church Notes." On organizing, see Collins, "1000 Bay Staters Joining March in Alabama."
80. Fripp, "Bay State Rights Band on Road to Washington"; McGrath, "'Berlin Rope' Falls in Selma"; Collins, "A Time of Change"; Dudley, "From Pulpit to Street."
81. Levey, "Clergy Interrupt School Board Meeting." One wonders if chaplains played a role in the busing crisis of the 1970s.
82. George M. Collins, "Students Defended: Chaplains Score 'Red' Name-Calling."

83. *BG*, "Fire Department Plans Memorial Mass May 16."
84. Very little historical work has been conducted about police chaplains to explore how they responded to cases of police brutality and when and if they were critical of the police.
85. Denvir, "Panel Looks at Obscenity." Interview 1/30/17.
86. Report of the Governor's Committee on Jails and Houses of Correction, 1965.
87. Dunstan, *A Light to the City: 150 Years of the City Missionary Society of Boston, 1816–1966*, 273.
88. Cadge and Skaggs, "Serving Seafarers in the Boston Harbor."
89. This act is Senate No. 694. A range of other acts related to chaplains came through the House of Representatives beginning in the mid-twentieth century. Senate No. 335 in 1946 stated, "Every public institution under the department of public welfare and department of mental health will have a Catholic, Protestant, and Jewish chaplain." In 1948 act No. 896 stated that the "Chaplain of the Senate and House will each receive a salary established by the committee on rules of the Senate and House." In 1954, No. 91 was passed by the Senate focusing on the salaries of officers and employees at the reformatory and prison, except the chaplain. In 1969, the House of Representatives passed act No. 3317 which allowed fire department chaplains to display flashing red lights on their vehicles. Several more acts related to flashing lights on chaplains' vehicles were passed in 1975, 1976, 1977, 1979, and 1995. In the 1970s there were sixteen new acts related to chaplaincy beginning with act No. 4274 that focused on placing the position of chaplain on the standard pay schedule for employees of state institutions.
90. Report on Campus Ministries, Episcopal Convention Journal, 1975. Peter Gomes, a theological moderate, came out as gay in 1991, thoroughly disliked the label, and was a prominent African American voice at Harvard until his death in 2011: *Harvard Gazette*, "Rev. Peter J. Gomes dies at 68"; *Harvard Crimson*, "Remembering Reverend Peter Gomes, Beloved Harvard Spiritual Leader"; Cherry, "Peter Gomes: Gay Black Harvard Minister Preached 'Scandalous Gospel.'"
91. E.g., *BG*, "150 at Graveyard Service for Lt. Edward F. Sherry."
92. Driscoll Jr. and Coughlin, "Rt. Rev. George V. Kerr, 63; Became 'All-American in Life'"; Turner, "Bludgeon Falls Lightly on Legislature's Budget."
93. See his "In Memoriam," n.d., http://stsebsclassof1966.blogspot.com/2016/04/in-memoriam-monsignor-james-j-keating.html and Long, "Msgr. J.J. Keating, Was Chaplain with Boston Firefighters; at 83."
94. November 24, 1998, letter from Martin Pierce, fire commissioner, to Cardinal Law, Boston City Archives. Lawrence, "Rev. James Lane, Police Chaplain, Pastor." For more general background, see Hammond and Linscott, "Probe Centers on Jet's Low Approach."
95. Johnson, "'The Quiet Revival.'"
96. Immigrants from Haiti, Syria, Lebanon, and Southeast Asia also arrived in Boston in the 1960s, joining existing religious organizations and starting their own. Maybe there is mention of chaplains in non-English sources that I hope future scholars will explore.

97. See Johnson, "'The Quiet Revival.'"
98. Catholic Directory, Archdiocese of Boston, 1990.
99. Episcopal Convention Journal, 1986.
100. See Our Lady of the Airwaves Archival Materials, Archdiocese of Boston Archives. Reprinted with permission: "Our Lady of the Airways Tour," n.d., https://brandeis.maps.arcgis.com/apps/MapJournal/index.html?appid=25e1a799ebd640d3a0506689aff8fde0. *BG*, "Logan Airport—a City within a City."
101. Richard, "The Unusual Becomes the Norm at Boston Waterfront Chapel."
102. Father Mahoney was appointed chief chaplain in 1991. He also served as spiritual director of the St. Florian Society and at St. Francis deSales Church in Charlestown. More information is in Radin, "A Fire with Faith." Also letters in the Boston City Archives from 1998.
103. See Richman, "Rare Breed of Officer." Rabbi Ira A. Korff, the Jewish chaplain, wrote a letter to the *Globe* on January 9, 1985, taking umbrage at the phrase "rare breed," calling it offensive to the Jewish community and to the police department.
104. The *Globe* reported that a group of African American clergy working through the Black Ecumenical Commission planned to sue the Department of Corrections in 1976 over discriminatory hiring practices and withdrew the suit when four minority chaplains were hired. In 1980 a promise was made to hire more minority chaplains for Massachusetts, and in 1983 a group of Black clergy criticized the Department of Corrections for not keeping that promise: *BG*, "Group Assails Lack of Minority Prison Chaplains."
105. E.g., Boston Police Department chaplains Rev. William Francis and Rev. Thomas Reill, led Mass at Mt. Hope Cemetery in 1983 to honor deceased police officers: *BG*, "Hub Police to Honor Deceased Members." And police chaplain George Farland took part in the burial ceremony for Michael J. Schlavina who was killed in the line of duty: Caldwell, "With a Volley of Rifles and Taps, a Patrolman Is Buried."
106. Cadge, *Paging God*.
107. Interview, 3/30/17.
108. Episcopal Convention Journal, 1995.
109. Ribadeneira, "A Times of Testing, Affirmation Rosh Hashanah a Renewal for Many Jewish Students"; Ribadeneira, "Diverse College Crowd Is Catching the Spirit: Religious Activism Is Back on Campus."
110. Cadge and Skaggs, "Serving Seafarers in the Boston Harbor."
111. Some claim the priests accused of sexual abuse were moved into chaplain positions to get them out of congregations. Others say this was not the case, particularly for chaplaincy positions funded by the state with equivalent pay and benefits. The analysis needed to evaluate these claims has not been conducted.
112. Winship, "End of a Miracle? Crime, Faith, and Partnership in Boston in the 1990s"; Braga, Hureau, and Winship, "Losing Faith? Police, Black Churches, and the Resurgence of Youth Violence in Boston."
113. Kelsey B. White et al., "Gender-Based Perspectives on Professional Healthcare Chaplaincy Board Certification."
114. Episcopal Convention Journal, 2000 and 2005.
115. MIT News, "A Dream Fulfilled."

116. Barlow, "At MIT, a New Dimension of Ministry; Chaplain Gives Ethical Guidance."
117. Barlow, "For Harvard Humanists, End of an Era"; Walsh, "Dust in the Wind"; Carroll, "Islamic Community at Odds Over Post; Court Dismisses Lawsuit Filed by Imam Fighting to Be Rehired."
118. Barlow, "Chapel Gives Airport Travelers a Lift."
119. Brown, "Port of Calling," *Boston Globe*, October 2, 2006.
120. Vanessa Jones, "A Study in Comfort: More Muslims Hear the Call to Chaplaincy as a Way to Share Their Faith yet Minister to All."
121. Barlow, "Chaplain's Calling Helps Muslims."
122. Bellah, "Civil Religion in America"; Gorski, *American Covenant: A History of Civil Religion from the Puritans to the Present.*
123. News Wise, "Catholic Prayer Book Designed for Military Personnel."
124. Michael Levenson, "For Heroes, Tributes and Treats; Bomb-Sniffing Dogs Honored for Service in Iraq."
125. Cullen, "God's Work on the Block."
126. According to state payroll records in 2010 there were forty chaplains ranging from part-time contractors to full-time staff. The majority worked for the Department of Corrections ($N = 23$) or the Sheriff's Department ($N = 8$). Others worked for the Department of Mental Health ($N = 4$), Department of Youth Services ($N = 2$), the Soldier's Home ($N = 2$), or the Department of Development Services ($N = 1$) (Open Payrolls, "52 Employee Records for Massachusetts Chaplain in 2010").

    In 2015, there were sixty-two chaplains on the state payroll: thirty-four worked for the Department of Corrections, twenty for the Sheriff's Department, four for the Department of Mental Health, and four other in other settings (one each in the Department of Developmental Services, the Soldier's Home, the Department of Public Health, and the Department of Youth Services) (Mass Live, "Massachusetts State Employee Salary Database 2015."). In 2019, there were fifty-four chaplains on the state payroll. The distribution by department is less clear (Mass Live, "Massachusetts State Employee Salary Database 2019").
127. E.g., Wangsness, "'You Are Not Forgotten about': Behind Bars, a Cardinal's Quiet Prison Ministry."
128. E.g., Veiga, "For I Have Sinned; With Guidance from Boston College Volunteers, Inmates at the State Prison in Norfolk Find a Path from the Past to Spirituality and 'Internal Freedom.'"
129. Burge, "A Better Kind of Care."
130. See, e.g., Nolan, "'He Needs to Talk!': A Chaplain's Case Study of Nonreligious Spiritual Care."
131. Maas, "Healing Mind and Soul: Chaplains Say More Hospice Patients Look Harder for Spiritual Care as Their Bodies Are Failing."
132. E.g., Viser, "Revere Bids Farewell to Fallen Officer: Five-Year Veteran Recalled as 'Best We Have to Offer'"; Collette, "Memorials and Longtime Ties: Retired Police Honor Comrades"; Nicas, "Boston's First Black Officer Receives His Long-Overdue Honors"; Nelson, "Farewell to Trooper Who 'Saw the Good in Everything': More Than 600 Attend Funeral"; Smalley, "Amid Turmoil, Davis Takes Police Reins."
133. Interview, 5/24/17.

134. Brown, "Port of Calling."
135. Wangsness, "Interfaith Group Rallies on Beacon Hill vs. Anti-Muslim Rhetoric."
136. Jarett Bencks, "Schools Review Gender Guide."
137. Andersen, "Clergy, Activists Rally for Initiatives: Back Casino Repeal, Sick Leave Proposal."
138. Hohler, "Faith Binds Many on Sox: Evangelical Christians Give Sport a Spiritual Context."
139. Shinzawa, "Return Engagements Pay Off; Cuts Overcame Sticky Situations"; *BG*, "Miami Hoping for a Miracle."
140. Dyer, "They Brake for Redemption: Truck-Stop Chapel Refuels Drivers in Battle against Sin."
141. English, "Her Mission: Helping Those Who Comfort Creatures."
142. Chaplains on the Way, "About Us."
143. Interview, 6/21/17.
144. Everett, *Holy Spokes: The Search for Urban Spirituality on Two Wheels.*
145. Mills, "Tirelessly, the Minister Goes to Where the Need Is: From Church to Shelter to Jail to Graveside, Rev. Laura Ahart Follows a Midlife Calling."
146. Interview, 5/2/15.
147. MacCormack, "Antiviolence Ministry Ordains First Group of Chaplains: 7 Members Train in Prevention."
148. For more on being a chaplain at Boston Medical Center, see Alberts, *A Hospital Chaplain at the Crossroads of Humanity.*

Chapter 3

1. He retired when I was working on this book and was not replaced.
2. The 192nd General Court of the Commonwealth of Massachusetts, chap. 265, sect. 17. See the full text here: https://malegislature.gov/Laws/GeneralLaws/PartIV/TitleI/Chapter265/section37.
3. See 192nd General Court, chap. 272, sect. 38, https://malegislature.gov/Laws/GeneralLaws/PartIV/TitleI/Chapter272/Section38.
4. See 192nd General Court, chap. 22c, sect. 32, https://malegislature.gov/laws/generallaws/parti/titleii/chapter22c/section32.
5. Interview, 1/30/17. His real name is used here with permission.
6. See 192nd General Court, chap. 233, sect. 20a, https://malegislature.gov/Laws/GeneralLaws/PartIII/TitleII/Chapter233/Section20A.
7. Documents in the archives of Boston's Catholic Archdiocese tell some of the history of a Catholic chapel at this site. Letters from the 1970s between Catholic leadership and leadership in the Department of Youth Services make clear that there was a Catholic chapel there at the time, and there were tensions about how it should be used, physically maintained, and whether youth should receive religious instruction while in the facility. See also Dorney, "Many Donate Time, Treasure to Erect Chapel for Troubled Youth an Island of Hope"; Tolfree, "Working to Curb Violence, One Youth at a Time."

8. Still Harbor website: https://www.stillharbor.org/.
9. Interview, 5/23/17. The organization has continued to evolve since we spoke, and some of how they describe their work now is slightly different from how it was at that time. I use Perry Dougherty's real name with permission.
10. I do not address gendered patterns in the work here. For an overview in healthcare, see White et al., "Gender-Based Perspectives on Professional Healthcare Chaplaincy Board Certification."
11. Interview, 3/30/17c.
12. Interview, 7/13/17b.
13. Interview, 3/6/17.
14. Interview, 5/3/17b.
15. Interview, 2/27/17.
16. Interview, 2/21/17a.
17. Interview, 2/8/17.
18. Interview, 5/22/17.
19. Interview, 5/15/17.
20. Interview, 12/9/16.
21. Interview, 9/1/16.
22. Interview, 3/13/17.
23. No one described working as a chaplain because they did not like or were not suited for work in a congregation—a claim that has often been made about chaplains historically.
24. Interview, 3//27/17.
25. Interview, 5/3/17b.
26. Cadge, Wang, and Rowe. "Perspectives from the Edge: Chaplains in Greater Boston, 1945–2015."
27. See also Stahl, *Enlisting Faith*. Gomulka, "The Boundaries of Chaplain Confidentiality."
28. Interview, 3/6/17.
29. Interview, 4/25/17.
30. Interview, 2/17/17.
31. Just over 80% are ordained as described in the methods appendix.
32. Interview, 3/30/17c.
33. Interview, 11/18/16.
34. Interview, 5/24/17a.
35. More on this gap is described in Cadge et al., "Training Chaplains and Spiritual Caregivers? The Emergence and Growth of Chaplaincy Programs in Theological Education." Clevenger et al., "Education for Professional Chaplaincy in the US." Cadge et al., "Training Healthcare Chaplains." Cadge and Rambo, *An Introduction to Chaplaincy and Spiritual Care*.
36. Lonsway, "Profiles of Ministry: History and Present Research."
37. Multiple organizations offer CPE and related forms of clinical training as described here: Chaplaincy Innovation Lab, "Clinical Training Organizations."

    The APCE is the oldest and largest in the United States: https://acpe.edu/. Clevenger et al., "Education for Professional Chaplaincy in the US"; Hall, *Head and*

Heart: The Story of the Clinical Pastoral Education Movement; Thomas, *A "Snap Shot" History (1975–2000) of the Association for Clinical Pastoral Education, Inc.* Hilsman, *How to Get the Most Out of Clinical Pastoral Education: A CPE Primer*.

38. Cadge, *Paging God*. The process and requirements of board certification—designed and regulated by professional associations of healthcare chaplains—are described in Board of Chaplaincy Certification, Inc., "Notice about BCCI Certification Verification." Description of the requirements for individual units of CPE and the hours requirements are described in ACPE, "Defining a Unit or a Half-Unit of CPE."
39. This is likely unique to Boston where the average education of residents is higher. In 2018, 89.8% of American adults aged twenty-five years or older had completed high school. About 35% had a bachelor's degree or higher. In Massachusetts, this was slightly higher with 90.8% having a high school diploma. The state ranks number one in the country for adults attaining a bachelor's degree or higher at 44%. See National Center for Education Statistics, tables 104.10 and 104.88. This may also be changing as more MA programs in chaplaincy and spiritual care are being started.
40. Interview, 7/13/17a.
41. Interview, 2/27/17.
42. Cadge et al., "Training Chaplains and Spiritual Caregivers?"
43. Details about the programs are here for the U.S. Army: https://www.goarmy.com/chaplain/become-an-army-chaplain/candidate-program.html. Here for the Air Force: https://www.afrc.af.mil/About-Us/Chaplain/Chaplain-Candidate/. And here for the Navy: https://www.navy.com/careers/navy-chaplain. Navy chaplains also serve the Marines and Coast Guard.
44. Interview, Paul Minor, 2/21/17a.
45. Personal correspondence, June 2013.
46. Interview, 3/30/17b.
47. Interview, 8/9/17.
48. International Fellowship of Chaplains: https://ifoc.org/.
49. Personal correspondence, May 2015.
50. MacCormack, "Antiviolence Ministry Ordains First Group of Chaplains."
51. Interview, 5/22/17.
52. Interview, 11/16/16.
53. More about these training requirements and how they changed over time is described in chapters 2 and 3 of Sullivan, *A Ministry of Presence*. Also in Cadge, "Healthcare Chaplaincy as a Companion Profession."
54. Bucher and Strauss, "Professions in Process."
55. E.g., Eiesland, *A Particular Place: Urban Restructuring and Religious Ecology in a Southern Exurb*; Cimino, "Neighborhoods, Niches, and Networks: The Religious Ecology of Gentrification"; Howell et al., "When Faith, Race, and Hate Collide: Religious Ecology, Local Hate Cultures, and Church Burnings"; Marshall and Olson, "Local Religious Subcultures and Generalized Social Trust in the United States."
56. Interview, 2/17/17.
57. Chaplains who do not also have paid positions in local congregations tend to belong to local congregations as members.

58. More research is needed, and I suspect it is increasing religious diversity alongside shifting population demographics that weakened or challenged some of the long-standing informal relationships between the Catholic Archdiocese of Boston and the Boston Police and Fire Departments for example and/or between healthcare organizations and local hospices whose chaplains used to belong to the same (Protestant) congregations and see one another on Sunday mornings but do not anymore.
59. Interview, 6/21/17.
60. Interview, 2/18/17.
61. Interview, 5/22/17. This is another way prisons are more porous than scholars have traditionally argued Ellis, "Prisons as Porous Institutions."
62. Antoine, Aja, Barbara Savage, and Wendy Cadge, "Black Chaplains in the United States, 1940–2021: The Role of Race and the Work of Chaplaincy and Spiritual Care."
63. Cadge et al., "Training Chaplains and Spiritual Caregivers?"

Chapter 4

1. Sharon Parks calls these experiences "shipwrecks" in her writing about young adult formation, Parks, *Big Questions, Worthy Dreams*.
2. The few that are paid receive annual stipends from the cities where they work. In Boston, e.g., the city paid three chaplains to the Boston Fire Department with salaries between $11,724.43 and $52,072.63 (Analyze Boston, "Employee Earnings Report 2019").
3. Group conversation, 5/3/17a. All quotes from fire chaplains who work in Massachusetts but not in the city of Boston.
4. Interview, 11/8/16.
5. See, e.g., section 3 of Fitchett, White, and Lyndes, *Evidence-Based Healthcare Chaplaincy*; Massey et al., "What Do I Do? Developing a Taxonomy of Chaplaincy Activities and Interventions for Spiritual Care in Intensive Care Unit Palliative Care"; Sharma, "Using the Taxonomy: A Standard Vocabulary of Chaplain Activities." Less outcomes-oriented research about prison and military chaplains is in the public domain.
6. Growing numbers of people seeking to become chaplains are not formally affiliated with religious organizations raising more challenges in some institutions than others in being trained and credentialed for the work as described and cited in chapter 1.
7. See Hansen, *Military Chaplains & Religious Diversity*; Sullivan, *A Ministry of Presence*; Cadge, *Paging God*; Paget and McCormack, *The Work of the Chaplain*.
8. Faber, *Pastoral Care in the Modern Hospital*, 6.
9. Katz, "Jazz in Social Interaction"; Whalen, Whalen, and Henderson, "Improvisational Choreography in Teleservice Work"; Carter, "Creative Providers: Counseling and Counselors in Family Planning and Reproductive Health"; Kapp, "I'll Think of Something: Improvisation in Small Church Service Programs."
10. Some of these are classically described by Goffman as total institutions in his *Asylums*.

11. Chaplains in some municipal and community settings also primarily do rituals. Fire chaplains call their (few) colleagues who only do this banquet chaplains. As one explained, "there are a class of chaplains we call banquet chaplains—not a compliment. They go to swearings-in but not to incidents." Some chaplains with civic organizations open meetings: "It is a volunteer position where I'm just sort of there as part of the opening and closing prayers . . . when there is a memorial service for one of our members who has died."
12. Interview, 4/28/17.
13. See Cadge, Wang, and Rowe, "Perspectives from the Edge: Chaplains in Greater Boston, 1945–2015."
14. Cadge, Wang, and Rowe, "Perspectives from the Edge."
15. Interview, 2/8/17.
16. Allen and Rosen, "Trooper Is Remembered as a Devoted Father of 7."
17. Seltz, "Easton Church to Honor Town's Police, Fire Departments."
18. Interview, 5/24/17b.
19. Interview, 12/15/16.
20. Interview, 5/24/17a. See also Dubler, *Down in the Chapel*. Beckford and Gilliat, *Religion in Prison*; Erzen, *God in Captivity*; Sullivan, *Prison Religion*; Ellis, "Prisons as Porous Institutions"; Pew Forum on Religion and Public Life, "Religion in Prisons: A 50 State Survey of Prison Chaplains."
21. Interview, 5/22/17.
22. Interview, 11/17/16.
23. Interview, 3/30/17b.
24. Interview, 5/24/17a.
25. Interview, 5/16/17.
26. Interview, 3/6/17.
27. Interview, 2/8/17.
28. Interview, 3/6/17.
29. Interview, 4/25/17.
30. Interview, 3/30/17c.
31. Interview, 4/24/17b.
32. Interview, 3/27/17c.
33. Interview, 3/27/17b.
34. Interview, 3/30/17a.
35. Interview, 4/7/17.
36. Cadge, *Paging God*; Cadge and Sigalow, "Negotiating Religious Differences."
37. Interview, 4/28/17.
38. Interview, 6/3/17.
39. Interview, 5/14/17.
40. Interview, 11/17/16.
41. Sullivan, *A Ministry of Presence*, 174.
42. Sullivan, *A Ministry of Presence*, 174.
43. Cadge et al., "Training Chaplains and Spiritual Caregivers? The Emergence and Growth of Chaplaincy Programs in Theological Education"; Cash, *A Table in the Presence*; Dzikus, Hardin, and Waller, "Case Studies of Collegiate Sport Chaplains,"

Jacobsen and Hustedt Jacobsen, *No Longer Invisible: Religion in University Education*; Miller, Ngunjiri, and Lorusso, "Human Resources Perceptions of Corporate Chaplains."

44. Sullivan, *A Ministry of Presence*, 174 and 191.
45. Physically showing up is usually straight-forward though not for chaplains who work with the unhoused. They spoke about walking the streets with people who are unhoused as well as accompanying them to McDonald's and then sometimes to doctor appointments and other places they might provide support. In the words of one such chaplain describing her time at McDonald's, "We're both hanging out and having conversations, but we're also listening for ways that we can hook people into other resources. . . . But the helping is mostly accompanying someone to something else. Just the other day I went with a guy . . . to the doctor's appointments just to make sure that everything goes smoothly for him. And boy was it complicated. . . . I was really glad that I had gone." Interview, 7/13/17a.
46. Interview, 1/9/17.
47. Interview, 2/21/17a.
48. Interview, 8/9/17.
49. Interview, 4/24/17b.
50. Cadge, "God on the Fly?"; Cadge, "Healthcare Chaplaincy as a Companion Profession."
51. Interview, 5/14/17.
52. Interview, 3/13/17.
53. Interview, 7/7/17.
54. Interview, 6/3/17.
55. Interview, 3/30/17a.
56. Cadge, *Paging God*; Cadge and Sigalow, "Negotiating Religious Differences."
57. Interview, 7/7/17.
58. Group conversation, 5/3/17a.
59. Interview, 5/3/17b. Chaplains are part of what Rachel Ellis describes as the porousness of prisons: Ellis, "Prisons as Porous Institutions."
60. Interview, 5/12/17.
61. See, e.g., the training the Faith Matters Network offers for social movement chaplains: https://www.faithmattersnetwork.org/daringcompassion. Maia, "The Protest Chaplains." Bucher and Strauss, "Professions in Process."
62. See also Cadge, *Paging God* for a description of variation among healthcare chaplains and the centrality of death in their work.
63. Abbott, *The System of Professions*; Cadge, " 'God on the Fly?"
64. Seigler and Cadge, "How Leaders Negotiate Religious Differences."
65. Interview, 4/25/17.
66. Interview, 6/3/17.
67. Interview, 5/22/17.
68. Interview, 3/27/17b.
69. Interview, 4/18/2017.
70. Interview, 4/3/17b.
71. For the history of these policies see Cadge, *Paging God*.

72. Interview, 4/18/2017.
73. Interview, 11/28/16.
74. Interview, 4/21/17.
75. Interview, 11/18/16.
76. Interview, 4/14/17.
77. Interview, 3/30/17a.
78. Interview, 3/30/17b.
79. Interview, 6/21/17.
80. Interview, 4/28/17.
81. Interview, 12/12/16.
82. Waggoner, "Taking Religion Seriously in the U.S. Military: The Chaplaincy as a National Strategic Asset."
83. Interview, 5/4/15.
84. See Fitchett, White, and Lyndes, *Evidence-Based Healthcare Chaplaincy*. Kestenbaum et al., "What Impact Do Chaplains Have? A Pilot Study of Spiritual AIM for Advanced Cancer Patients in Outpatient Palliative Care." Labuschagne et al., "Chaplaincy Care in the MICU: Examining the Association Between Spiritual Care and End-of-Life Outcomes"; Damen et al., "Examining the Association Between Chaplain Care and Patient Experience."
85. See Cadge et al., "Training Healthcare Chaplains"; Cadge et al., "Training Chaplains and Spiritual Caregivers?" Particularly in healthcare organizations influenced by more traditional causal frameworks, there is a dialectic between a perceived need, actions to respond to that need, and naming the presumed outcomes of that response (and then measuring them).
86. Antoine et al., "What Organizational and Business Models Underlie the Provision of Spiritual Care in Healthcare Organizations?"; Antoine et al., "How Do Healthcare Executives Understand and Make Decisions about Spiritual Care Provision?"
87. Barton, Cadge, and Van Stee, "Caring for the Whole Student: How Do Chaplains Contribute to Campus Life?"; Van Stee et al., "What Effect Do Chaplains Have on Students? A Pilot Study from a Residential Liberal Arts College."
88. Interview, 5/22/17.
89. Group conversation, 5/3/17a.

Chapter 5

1. Interview, 5/24/17.
2. Interview, 9/1/16.
3. Interview, 4/24/17a.
4. Paget and McCormack, *The Work of the Chaplain*.
5. Spillman and Brophy, "Professionalism as a Cultural Form: Knowledge, Craft, and Moral Agency." For an example of how these claims have changed over time among healthcare chaplains see Bernau, "From Christ to Compassion: The Changing Language of Pastoral Care."

6. Also others on healthcare teams ask these questions, see Cunningham et al., "Perceptions of Chaplains' Value and Impact within Hospital Care Teams."
7. Antoine et al., "What Organizational and Business Models Underlie the Provision of Spiritual Care in Healthcare Organizations?"; Antoine et al., "How Do Healthcare Executives Understand and Make Decisions about Spiritual Care Provision?"
8. Abbott, "Things of Boundaries"; Abbott, "Boundaries of Social Work or Social Work of Boundaries? The Social Service Review Lecture"; Halpern, "Dynamics of Professional Control: Internal Coalitions and Cross-Professional Boundaries"; Kronus, "The Evolution of Occupational Power: An Historical Study of Task Boundaries between Physicians and Pharmacists"; Lamont and Molnar, "The Study of Boundaries in the Social Sciences."
9. This is consistent with what I found in the interviews I conducted with chaplains across the country that informed *Paging God*. I suspect chaplains talk more with those they serve than with me as an interviewer about questions of theodicy. It is also possible that, as a sociologist, my ear is not trained to hear nuances that a theologian or other scholar with explicit training in theodicy would hear.
10. Interview, 7/13/17a.
11. Interview, 5/23/17.
12. Interview, 3/30/17b.
13. Interview, 12/9/16.
14. Interview, 11/8/16.
15. Interview, 11/16/16a.
16. This example is interesting because when we interviewed healthcare executives in hospitals in other cities, they saw staff support as central to what chaplains uniquely contribute. See Antoine et al., "What Organizational and Business Models Underlie the Provision of Spiritual Care in Healthcare Organizations?; Antoine et al., "How Do Healthcare Executives Understand and Make Decisions about Spiritual Care Provision?"
17. Cadge, *Paging God*.
18. Interview, 12/9/16.
19. Interview, 5/16/17.
20. Histories and perspectives on this kind of pastoral care are evident in Gerkin, *An Introduction to Pastoral Care*; Holst, "The Hospital Chaplain between Worlds."
21. Interview, 3/15/17a.
22. Interview, 4/14/17.
23. Interview, 2/17/17.
24. Interview, 4/25/17.
25. Interview, 11/17/16.
26. Interview 3/30/17a.
27. Interview, 4/18/17.
28. Interview, 2/8/17.
29. The term "moral injury" was originally coined in the military, but it has since been used across different contexts, including healthcare and medicine, as well as chaplaincy and spiritual care. The term has no universal definition, and it is used differently across these settings. As morality is typically rooted in one's spiritual beliefs,

chaplains often play key roles in addressing moral injury. Scholars note that mental health services and psychological treatments are not sufficient or holistic for healing these wounds that are often deep and spiritual, calling for further support from figures like chaplains. See Carey and Hodgson, "Chaplaincy, Spiritual Care and Moral Injury: Considerations Regarding Screening and Treatment"; Kopacz et al., "Moral Injury: A New Challenge for Complementary and Alternative Medicine"; Drescher et al., "A Qualitative Examination of VA Chaplains' Understandings and Interventions Related to Moral Injury in Military Veterans." See also Carey et al., "Moral Injury, Spiritual Care and the Role of Chaplains: An Exploratory Scoping Review of Literature and Resources."

30. Interview, 4/14/17.
31. Handzo et al., "Outcomes for Professional Health Care Chaplaincy: An International Call to Action"; Damen, "Can Outcome Research Respect the Integrity of Chaplaincy? A Review of Outcome Studies."
32. Interview, 3/13/17.
33. Interview, 3/15/17a.
34. Interview, 3/22/17.
35. Interview, 7/25/17.
36. Interview, 11/16/16a.
37. Interview, 5/22/17.
38. Interview, 7/25/17.
39. Group conversation, 5/3/17a.
40. Interview, 12/6/16.
41. Interview, 4/28/17.
42. Interview, 2/21/17a.
43. Interview, 11/17/16.
44. Interview, 7/25/17.
45. See Duncombe, "Prophetic Dimensions of Ministry in Clinical Pastoral Education"; McWilliams, "Voices Crying in the Wilderness: Prophetic Ministry in Clinical Pastoral Education"; Buhuro, *Spiritual Care in an Age of #BlackLivesMatter: Examining the Spiritual and Prophetic Needs of African Americans in a Violent America*.
46. Interview, 11/17/16.
47. Interview, 2/17/17.
48. Interview, 5/3/17b.
49. Interview, 4/3/17b.
50. Interview, 11/16/16a.
51. Interview, 3/22/17.
52. Interview, 6/3/17.
53. Interview, 12/15/16.
54. Evangelism by religious prison volunteers has a long history dating to the religious founding of many jails and prisons in the United States. Erzen, *God in Captivity: The Rise of Faith-Based Prison Ministries in the Age of Mass Incarceration*; Dubler, *Down in the Chapel: Religious Life in an American Prison*; Sullivan, *Prison Religion: Faith-Based Reform and the Constitution*; Ellis, "Prisons as Porous Institutions."

55. Interview, 12/15/16.
56. Interview, 6/3/17.
57. Interview, 2/8/17.
58. Interview, 3/13/17.
59. Interview, 7/25/17.
60. Interview, 3/23/17.
61. Interview, 4/24/17b.
62. Interview, 7/7/17.
63. Interview, 7/13/17a.
64. Interview, 3/30/17b.
65. Interview, 3/15/17a.

Chapter 6

1. See Black and Rubinstein, "Direct Care Workers' Response to Dying and Death in the Nursing Home: A Case Study."
2. A few of the prison chaplains also spoke about how they have gone to memorial services and funerals to represent prisoners who were not granted permission to be there. In one case, a judge deemed it too dangerous for a prisoner to attend so the chaplain went in his place. "The family cussed me out," the chaplain remembered, "and I said I just came to represent. And then they asked me to do a prayer" (interview, 5/22/17).
3. Interview, 3/30/17a.
4. Interview, 5/22/17.
5. Erickson, "Knowing Death Well: Intimate and Contextual Death Competence among End-of-Life Laborers."
6. Hughes, "Good People and Dirty Work"; and Kreiner, " 'How Can You Do It?': Dirty Work and the Challenge of Constructing a Positive Identity"; Ashforth, and Kreiner, "Dirty Work and Dirtier Work: Differences in Countering Physical, Social, and Moral Stigma"; Ashforth et al., "Normalizing Dirty Work: Managerial Tactics for Countering Occupational Taint." For good recent overviews of social scientific thinking about death also see Engelke, "The Anthropology of Death Revisited." Carr and Luth, "Well-Being at the End of Life." Kaufman and Morgan, "The Anthropology of the Beginnings and Ends of Life."
7. Glaser and Strauss, *Awareness of Dying*; Sudnow, *Passing On: The Social Organization of Death*; Hughes, *The Sociological Eye*; Bosk, *All God's Mistakes: Genetic Counseling in a Pediatric Hospital*; Engelke, "The Anthropology of Death Revisited"; Charmaz, *The Social Reality of Death*; Sudnow, *Passing On*; Christakis, *Death Foretold: Prophecy and Prognosis in Medical Care.*
8. As part of hospice and palliative care efforts that he calls "social movements"—pushing back against medicalized death in hospitals—whether these chaplains are the "medical authorities" Timmermans asserts in his conception of death brokers is arguable. Timmermans, "Death Brokering: Constructing Culturally Appropriate Deaths."

9. They are contextually competent around death as described in Erickson, "Knowing Death Well."
10. Chaplains and religious leaders have long been perceived as death experts, though some claim they need more training, e.g., Lloyd-Williams, Cobb, and Taylor, "How Well Trained Are Clergy in Care of the Dying Patient and Bereavement Support?"
11. Hochschild, *The Managed Heart: The Commercialization of Human Feeling.*
12. Cadge, Fox, and Lin, "Watch over Us Sweet Angels: How Loved Ones Remember Babies in a Hospital Memory Book."
13. The pandemic brought this work into the public eye in hundreds of media pieces showing chaplains with victims of COVID-19, facilitating goodbyes with loved ones through Facetime and Zoom, and supporting healthcare staff steeped in death. For a sample of national articles, see the following: Brogan, "Cony High School Graduate, Now Chaplain at Boston Hospital, Offers Comfort, Hope to Coronavirus, COVID-19 Patients, Families"; Brunk, "Undeterred during COVID-19, Hospital Chaplains Transform Delivery of Spiritual Care"; Cadge, "The Rise of the Chaplains"; Cardillo, "Coronavirus Has Shut Down Most Places of Worship. Now What?"; Cardillo, "Via Social Media, Simona Shuman '22 Supports Chaplains on the Front Lines of Coronavirus"; Cawley and Precey, "Coronavirus: The Chaplains at the Front Line of End-of-Life Care"; Cornelius, "For Chaplains on the Front Lines, the Job Remains the Same, but the Circumstances Are Different"; Jenkins, "For Hospital Chaplains, Being Vaccinated First Brings a Mix of Emotions"; Kuruvilla, "Hospital Chaplains Grapple with COVID-19's 'Tsunami' of Grief"; Massari, "A Joyful Sorrow"; Mealer, "'You're Not Alone. I Am with You': The Chaplains Tending to Those Dying from Covid-19"; Ruggiero, "The Chaplain's Job"; Sikora, "The Case for Music in Times of Loss"; *The Economist*, "Civil Rites: As Fewer Americans Go to Church, Chaplains Are Finding Work Elsewhere"; Walker, "Hospital Chaplains Are Bridging the Gap between Patients and Grieving Families Who Can't Stay by Their Bedside."
14. Interview, 5/24/17a.
15. Interview, 5/22/17.
16. Interview, 3/6/17.
17. Interview, 3/6/17.
18. Interview, 4/28/17.
19. Interview, 2/21/17a.
20. As described in Molna, "As Americans Become Less Religious, the Role of Chaplains May Grow."
21. Interview, 2/27/17.
22. For an overview of what chaplains who work for hospices and palliative care do see Jeuland et al., "Chaplains Working in Palliative Care: Who They Are and What They Do." Nolan, "Hope beyond (Redundant) Hope: How Chaplains Work with Dying Patients." See also Emanuel et al., "Workings of the Human Spirit in Palliative Care Situations: A Consensus Model from the Chaplaincy Research Consortium."
23. Interview, 3/15/17a.
24. Interview, 5/3/17a.

25. Interview, 5/24/17b. See Allen, "Prayers, Offerings Pour in as 2 of City's Fallen Are Mourned"; MacQuarrie, "For Longtime Chaplain, a Duty That Never Gets Easier."
26. Interview, 2/8/17.
27. Interview, 5/22/17.
28. Interview, 2/8/17.
29. Interview, 5/16/17.
30. This includes having chaplains sit on ethics committees in healthcare organizations. Courtwright et al., "The Changing Composition of a Hospital Ethics Committee: A Tertiary Care Center's Experience"; Eyer, "Clergy's Role on Medical Ethics Committees"; Cadge et al., "The Role of Religious Beliefs in Ethics Committee Consultation for Conflict over Life-Sustaining Treatments." See also Labuschagne et al., "Chaplaincy Care in the MICU: Examining the Association Between Spiritual Care and End-of-Life Outcomes."
31. Glaser and Strauss, *Awareness of Dying*; Sudnow, *Passing On*.
32. See Kwak et al., "The Role and Activities of Board-Certified Chaplains in Advanced Care Planning"; Wittenberg-Lyles et al., "Communication Dynamics in Hospice Teams: Understanding the Role of the Chaplain in Interdisciplinary Team Collaboration"; Labuschagne et al., "Chaplaincy Care in the MICU."
33. Interview, 4/7/17. Choi, Curlin, and Cox, "'The Patient Is Dying, Please Call the Chaplain:' The Activities of Chaplains in One Medical Center's Intensive Care Units."
34. Interview, 3/13/17.
35. Interview, 4/7/17.
36. Interview, 7/7/17. Chaplain researcher Kate Piderman developed a spiritual life review intervention called Hear My Voice as described in several articles: Piderman, "On These Holy Mountains"; Piderman et al., "Hearing and Heeding the Voices of Those with Advanced Illnesses"; Piderman et al., "The Feasibility and Educational Value of Hear My Voice, a Chaplain-Led Spiritual Life Review Process for Patients with Brain Cancers and Progressive Neurologic Conditions."
37. Interview, 7/7/17.
38. Interview, 6/21/17.
39. Interview, 7/7/17.
40. Interview, 7/7/17.
41. Interview, 3/13/17. Many case studies have been published about the work of chaplains, including a number focused on how they care for people who are dying and their loved ones, e.g., Cooper, "Case Study of a Chaplain's Spiritual Care for a Patient with Advanced Metastatic Breast Cancer." Fitchett and Nolan, *Spiritual Care in Practice: Case Studies in Healthcare Chaplaincy*.
42. Interview, 4/18/17.
43. Interview, 7/7/17.
44. Interview, 3/27/17b.
45. Interview, 3/27/17b.
46. This is described in Broccolo and VandeCreek, "How Are Health Care Chaplains Helpful to Bereaved Family Members? Telephone Survey Results." Clergy—at least in a study in the UK—do not feel they receive enough training around death and

dying in their education: Lloyd-Williams, Cobb, and Taylor, "How Well Trained Are Clergy in Care of the Dying Patient and Bereavement Support?"; Goodhead, Speck, and Selman, "'I Think You Just Learnt as You Went Along'—Community Clergy's Experiences of and Attitudes towards Caring for Dying People: A Pilot Study."

47. Interview, 9/1/16.
48. Interview, 3/13/17.
49. Interview, 3/30/17a.
50. Interview, 8/8/17.
51. Interview, 4/21/17.
52. Interview, 11/18/16.
53. Interview, 6/21/17.
54. Interview, 4/7/17.
55. Interview, 7/13/17a.
56. Interview, 4/24/17b.
57. Interview, 4/18/17.
58. Interview, 7/17/17.
59. Interview, 3/30/17a.
60. See Olsen, Buenefe, and Falco, "Death in the Emergency Department."
61. Interview, 5/3/17a.
62. Johnson, 4/21/17.
63. See also Rawlings et al., "What Role for Death Doulas Play in End-of-Life Care? A Systematic Review."
64. Interview, 7/17/17.
65. There is a growing empirical literature on these questions, see, e.g.,Carr, "A 'Good Death' for Whom? Quality of Spouse's Death and Psychological Distress among Older Widowed Persons";Wakenshaw, "From a Good Death to a Better Bereavement? The Impact of the End of Life Experience on Bereavement Adjustment, a Thematic Analysis."

Chapter 7

1. Interview, 8/9/17.
2. For two examples written for teaching see https://pluralism.org/a-call-to-prayer, https://pluralism.org/invocation-or-provocation. These issues are often debated in what military chaplains can and cannot say in public prayers as described in Hansen, *Military Chaplains & Religious Diversity*. See also Reimer-Kirkham et al., *Prayer as Transgression? The Social Relationship of Prayer in Healthcare Settings*.
3. Interview, 4/5/17.
4. Interview, 11/21/15.
5. Related tensions are described by Braunstein, Fulton, and Wood, "The Role of Bridging Cultural Practices in Racially and Socioeconomically Diverse Civic Organizations"; Lichterman, "Religion in Public Action: From Actors to Settings."

6. There is a limited military and federal prison presence in Boston and Massachusetts, leading me not to have the kind of comprehensive data at the local level required to fill this out. For national perspectives see Stahl, *Enlisting Faith: How the Military Chaplaincy Shaped Religion and State in Modern America*; Hansen, *Military Chaplains & Religious Diversity*.
7. Reimer-Kirkham et al., *Prayer as Transgression?* See especially chapter 2, "Creating an Inclusive Public Sphere: Healthcare and the Role of Prayer."
8. Cadge and Sigalow, "Negotiating Religious Differences: The Strategies of Interfaith Chaplains in Healthcare."
9. A growing literature explores spirituality in workplaces, particularly corporate workplaces including Hicks, *Religion and the Workplace: Pluralism, Spirituality, Leadership*; Miller, *God at Work: The History and Promise of the Faith at Work Movement*.
10. Bunting, *Portrait of a Port: Boston, 1852–1914*; Morison, *The Maritime History of Massachusetts 1783–1860*; Knickerbocker, *Bard of the Bethel*; Deems, *A Home Away from Home: The Boston Seaman's Friend Society, Inc. 1827–1975*.
11. Day, "The Scandinavian Seamen's Mission: An Historical Approach toward a Covenant Theology of Missions."
12. Cadge and Skaggs, "Serving Seafarers in the Boston Harbor: Local Adaptation to Global Economic Change, 1820–2015"; Leehey, "A History of Mariner's House, 11 North Square, Boston, MA"; Rousmaniere, *Anchored within the Veil*.
13. Sampson and Wu, "Compressing Time and Constraining Space: The Contradictory Effects of ICT and Containerization on International Shipping Labour"; Cudahy, *Box Boats: How Container Ships Changed the World*; Levinson, *The Box: How the Shipping Container Made the World Smaller and the World Economy Bigger*.
14. Inc Billings & Reece Inc., "Proposal for Survey of Needs of Mariners in the Boston Area for Boston Port and Seamen's Aid Society."
15. Allison, *A Short History of Boston*.
16. For a fuller account of the history of port chaplaincy in Boston see Cadge and Skaggs, "Serving Seafarers in the Boston Harbor." There have also been several recent radio pieces about the New England Seafarers Mission: Wuthman, "For Nearly 140 Years, A Seaside Mission Has Offered Ship Workers Small Comforts And Spiritual Support"; Wuthman, "For Seafaring Workers, The Pandemic Could Mean Even More Time Away from Home." Reimer-Kirkham, et al., *Prayer as Transgression?*
17. *Boston Globe* (hereafter *BG*), "Boston City Council."
18. *BG*, "Firemen's Spiritual Welfare: Leo Club Organized in Boston Department and Chaplains Appointed."
19. *BG*, "Rev. Pomeroy"; *BG*, "Rev. H.E. Pomeroy Protestant Chaplain of Fire Department."
20. These numbers are based on employment records shared by Paul Christian former chief of the BFD.
21. Email, Paul Christian, 3/8/21.
22. *Boston Firefighters Digest*, "Department Has New Catholic Chaplain." Long, "Obituaries: Msgr. J.J. Keating, Was Chaplain with Boston Firefighters; at 83."

23. Chaplains were present at the Coconut Grove fire and served in its aftermath as described in Stack, "Memory Dies Hard: Cocoanut Grove—Visions of Hell"; Benzaquin, "Holocaust!—The Story of the Cocoanut Grove Fire-VI: Priest Burns Finger Giving Last Rites to Hundreds"; Potter, "Hero Priest at Club Fire Tells of 'Terrible Sights'"; *DBG*, "'Night of Panic' on WBZ Next Wednesday Marks 17th Anniversary of Grove Fire"; *BG*, "Firefighters Crowd Rites for Retired Hub Chief Pope"; Flynn, "Priest Describes Giving Last Rites to Victims."
24. Abbott and Kindleberger, "Two Missing, Eight Hurt after Hotel Wall Collapses: 7 Firemen Killed in Vendome Blaze"; *DBG*, "Cocoanut Grove Fire City's Worst Tragedy"; SCutler, "400 Dead In Hub Night Club Fire: Hundreds Hurt in Panic as the Cocoanut Grove Becomes Wild Inferno," *DBG*, "Even 500 Now Death Toll in Tragic Fire of Cocoanut Grove"; Botwright, "State Investigation Fails to Establish Cause of Hotel Vendome Fire"; Cutler, "400 DEAD IN HUB NIGHT CLUB FIRE."
25. E.g., *BG*, "Harold Matulaitis"; *BG*, "Fumes Kill Elderly Hub Brothers"; *BG*, "Memorial Services Held for Boston's Firefighters." Also, a service is held on the second Sunday of June at the Fireman's Lot in the Forest Hills Cemetery to recognize firefighters who had died. A statue was erected in 1909, and the chaplains rotate responsibility for the service.
26. Unpublished book manuscript, Father James Keating, p. 30.
27. Abbott and Kindleberger, "Two Missing, Eight Hurt after Hotel Wall Collapses"; Botwright, "State Investigation Fails to Establish Cause of Hotel Vendome Fire."
28.. Curran, "A Sincere Tribute to Fallen Firefighters."
29. Unpublished book manuscript, Father James Keating, p. 56.
30. Curran, "A Sincere Tribute to Fallen Firefighters."
31. Mieth, *All Hands Herald: Massachusetts Department of Fire Services*, 2014.
32. Mieth, *All Hand Herald: Massachusetts Department of Fire Services*, 2016.
33. Each chaplain is paid a stipend by the city with the Catholic chaplain paid much more than the other two (Analyze Boston, "Employee Earnings Report 2019").
34. eTreadwell, "MGH History." Rosenberg, *The Care of Strangers: The Rise of America's Hospital System*.
35. Records from the archives at MGH suggest some early trustees were concerned about religion and wished to have daily religious services in the hospital and a sermon on Sundays offered by a rotating set of local clergy.
36. Cadge, *Paging God*.
37. Fifty Years of Chaplaincy and Clinical Pastoral Education at the Massachusetts General Hospital.
38. Fifty Years of Chaplaincy and Clinical Pastoral Education at the Massachusetts General Hospital.
39. For more information and photos see Boston's Sacred Spaces, "Massachusetts General Hospital," n.d. http://www.hiddensacredspaces.org/massachusetts-general-hospital-2.
40. Interview, 12/9/16.
41. This approach has been critiqued, see, e.g., Coble, *The Chaplain's Presence and Medical Power: Rethinking Loss in the Hospital*; Beaman, "The Will to Religion: Obligatory Religious Citizenship." Case studies of chaplains working across religious traditions are described in Fitchett and Nolan, *Spiritual Care in Practice*.
42. Interview, 12/9/16.
43. Interview, 2/21/17a.

44. Interview, 7/13/17b.
45. Interview, 11/8/16.
46. Interview, 5/23/17.
47. Interview, 4/14/17.
48. Interview, 2/21/17a.
49. Interview, 2/21/17a.
50. Interview, 4/28/17.
51. Interview, 4/25/17.
52. Interview, 4/25/17
53. Interview, 4/25/17.
54. Seigler and Cadge, "How Leaders Negotiate Religious Differences."
55. Interview, 5/24/17a.
56. Cadge, *Paging God.*
57. A summary document, "Medicare Hospice Conditions of Participation, Spiritual Care Giver" prepared by the National Hospice and Palliative Care Organization summarizes these guidelines including the language about a "pastoral or other counselor" (i.e., not a chaplain) needing to be on the core hospice team. The federal guidelines are in Part II Department of Health and Human Services, Centers for Medicare and Medicaid Services, 42 CFR Part 418, Medicare and Medicaid Programs: Hospice Conditions and Participation; Proposed Rule, May 27, 2005.
58. Cadge and Sigalow, "Negotiating Religious Differences."
59. Interview, 7/13/17b.
60. Interview, 3/20/17.
61. Interview, 3/30/17a.
62. Interview, 3/30/17b.
63. Interview, 3/13/17.
64. Interview, 3/30/17b.
65. Interview, 3/22/17.
66. Interview, 4/18/17.
67. Interview, 3/27/17b.
68. Interview, 4/7/2017.
69. Interview, 3/27/17b
70. Interview, 7/7/17.
71. Interview, 3/6/17.
72. Interview, 3/6/17.
73. Interview, 11/17/16. See also Tobak, "A Theological Reflection on Baptism by a Jewish Chaplain."
74. I have changed minor demographic details in this exchange and am not identifying which interview it came from out of respect for the chaplain in question.
75. Interview, 3/27/17a.

Chapter 8

1. Weiss, "The Men and Women Who Run Toward the Dying." For a sample of national articles, also see the following: Brogan, "Cony High School Graduate, Now

Chaplain at Boston Hospital, Offers Comfort, Hope to Coronavirus, COVID-19 Patients, Families"; Brunk, "Undeterred during COVID-19, Hospital Chaplains Transform Delivery of Spiritual Care"; Cadge, "The Rise of the Chaplains"; Cardillo, "Coronavirus Has Shut down Most Places of Worship. Now What?"; Cardillo, "Via Social Media, Simona Shuman '22 Supports Chaplains on the Front Lines of Coronavirus"; Cawley and Precey, "Coronavirus"; Cornelius, "For Chaplains on the Front Lines, the Job Remains the Same, but the Circumstances Are Different"; Jenkins, "For Hospital Chaplains, Being Vaccinated First Brings a Mix of Emotions"; Kuruvilla, "Hospital Chaplains Grapple With COVID-19's 'Tsunami' Of Grief"; Massari, "A Joyful Sorrow"; Mealer, " 'You're Not Alone. I Am with You' "; Ruggiero, "The Chaplain's Job"; Sikora, "The Case for Music in Times of Loss"; *The Economist*, "Civil Rites: As Fewer Americans Go to Church, Chaplains Are Finding Work Elsewhere"; Walker, "Hospital Chaplains Are Bridging the Gap between Patients and Grieving Families Who Can't Stay by Their Bedside."

2. See Bard, "COVID-19 and Chaplains"; Best, Rajaee, and Vandenhoeck, "A Long Way to Go Understanding the Role of Chaplaincy? A Critical Reflection on the Findings of the Survey Examining Chaplaincy Responses to Covid-19"; Tan et al., " 'Essential Not Optional:' Spiritual Care in Australia during a Pandemic"; Zollfrank, "Chaplaincy in a Free-Standing Psychiatric Hospital During the COVID-19 Pandemic"; Vandenhoeck, "The Impact of the First Wave of the Covid-19 Pandemic on Chaplaincy in Health Care: Introduction to an International Survey"; Vandenhoeck et al., " 'The Most Effective Experience Was a Flexible and Creative Attitude'—Reflections on Those Aspects of Spiritual Care That Were Lost, Gained, or Deemed Ineffective during the Pandemic"; Haythorn, "Conclusion: What We Learned and Next Steps"; Snowden, "What Did Chaplains Do during the Covid Pandemic? An International Survey"; Desjardins et al., "Scared but Powerful: Healthcare Chaplains' Emotional Responses and Self-Care Modes during the SARS Cov-19 Pandemic"; Tata et al., "Staff-Care by Chaplains during COVID-19."
3. Sullivan, *A Ministry of Presence*, 196.
4. Interview, 5/2/15.
5. Warner, "Work in Progress: Toward a New Paradigm for the Sociological Study of Religion in the United States." Comparisons to other national contexts are also very insightful, e.g., McCarroll and Schmidt, "The Present and Future of Spiritual Care and Chaplaincy in Canada."
6. Konieczny and Rogers, "Religion, Secular, Humanism and Atheism: USAFA and the Cadet Freethinkers Group."
7. Representatives from the Veterans Administration shared with me their total number of chaplains. They would not share data broken down by gender and race. VA chaplains speak often, off the record, about demographic disparities.
8. Interview, 5/24/17b.
9. Perry and Schleifer, "Are Bi-Vocational Clergy Becoming the New Normal? An Analysis of the Current Population Survey, 1996–2017."
10. Antoine et al., "What Organizational and Business Models Underlie the Provision of Spiritual Care in Healthcare Organizations?"; Antoine et al., "How Do Healthcare

Executives Understand and Make Decisions about Spiritual Care Provision? A Pilot Study."

11. Interview, 12/9/16.
12. Interview, 2/27/17.
13. Holst, "The Hospital Chaplain between Worlds."
14. Interview, 2/8/17.
15. Interview, 3/13/17a.
16. Interview, 2/21/17a.
17. Interview, 3/30/17b
18. Chaves, *American Religion: Contemporary Trends*, 58.
19. NORC, "National Survey of Religious Leaders (NSRL)." Details here provided by March Chaves, personal communication, spring 2021.
20. Interview, 3/30/17b.
21. Chaves, *American Religion*, chapter 6.
22. Cadge et al., "Training Chaplains and Spiritual Caregivers? The Emergence and Growth of Chaplaincy Programs in Theological Education"; Cadge et al., "Training Healthcare Chaplains: Yesterday, Today and Tomorrow."
23. Cadge and Rambo, *An Introduction to Chaplaincy and Spiritual Care*.
24. Interview, 5/2/15.
25. See also Buhuro, *Spiritual Care in an Age of #BlackLivesMatter: Examining the Spiritual and Prophetic Needs of African Americans in a Violent America*.
26. See, e.g., Damen, Delaney, and Fitchett, "Research Priorities for Healthcare Chaplaincy: Views of U.S. Chaplains"; Fitchett et al., "Evidence-Based Chaplaincy Care: Attitudes and Practices in Diverse Healthcare Chaplain Samples."
27. Interview, 2/12/16.
28. Interview, 7/13/17b.
29. Emotional exhaustion is a challenge for chaplains even under "normal" circumstances White et al., "Distress and Self-Care among Chaplains Working in Palliative Care." Carter, Trungale, and Barnes, "From Bedside to Graveside: Increased Stress among Healthcare Chaplains."
30. See, e.g., map of COVID-19 storytelling initiatives: https://www.google.com/maps/d/u/0/viewer?mid=1FMGFrGeIoxVNCxESEVkII9sPP5ZIC3Pb&ll=29.41321993849139%2C-74.31292491321403&z=2.
31. a chapter titled "The Commissioning" co-authored with Jason Callahan in this book: https://uncpress.org/book/9781469667607/chaplaincy-and-spiritual-care-in-the-twenty-first-century/.
32. Holst and Kurtz, *Toward a Creative Chaplaincy*, 150.

Appendix

1. Many others have commented on the physical components of ethnographic work and how they have engaged around personal experiences such as pregnancy, chronic and genetic illnesses, and other factors, e.g., Turco, *The Conversational Firm*; Reich, "Pregnant with Possibility: Reflections on Embodiment, Access, and Inclusion in

Field Research." An excellent anthology is Muhammad and Neuilly, *Mothering from the Field: The Impact of Motherhood on Site-Based Research.*

2. Information about the collaborative project is on my website, "Religion in Multi-Ethnic Contexts: A Multi-Disciplinary Case Study of Global Seafaring," n.d., https://wendycadge.com/research/religion-in-multi-ethnic-contexts/.
3. Cadge, "'God on the Fly? The Professional Mandates of Airport Chaplains'"; Cadge, "The Evolution of American Airport Chapels: Local Negotiations in Religiously Pluralistic Contexts."
4. Cadge, Clendenen, and Olson, "Idiosyncratic Prophets: Personal Style in the Prayers of Congressional Chaplains, 1990–2010."
5. Anthropologists are newly calling these dilemmas "patchwork ethnography": Gökçe Varma, and Watanabe, "A Manifesto for Patchwork Ethnography," Society for Cultural Anthropology.
6. Hidden Sacred Spaces website: http://www.hiddensacredspaces.org/.
7. Cadge et al., "Sacred Space in a Secular Nation of Believers: A Working Paper."
8. Stahl, *Enlisting Faith: How the Military Chaplaincy Shaped Religion and State in Modern America*; Hansen, *Military Chaplains & Religious Diversity*; Dubler, *Down in the Chapel: Religious Life in an American Prison*, 2013; Schmalzbauer and Mahoney, *The Resilience of Religion in Higher Education.*
9. Cadge, Wang, and Rowe, "Perspectives from the Edge: Chaplains in Greater Boston, 1945–2015."
10. Seigler and Cadge, "How Leaders Negotiate Religious Differences: Frameworks of Mandate and Interpersonal Care."
11. See the final report for the project funded by a $4.5 million grant from the John Templeton Foundation, Transforming Chaplaincy, "Phase 1 Final Report."
12. These continue after the grant ended in 2019 as described here https://www.transformchaplaincy.org/. I transitioned to be an advisor (rather than co-director) of the effort after the grant ended.
13. The Lab continues to evolve as described here: https://chaplaincyinnovation.org/.
14. Much of this is described in the Lab's first annual report: https://chaplaincyinnovation.org/resources/annual-report-fy-2020. COVID-19 resources are here: https://chaplaincyinnovation.org/2020/05/chaplaincy-coronavirus. And the offerings made possible by the Henry Luce Foundation's support during the pandemic are here: https://chaplaincyinnovation.org/projects/resilience-frontline-spiritual-providers
15. For a full list, see https://chaplaincyinnovation.org/about/our-partners.

References

"1st Jewish Rites Held in Chelsea Naval Chapel." *Daily Boston Globe*, July 28, 1945.

"$2 Million Campus, Religious Center to Be Dedicated at M.I.T. Today." *Daily Boston Globe*, May 8, 1955.

"13 Chaplains to Get Diplomas at Devens." *Daily Boston Globe*, April 20, 1945.

"74 Bay State Nurses Graduate at Fort Devens." *Daily Boston Globe*, June 17, 1945.

"150 at Graveyard Service for Lt. Edward F. Sherry." *Boston Globe*, March 4, 1975.

"A Dream Fulfilled." MIT News. October 1, 2007. https://news.mit.edu/2007/chaplain-1001.

Abbott, Andrew. "Boundaries of Social Work or Social Work of Boundaries? The Social Service Review Lecture." *Social Service Review* 69, no. 4 (1995): 545–62.

Abbott, Andrew. *The System of Professions: An Essay on the Division of Expert Labor*. Chicago: University of Chicago Press, 1988.

Abbott, Andrew. "Things of Boundaries." *Social Research* 62 (1995): 857–82.

Abbott, John, and Richard Kindleberger. "Two Missing, Eight Hurt after Hotel Wall Collapses: 7 Firemen Killed in Vendome Blaze." *Boston Globe*, June 18, 1972.

ACPE. "Defining a Unit or a Half-Unit of CPE." N.d. https://www.manula.com/manuals/acpe/acpe-manuals/2016/en/topic/defining-a-unit-or-a-half-unit-of-cpe?q=hours.

Alberts, William E. *A Hospital Chaplain at the Crossroads of Humanity*, 2012. https://www.amazon.com/Hospital-Chaplain-Crossroads-Humanity/dp/1470092433

Allen, Evan. "Prayers, Offerings Pour in as 2 of City's Fallen Are Mourned." *Boston Globe*, March 29, 2014.

Allen, Evan, and Andy Rosen. "Trooper Is Remembered as a Devoted Father of 7." *Boston Globe*, March 23, 2016.

Allison, Robert J. *A Short History of Boston*. Beverly, MA: Commonwealth Editions, 2004.

Analyze Boston. "Employee Earnings Report 2019." (Dataset.) https://data.boston.gov/dataset/employee-earnings-report/resource/3bdfe6dc-3a81-49ce-accc-22161e2f7e74.

Andersen, Travis. "Clergy, Activists Rally for Initiatives: Back Casino Repeal, Sick Leave Proposal." *Boston Globe*, October 23, 2014.

Antoine, Aja, Barbara Savage, and Wendy Cadge. 2021. "Black Chaplains in the United States, 1940–2021: The Role of Race and the Work of Chaplaincy and Spiritual Care." *Chaplaincy Innovation Lab*. https://chaplaincyinnovation.org/resources/working-papers/black-chaplains.

Antoine, Aja, George Fitchett, Deborah Marin, Vanshdeep Sharma, Andrew Garman, Trace Haythorn, Kelsey White, and Amy Greene. "How Do Healthcare Executives Understand and Make Decisions about Spiritual Care Provision? A Pilot Study." *Southern Medical Journal* 114, no. 4(2021): 207–12.

Antoine, Aja, George Fitchett, Deborah Marin, Vanshdeep Sharma, Andrew Garman, Trace Haythorn, Kelsey White, Amy Greene, and Wendy Cadge. "What Organizational and Business Models Underlie the Provision of Spiritual Care in Healthcare

Organizations? An Initial Description and Analysis." *Journal of Health Care Chaplaincy* 28, no. 2 (December 28, 2020): 1–13.

Ashforth, Blake E., and Glen Kreiner. "Dirty Work and Dirtier Work: Differences in Countering Physical, Social, and Moral Stigma." *Management and Organization Review* 10, no. 1 (2014): 81–108.

Ashforth, Blake E., and Glen Kreine. "'How Can You Do It?': Dirty Work and the Challenge of Constructing a Positive Identity." *Academy of Management Review* 24, no. 3 (1999): 413–34.

Ashforth, Blake E., Glen Kreiner, Mark Klark, and Mel Fugate. "Normalizing Dirty Work: Managerial Tactics for Countering Occupational Taint." *Academy of Management Journal* 50, no. 1 (2007): 149–74.

Autry, Jerry. *Gun-Totin' Chaplain: A True Memoir.* San Francisco: Airborne Press, 2006.

Baltzell, E. Digby. *Puritan Boston and Quaker Philadelphia.* New York: Routledge, 1996.

Bard, Terry R. "COVID-19 and Chaplains." *Journal of Pastoral Care & Counseling* 75, no. 1 (2021): 3.

Barlow, Rich. "At MIT, a New Dimension of Ministry; Chaplain Gives Ethical Guidance." *Boston Globe*, May 28, 2005.

Barlow, Rich. "Chapel Gives Airport Travelers a Lift." *Boston Globe*, December 10, 2005.

Barlow, Rich. "Chaplain's Calling Helps Muslims." *Boston Globe*, September 29, 2007.

Barlow, Rich. "For Harvard Humanists, End of an Era." *Boston Globe*, May 14, 2005.

Barton, Rebecca, Wendy Cadge, and Elena G. van Stee. "Caring for the Whole Student: How Do Chaplains Contribute to Campus Life?" *Journal of College and Character* 21, no. 2 (April 2, 2020): 67–85.

Beaman, Lori G. "The Will to Religion: Obligatory Religious Citizenship." *Critical Research on Religion* 1, no. 2 (2013): 141–57.

Beckford, James, and Ilona Cairns. "Muslim Prison Chaplains in Canada and Britain." *Sociological Review* 63 (2015): 36–56.

Beckford, James, and Sophie Gilliat. *Religion in Prison: Equal Rites in a Multi-Faith Society.* New York: Cambridge University Press, 1998.

Bellah, Robert. "Civil Religion in America." *Daedalus* 96, no. 1 Winter (1967): 1–21.

Bencks, Jarett. "Schools Review Gender Guide." *Boston Globe*, March 3, 2013.

Bendroth, Margaret. *The Last Puritans: Mainline Protestants and the Power of the Past.* Chapel Hill: University of North Carolina Press, 2015.

Bendroth, Margaret. *A School of the Church: Andover Newton across Two Centuries.* Grand Rapids, MI: Eerdmans, 2008.

Benimoff, Roger, with Eve Conant. *Faith under Fire: An Army Chaplain's Memoir.* New York: Crown, 2009.

Benzaquin, Paul. "Holocaust!—The Story of the Cocoanut Grove Fire-VI: Priest Burns Finger Giving Last Rites to Hundreds." *Daily Boston Globe*, January 16, 1960.

Bergen, Doris L. *The Sword of the Lord: Military Chaplains from the First to the Twenty-First Century.* South Bend: University of Notre Dame Press, 2004.

Berlinger, Nancy. "From Julius Varwig to Julie Dupree: Professionalizing Hospital Chaplains." *Bioethics Forum*, 2, no. 6 (January 25, 2008). http://www.bioethicsforum.org/hospital-chaplains-Julie-Dupree.asp.

Bernau, John A. "From Christ to Compassion: The Changing Language of Pastoral Care." *Journal for the Scientific Study of Religion* 60, no. 2 (2021): 362–81.

Best, Megan, Geila Rajaee, and Anne Vandenhoeck. "A Long Way to Go Understanding the Role of Chaplaincy? A Critical Reflection on the Findings of the Survey Examining

Chaplaincy Responses to Covid-19." *Journal of Pastoral Care & Counseling* 75, no. 1 (2021): 46–48.

Billings & Reece, Inc. "Proposal for Survey of Needs of Mariners in the Boston Area for Boston Port and Seamen's Aid Society." June 11, 1970.

Black, Helen K., and Robert L. Rubinstein. "Direct Care Workers' Response to Dying and Death in the Nursing Home: A Case Study." *Journal of Gerontology* 60B, no. 1 (2004): S3–10.

Board of Chaplaincy Certification, Inc. "Notice about BCCI Certification Verification." N.d. https://bcci.professionalchaplains.org/content.asp?pl=25&contentid=25.

Bosk, Charles. *All God's Mistakes: Genetic Counseling in a Pediatric Hospital.* Chicago: University of Chicago Press, 1992.

"Boston City Council." *Boston Globe*, January 16, 1902.

Boston University. "Aftermath of Marathon Bombings: Anxiety, Fear Persist for Some." BU Today. April 24, 2013. http://www.bu.edu/articles/2013/aftermath-of-marathon-bombings-anxiety-fear-persist-for-some/.

Botwright, Ken. "State Investigation Fails to Establish Cause of Hotel Vendome Fire." *Boston Globe*, July 13, 1972.

Bradfield, Cecil, Mary Lou Wylie, and Lennis G. Echterling. "After the Flood: The Response of Ministers to a Natural Disaster." *Sociological Analysis* 49, no. 4 (1989): 397–407.

Braga, Anthony A., David Hureau, and Christopher Winship. "Losing Faith? Police, Black Churches, and the Resurgence of Youth Violence in Boston." *Ohion State Journal of Criminal Law* 6 (2008): 141–72.

Brauer, Simon G. "How Many Congregations Are There? Updating a Survey-Based Estimate." *Journal for the Scientific Study of Religion* 56, no. 2 (2017): 438–48.

Brauer, Simon G. "The Surprising Predictable Decline of Religion in the United States." *Journal for the Scientific Study of Religion* 57, no. 4 (2018): 654–75.

Braunstein, Ruth, Brad R. Fulton, and Richard L. Wood. "The Role of Bridging Cultural Practices in Racially and Socioeconomically Diverse Civic Organizations." *American Sociological Review* 79, no. 4 (2014): 705–25.

Brinsfield, John W. "The U.S. Military Chaplaincy, Then and Now." *The Review of Faith & International Affairs* 7, no. 4 (2010): 17–24.

Broccolo, Gerard T., and Larry VandeCreek. "How Are Health Care Chaplains Helpful to Bereaved Family Members? Telephone Survey Results." *The Journal of Pastoral Care and Counseling* 58, no. 1–2 (2004): 31–39.

Brogan, Beth. "Cony High School Graduate, Now Chaplain at Boston Hospital, Offers Comfort, Hope to Coronavirus, COVID-19 Patients, Families." News Center Maine, May 11, 2020. https://www.newscentermaine.com/article/news/health/coronavirus/cony-high-school-graduate-now-chaplain-at-boston-hospital-offers-comfort-hope-to-coronavirus-covid-19-patients-families/97-170a5ab9-30b7-4d1a-8217-5821af2a1270.

Brown, Joel. "Port of Calling." *Boston Globe*, October 2, 2006.

Brudnick, Ida A. "House and Senate Chaplains: An Overview." Congressional Research Service, 2011.

Brunk, Doug. "Undeterred during COVID-19, Hospital Chaplains Transform Delivery of Spiritual Care." MDedge Hematology and Oncology, April 27, 2020. https://www.mdedge.com/hematology-oncology/article/221320/coronavirus-updates/undeterred-during-covid-19-hospital-chaplains?sso=true.

Bucher, Rue, and Anselm Strauss. "Professions in Process." *American Journal of Sociology* 66, no. 4 (1961): 325–34.

Bucheri, Marilyn. "Chaplain at Newtown and Boston Knew She Wasn't Alone." National Association of Catholic Chaplins, n.d. https://www.nacc.org/vision/2014-mar-apr/chaplain-at-newtown-and-boston-knew-she-wasnt-alone-by-marilyn-bucheri/.

Buhuro, Danielle J. *Spiritual Care in an Age of #BlackLivesMatter: Examining the Spiritual and Prophetic Needs of African Americans in a Violent America*. Eugene, OR: Cascade Books, 2019. https://www.amazon.com/Spiritual-Care-Age-BlackLivesMatter-Examining/dp/1532648081.

Bunting, W. H. *Portrait of a Port: Boston, 1852–1914*. Cambridge: Harvard University Press, 1971.

Burge, Kathleen. "A Better Kind of Care." *Boston Globe*, July 24, 2011.

Cadge, Wendy. "The Evolution of American Airport Chapels: Local Negotiations in Religiously Pluralistic Contexts." *Religion and American Culture: A Journal of Interpretation* 28, no. 1 (2018): 135–65.

Cadge, Wendy. "God on the Fly? The Professional Mandates of Airport Chaplains." *Sociology of Religion* 78, no. 4 (2018): 437–55.

Cadge, Wendy. "Healthcare Chaplaincy as a Companion Profession: Historical Developments." *Journal of Health Care Chaplaincy* 25 (2019): 45–60.

Cadge, Wendy. *Paging God: Religion in the Halls of Medicine*. Chicago: University of Chicago Press, 2012.

Cadge, Wendy. "The Rise of the Chaplains." *The Atlantic*, May 17, 2020. https://www.theatlantic.com/ideas/archive/2020/05/why-americans-are-turning-chaplains-during-pandemic/611767/.

Cadge, Wendy, Julia Bandini, Ellen Robinson, Andrew Courtwright, and Angelika Zollfrank. "The Role of Religious Beliefs in Ethics Committee Consultation for Conflict over Life- Sustaining Treatments." *Journal of Medical Ethics* 43, no. 6 (2017): 353–58.

Cadge, Wendy, Margaret Clendenen, and Laura Olson. "Idiosyncratic Prophets: Personal Style in the Prayers of Congressional Chaplains, 1990–2010." *Journal of Church and State* 61, no. 4 (2015): 680–701.

Cadge, Wendy, George Fitchett, Trace Haythorn, Patricia Palmer, Shelly Rambo, Casey Clevenger, and Irene Elizabeth Stroud. "Training Healthcare Chaplains: Yesterday, Today and Tomorrow." *Journal of Pastoral Care and Counseling* 73, no. 4 (2019): 211–21.

Cadge, Wendy, Nicole Fox, and Qiong Lin. "Watch over Us Sweet Angels: How Loved Ones Remember Babies in a Hospital Memory Book." *Omega: Journal of Death and Dying* 73 (2015): 287–307.

Cadge, Wendy, Jeremy Freese, and Nicholas Christakis. "Hospital Chaplaincy in the United States: A National Overview." *Southern Medical Journal* 101, no. 6 (June 2008): 626–30.

Cadge, Wendy, Alice F. Friedman, Karla Johnson, and Margaret Clendenen. "Sacred Space in a Secular Nation of Believers: A Working Paper." 2012.

Cadge, Wendy, and Shelly Rambo, eds. *An Introduction to Chaplaincy and Spiritual Care*. Chapel Hill: University of North Carolina Press, 2022.

Cadge, Wendy, and Emily Sigalow. "Negotiating Religious Differences: The Strategies of Interfaith Chaplains in Healthcare." *Journal for the Scientific Study of Religion* 52, no. 1 (2013): 146–58.

Cadge, Wendy, and Michael Skaggs. "Chaplaincy? Spiritual Care? Innovation? A Case Statement." Working Paper, Department of Sociology, Brandeis University, 2018.

Cadge, Wendy, and Michael Skaggs. "Humanizing Agents of Modern Capitalism? The Daily Work of Port Chaplains." *Sociology of Religion* 80, no. 1 (2018): 83–106.

Cadge, Wendy, and Michael Skaggs. "Serving Seafarers in the Boston Harbor: Local Adaptation to Global Economic Change, 1820–2015." *International Journal of Maritime History* 30, no. 2 (2018): 252–65.

Cadge, Wendy, Irene Elizabeth Stroud, Patricia K. Palmer, George Fitchett, Trace Haythorn, and Casey Clevenger. "Training Chaplains and Spiritual Caregivers? The Emergence and Growth of Chaplaincy Programs in Theological Education." *Pastoral Psychology* 69, no. 4 (2020): 187–208.

Cadge, Wendy, Katherine Wang, and Mary Rowe. "Perspectives from the Edge: Chaplains in Greater Boston, 1945–2015." *Journal for the Scientific Study of Religion* 58, 269–86 (2019).

Cadge, Wendy, Taylor Winfield, and Michael Skaggs. "The Social Significance of Chaplains: Evidence from a National Survey." *Journal of Health Care Chaplaincy* 28, no. 2 (2020): 208–17.

Caldwell, Jean. "With a Volley of Rifles and Taps, a Patrolman Is Buried." *Boston Globe*, November 17, 1985.

Callahan, William R. "South Station Chapel to Be Opened Monday." *Boston Globe*, February 19, 1955.

Cardillo, Julian. "Coronavirus Has Shut Down Most Places of Worship. Now What?" Phys.org, April 2, 2020. https://phys.org/news/2020-04-coronavirus-worship.html.

Cardillo, Julian. "Via Social Media, Simona Shuman '22 Supports Chaplains on the Front Lines of Coronavirus." BrandeisNOW, April 29, 2020. https://www.brandeis.edu/now/2020/april/simona-shuman-coronavirus.html.

Carey, Lindsay B., and Timothy J. Hodgson. "Chaplaincy, Spiritual Care and Moral Injury: Considerations Regarding Screening and Treatment." *Frontiers in Psychiatry* 9 (December 5, 2018): 1–10.

Carey, Lindsay B., Timothy J. Hodgson, Lillian Krikheli, Rachel Y. Soh, Annie-Rose Armour, Taranjeet K. Singh, and Cassandra G. Impiombato. "Moral Injury, Spiritual Care and the Role of Chaplains: An Exploratory Scoping Review of Literature and Resources." *Journal of Religion and Health* 55, no. 4 (August 1, 2016): 1218–45.

Carr, Deborah. "A 'Good Death' for Whom? Quality of Spouse's Death and Psychological Distress among Older Widowed Persons." *Journal of Health and Social Behavior* 44, no. 2 (2003): 215–32.

Carr, Deborah, and Elizabeth A. Luth. "Well-Being at the End of Life." *Annual Review of Sociology* 45 (2019): 515–34.

Carroll, Matt. "Islamic Community at Odds over Post; Court Dismisses Lawsuit Filed by Imam Fighting to Be Rehired." *Boston Globe*, August 26, 2005.

Carter, Anthony. "Creative Providers: Counseling and Counselors in Family Planning and Reproductive Health." *Demographic Research* 19 (2008): 1969–2010.

Carter, Jerry L., Kelli R. Trungale, and Sunni A. Barnes. "From Bedside to Graveside: Increased Stress among Healthcare Chaplains." *Journal of Pastoral Care & Counseling* 67, no. 4 (December 1, 2013): 1–8.

Cash, Carey H. *A Table in the Presence*. Nashville: W. Publishing Group, 2004.

"Catholic Prayer Book Designed for Military Personnel." News Wise, May 13, 2005. https://www.newswise.com/articles/catholic-prayer-book-designed-for-military-personnel.

Cawley, Laurence, and Matt Precey. "Coronavirus: The Chaplains at the Front Line of End-of-Life Care." BBC News, June 7, 2020, sec. Norfolk. https://www.bbc.com/news/uk-england-norfolk-52820028.

Center for Spiritual Life. "Sacred Places." N.d. https://www.brandeis.edu/spiritual-life/sacred-places/index.html.
Chander, Vineet. "A Room with a View: Accommodating Hindu Religious Practice on a College Campus." *Journal of College and Character* 14, no. 2 (2013): 105–16.
Chander, Vineet, and Lucinda Mosher, eds. *Hindu Approaches to Spiritual Care.* Philadelphia, PA: Jessica Kingsley, 2019.
"Chaplain Braves Guns of Convicts to Aid Hostages." *Daily Boston Globe*, January 19, 1955.
Chaplains on the Way. "About Us." n.d. https://www.chaplainsontheway.us/about.
Chaplaincy Innovation Lab. "Beginner's Guide to Spiritual Care." N.d. https://chaplaincyinnovation.org/resources/beginners-guide.
Chaplaincy Innovation Lab. "Clinical Training Organizations." N.d. https://chaplaincyinnovation.org/training-credentials/clinical-training-organizations.
Chaplaincy Innovation Lab. "Meditations on Chaplaincy and Spiritual Care." N.d. https://chaplaincyinnovation.org/resources/meditations.
"Chaplains in Great Demand in Aftermath of Boston Marathon Bombing." HuffPost, April 19, 2013. https://www.huffpost.com/entry/chaplains-in-great-demand-in-aftermath-of-boston-marathon-bombing_n_3119425.
Charmaz, Kathy. *The Social Reality of Death*. Reading, MA: Addison Wesley, 1980.
Chaves, Mark. *American Religion: Contemporary Trends.* 2nd ed. Princeton: Princeton University Press, 2017.
Cherry, Conrad, Betty DeBerg, and Amanda Porterfield. *Religion on Campus.* Chapel Hill: University of North Carolina Press, 2001.
Cherry, Kitteredge. "Peter Gomes: Gay Black Harvard Minister Preached 'Scandalous Gospel.'" *Spirit*, February 28, 2022. https://qspirit.net/peter-gomes/.
Choi, Philip J., Farr Curlin, and Christopher Cox. "'The Patient Is Dying, Please Call the Chaplain:' The Activities of Chaplains in One Medical Center's Intensive Care Units." *Journal of Pain and Symptom Management* 50, no. 4 (2015): 501–06.
Christakis, Nicholas. *Death Foretold: Prophecy and Prognosis in Medical Care.* Chicago: University of Chicago Press, 1999.
"Church Notes." *Boston Globe*, March 6, 1965.
Cimino, Richard. "Neighborhoods, Niches, and Networks: The Religious Ecology of Gentrification." *City & Community* 10, no. 2 (2011): 157–81.
"Citizens Committee Settles Charlestown Prison Riot." *Daily Boston Globe*, January 22, 1955.
Clevenger, Casey, Wendy Cadge, Irene Elizabeth Stroud, Patricia K. Palmer, Trace Haythorn, and George Fitchett. "Education for Professional Chaplaincy in the US: Mapping Current Practice in Clinical Pastoral Education (CPE)." *Journal of Health Care Chaplaincy* 27, no. 4 (February 7, 2020): 222–37.
Coble, Richard. *The Chaplain's Presence and Medical Power: Rethinking Loss in the Hospital.* Lanham, MD: Lexington Books, 2018.
"Cocoanut Grove Fire City's Worst Tragedy." *Daily Boston Globe*, November 29, 1942.
Collette, Matt. "Memorials and Longtime Ties: Retired Police Honor Comrades." *Boston Globe*, June 2, 2008.
Collins, George M. "1000 Bay Staters Joining March in Alabama." *Boston Globe*, March 22, 1965.
Collins, George M. "Students Defended: Chaplains Score 'Red' Name-Calling." *Boston Globe*, October 23, 1965.

Collins, George M. "A Time of Change." *Boston Globe*, March 27, 1965.

Cooper, Rhonda. "Case Study of a Chaplain's Spiritual Care for a Patient with Advanced Metastatic Breast Cancer." *Journal of Health Care Chaplaincy* 17, no. 1 (2011): 19–37.

Cooperman, Alan. "America's Changing Religious Landscape: Christians Decline Sharply as Share of Population; Unaffiliated and Other Faiths Continue to Grow." Pew Research Center, 2015.

Cornelius, Earle. "For Chaplains on the Front Lines, the Job Remains the Same, but the Circumstances Are Different." LancasterOnline, April 25, 2020. https://lancasteronline.com/features/for-chaplains-on-the-front-lines-the-job-remains-the-same-but-the-circumstances-are/article_63e061ea-858f-11ea-b98e-836ff69be0d0.html.

Courtwright, Andrew, Sharon Brackett, Alexandra Cist, Cornelia Cremens, Eric Krakauer, and Ellen Robinson. "The Changing Composition of a Hospital Ethics Committee: A Tertiary Care Center's Experience." HealthCare Ethics Committee Forum, 2013.

Cress, Mark, Dwayne Reece, and Chris Hobgood. *The Complete Community Chaplains Handbook*. Lanphier Press, 2006.

"Crosscup Post to Install Officers Friday Night." *Daily Boston Globe*, October 17, 1945.

Cudahy, Brian J. *Box Boats: How Container Ships Changed the World*. New York: Fordham University Press, 2006.

Cullen, Kevin. "God's Work on the Block." *Boston Globe*, November 26, 2009.

Cunningham, Christopher J. L., Mukta Panda, Jeremy Lambert, Greg Daniel, and Kathleen DeMars. "Perceptions of Chaplains' Value and Impact within Hospital Care Teams." *Journal of Religion and Health* 56, no. 4 (August 1, 2017): 1231–47.

Curran, Charles C. "A Sincere Tribute to Fallen Firefighters." *Wakefield Daily Item*, June 23, 1972.

Cutler, John Henry. *Cardinal Cushing of Boston*. New York: Hawthorn Books, 1970.

Cutler, Samuel B. "400 Dead in Hub Night Club Fire: Hundreds Hurt in Panic as the Cocoanut Grove Becomes Wild Inferno." *Daily Boston Globe*, November 29, 1942. https://search.proquest.com/hnpnewyorkbostonglobe/docview/817086842/abstract/E97E3E25FE9247F8PQ/1.

Damen, Annelieke, Allison Delaney, and George Fitchett. "Research Priorities for Healthcare Chaplaincy: Views of U.S. Chaplains." *Journal of Health Care Chaplaincy* 24, no. 2 (2017): 57–66.

Damen, Annelieke, Patricia Murphy, Francis Fullam, Deirdre Mylod, Raj C Shah, and George Fitchett. "Examining the Association between Chaplain Care and Patient Experience." *Journal of Patient Experience* 7, no. 6 (April 19, 2020): 1–7.

Damen, Schuhmann. "Can Outcome Research Respect the Integrity of Chaplaincy? A Review of Outcome Studies." *Journal of Health Care Chaplaincy* 26, no. 4 (2020): 131–58.

"Daring Compassion: The Role of Movement Chaplaincy in Social Change." Faith Matters Network, 2019.

Day, Paul. "The Scandinavian Seamen's Mission: An Historical Approach toward a Covenant Theology of Missions." Eastern Nazarene College, 1975.

De Lue, Willard. "Life under the Japs: From Bataan's Fall to Miraculous Rescue at Cabanatuan by Yanks." *Daily Boston Globe*, April 1, 1945.

Deems, Mervin M. *A Home away from Home: The Boston Seaman's Friend Society, Inc. 1827–1975*. Bangor, Maine: Furbush-Roberts, 1978.

Denney, Andrew S. "Prison Chaplains: Perceptions of Criminality, Effective Prison Programming Characteristics, and the Role of Religion in the Desistance from Crime." *American Journal of Criminal Justice* 43, no. 3 (2017): 694–723.

Denvir, Philip J. "Panel Looks at Obscenity." *Boston Globe*, March 27, 1965.
Denvir, Robert F. "Boston Bows Its Head in Grief for F.D.R." *Boston Globe*, April 15, 1945.
"Department Has New Catholic Chaplain." *Boston Firefighters Digest*, August 1969.
Desjardins, Cate Michelle, Anne Bovo, Mario Cagna, Martijn Steegen, and Anne Vandenhoeck. "Scared but Powerful: Healthcare Chaplains' Emotional Responses and Self-Care Modes during the SARS Cov-19 Pandemic." *2021*, 75, no. 1 (April 2021): 30–36.
Devine, M. C. *The World's Cardinal*. Boston: Daughters of St. Paul, 1964.
Dorney, Meghan. "Many Donate Time, Treasure to Erect Chapel for Troubled Youth an Island of Hope." *The Pilot*, July 18, 2003.
Drescher, Kent D., Joseph M. Currier, Jason A. Nieuwsma, Wesley McCormick, Timothy D. Carroll, Brook M. Sims, and Christine Cauterucio. "A Qualitative Examination of VA Chaplains' Understandings and Interventions Related to Moral Injury in Military Veterans." *Journal of Religion and Health* 57, no. 6 (December 1, 2018): 2444–60.
Driscoll, Edgar J., Jr., and William P. Coughlin. "Rt. Rev. George V. Kerr, 63; Became 'All-American in Life.'" *Boston Globe*, January 24, 1983.
Dubler, Joshua. *Down in the Chapel: Religious Life in an American Prison*. New York: Farrar, Straus & Giroux, 2013.
Dudley, Uncle. "From Pulpit to Street." *Boston Globe*, March 21, 1965.
Duncombe, David C. "Prophetic Dimensions of Ministry in Clinical Pastoral Education." *The Journal of Pastoral Care* 44, no. 4 (1990): 317–28.
Dunstan, J. Leslie. *A Light to the City: 150 Years of the City Missionary Society of Boston, 1816–1966*. Boston: Beacon Press, 1966.
Dyer, John. "They Brake for Redemption: Truck-Stop Chapel Refuels Drivers in Battle against Sin." *Boston Globe*, November 23, 2008.
Dzikus, Lars, Robin Hardin, and Steven N. Waller. "Case Studies of Collegiate Sport Chaplains." *Journal of Sport & Social Issues 36*, no. 3 (2012): 268–94.
Eck, Diana L. *A New Religious America: How a "Christian Country" Has Now Become the World's Most Religiously Diverse Nation*. New York: Harper Collins, 2001.
Eiesland, Nancy. *A Particular Place: Urban Restructuring and Religious Ecology in a Southern Exurb*. New Brunswick: Rutgers University Press, 1999.
Eisenstadt, Peter. *Against the Hounds of Hell: A Life of Howard Thurman*. Charlottesville: University of Virginia Press, 2021.
Ellis, Rachel. "Prisons as Porous Institutions." *Theory and Society* 50, no. 2 (2021): 175–99.
Emanuel, Linda, George Handzo, George Grant, Kevin Massey, Angelika Zollfrank, Diana Wilke, Richard Powell, Walter Smith, and Kenneth Pargament. "Workings of the Human Spirit in Palliative Care Situations: A Consensus Model from the Chaplaincy Research Consortium." *BMC Palliative Care* 14, no. 1 (June 2, 2015): 29.
Engelke, Matthew. "The Anthropology of Death Revisited." *Annual Review of Anthropology* 48 (2019): 29–44.
English, Bella. "Her Mission: Helping Those Who Comfort Creatures." *Boston Globe*, April 8, 2012.
Erickson, Karla A. "Knowing Death Well: Intimate and Contextual Death Competence among End-of-Life Laborers." *Journal of Contemporary Ethnography* 46, no. 6 (2017): 647–72.
Ernst, Margaret, and Lindsey Krinks. "A Guide for Movement Chaplains: Spiritual and Emotional Care during Counter-Actions to White Supremacist Hate Rallies." Faith Matters Network, 2017. https://static1.squarespace.com/static/53f25c8fe4b0014b3

798ea58/t/5a394145e2c48325eff88c5a/1513701726612/FMN-Guide-for-Movement-Chaplains.pdf.

Erzen, Tanya. *God in Captivity: The Rise of Faith-Based Prison Ministries in the Age of Mass Incarceration*. Boston: Beacon Press, 2017.

eTreadwell, "MGH History." N.d. Virtual Library of Massachusetts General Hospital. https://libguides.massgeneral.org/mghhistory

"Even 500 Now Death Toll in Tragic Fire of Cocoanut Grove." *Daily Boston Globe*, December 8, 1942.

Everett, Laura. *Holy Spokes: The Search for Urban Spirituality on Two Wheels*. Grand Rapids, MI: Eerdmans, 2017.

Eyer, Richard C. "Clergy's Role on Medical Ethics Committees." *The Journal of Pastoral Care* 39, no. 3 (1985): 208–12.

Faber, Heije. *Pastoral Care in the Modern Hospital*. Philadelphia: Westminster Press, 1971.

Faith Matters Network. "Movement Chaplaincy." N.d. https://www.faithmattersnetwork.org/daringcompassion.

Faust, Drew Gilpin. *The Republic of Suffering: Death and the American Civil War*. New York: Vintage Books, 2008.

Fawcett, Rachelle. "Muslim Women Chaplains in America." *Azizah Magazine*, 2014. http://www.azizahmagazine.com/Features/Feature_7-4_Chaplain.html.

Fenton, John H. *Salt of the Earth: An Informal Profile of Richard Cardinal Cushing*. New York: Coward-McCann, 1965.

"Fire Department Plans Memorial Mass May 16." *Boston Globe*, May 9, 1965.

"Firefighters Crowd Rites for Retired Hub Chief Pope." *Boston Globe*, January 9, 1973.

"Firemen's Spiritual Welfare: Leo Club Organized in Boston Department and Chaplains Appointed." *Boston Globe*, January 7, 1906.

Fisher, Daniel Clarkson. *Benefit Beings!: The Buddhist Guide to Professional Chaplaincy*. University of the West, 2013. https://www.amazon.com/Benefit-Beings-Buddhist-Professional-Chaplaincy/dp/0615796494

Fitchett, George, Jason Nieuwsma, Mark K. Bates, Jeffrey E. Rhodes, and Keither Meador. "Evidence-Based Chaplaincy Care: Attitudes and Practices in Diverse Healthcare Chaplain Samples." *Journal of Health Care Chaplaincy* 20, no. 4 (2014): 144–60.

Fitchett, George, and Steve Nolan. *Spiritual Care in Practice: Case Studies in Healthcare Chaplaincy*. Philadelphia: Jessica Kingsley, 2015.

Fitchett, George, Kelsey B. White, and Kathryn Lyndes. *Evidence-Based Healthcare Chaplaincy*. London: Jessica Kingsley, 2018.

Flynn, Frank. "Priest Describes Giving Last Rites to Victims." *Daily Boston Globe*, November 30, 1942.

"For Hospital Chaplains, Delicate Work After Marathon Bombings." wbur, April 23, 2014. https://www.wbur.org/news/2013/04/23/hospital-chaplains-marathon-bombs.

Forster-Smith, Lucy A. *College & University Chaplaincy in the 21st Century: A Multifaith Look at the Practice of Ministry on Campuses Across America*. Woodstock, VT: SkyLight Paths, 2013. https://books.google.com/books?id=BRbXnAEACAAJ&dq=forster+smith+chaplain&hl=en&newbks=1&newbks_redir=0&sa=X&ved=2ahUKEwjt2OrAs9_qAhVJ7qwKHSjpBZEQ6AEwAXoECAIQAg.

Friedman, Dayle. *Jewish Pastoral Care: A Practical Handbook from Traditional and Contemporary Sources*. Woodstock, VT: Jewish Lights, 2005.

Fripp, William J. "Bay State Rights Band on Road to Washington." *Boston Globe*, March 12, 1965.

"Fumes Kill Elderly Hub Brothers." *Boston Globe*, December 9, 1984.
Gamm, Gerald. *Urban Exodus: Why the Jews Left Boston and the Catholics Stayed*. Cambridge: Harvard University Press, 2001.
Gauthier, Tina Jitsujo. "Formation and Supervision in Buddhist Chaplaincy." *Reflective Practice: Formation and Supervision in Ministry* 37 (2017): 185–201.
Gerkin, Charles V. *An Introduction to Pastoral Care*. Nashville: Abingdon Press, 1997.
Giles, Cheryl A., and Willa Miller, eds. *The Arts of Contemplative Care: Pioneering Voices in Buddhist Chaplaincy and Pastoral Work*. Boston: Wisdom, 2012.
Glaser, Barney G., and Anselm L. Strauss. *Awareness of Dying*. Chicago: Aldine, 1965.
Goffman, Erving. *Asylums: Essays on the Social Situation of Mental Patients and Other Inmates*. New York City, NY: Anchor Books, 1961.
Gomulka, Leila. "The Boundaries of Chaplain Confidentiality." *U.S. Naval Institute Proceedings* 139, no. 12 (2013). https://ezinearticles.com/?The-Boundaries-of-Chaplain-Confidentiality&id=8911292
Goodhead, Andrew, Peter Speck, and Lucy Selman. "'I Think You Just Learnt as You Went Along'—Community Clergy's Experiences of and Attitudes towards Caring for Dying People: A Pilot Study." *Palliative Medicine* 30, no. 7 (2016): 674–83.
Gorski, Philip. *American Covenant: A History of Civil Religion from the Puritans to the Present*. Princeton: Princeton University Press, 2017.
Gouse, Valerie. "An Investigation of an Expanded Police Chaplaincy Model: Police Chaplains' Communications with Local Citizens in Crisis." *Journal of Pastoral Care & Counseling* 70, no. 3 (2016): 195–202.
"Grand Rabbi Korff Escorted with Band." *Boston Globe*, September 1, 1926.
Greene, David. "'Mourning in Isolation'': Chaplain Tries to Comfort Families of COVID-19 Patients." NPR, April 10, 2020. https://www.npr.org/transcripts/831480517.
Greene, Lauren. "Hospital Chaplain Who Fought in Desert Storm Faithfully Serves on the Front Lines of Coronavirus Battle." Fox News, April 27, 2020. https://www.foxnews.com/faith-values/coronavirus-hospital-chaplain-combat-veteran.
"Ground Broken for Dooley Chapel at Deaconess." *Boston Globe*, September 13, 1955.
"Group Assails Lack of Minority Prison Chaplains." *Boston Globe*, August 11, 1983.
Grouse, Valerie. *Ministry of Presence: An Investigation of Communication between Police Chaplains Ad Local Civilians in Crisis*, Regent University, School of Communication and the Arts, 2017.
Günel, Gökçe, Saiba Varma, and Chika Watanabe. "A Manifesto for Patchwork Ethnography." Society for Cultural Anthropology, June 9, 2020. https://culanth.org/fieldsights/a-manifesto-for-patchwork-ethnography.
Gutierrez, Ian, Elizabeth Alders, Zainah Abulhawa, and Patricia Deuster. "Victors: A Conceptual Framework for Implementing and Measuring Military Spiritual Fitness." *Military Behavioral Health* 9, no. 4 (2021): 375–89.
Hadden, Jeffrey K. *The Gathering Storm in the Churches*. Garden City: Doubleday, 1969.
Hall, Charles. *Head and Heart: The Story of the Clinical Pastoral Education Movement. Journal of Pastoral Care Publications*, 1992.
Halpern, Sydney A. "Dynamics of Professional Control: Internal Coalitions and Cross-Professional Boundaries." *American Journal of Sociology* 97 (1992): 994–1021.
Hammond, James H. "85-Hour Revolt Ends: Prison Rebels Surrender to 7-Man Citizens' Group." *Boston Globe*, January 22, 1955.
Hammond, James H. "Riot-Ending Drive Hinted: Alternate Plan Set If Peaceful Means Fail in Prison Revolt." *Boston Globe*, January 20, 1955.

Hammond, James, and Seymour Linscott. "Probe Centers on Jet's Low Approach." *Boston Evening Globe*, August 1, 1973.

Handzo, George. F., Mark Cobb, Cheryl Holmes, Ewan Kelly, and Shane Sinclair. "Outcomes for Professional Health Care Chaplaincy: An International Call to Action." *Journal of Health Care Chaplaincy* 20, no. 2 (2014): 43–53.

Hansen, Kim Philip. *Military Chaplains & Religious Diversity*. New York: Palgrave Macmillan, 2012.

"Harold Matulaitis." *Boston Globe*, October 11, 1984.

Harris, John. "5-Hour Walkout Ties Up Ten of City's Docks." *Daily Boston Globe*, May 18, 1955.

Harvard Crimson. "Remembering Reverend Peter Gomes, Beloved Harvard Spiritual Leader." March 2, 2001. https://www.thecrimson.com/article/2011/3/2/gomes-harvard-university-cox/.

Harvard Gazette. "Rev. Peter J. Gomes Dies at 68." March 1, 2001. https://news.harvard.edu/gazette/story/2011/03/rev-peter-j-gomes-dies-at-68/.

"Harvard to Note Founding of Navy Chaplain Corps." *Daily Boston Globe*, November 27, 1955.

Harvey, Paul. *Howard Thurman and the Disinherited: A Religious Biography*. Grand Rapids: Eerdmans, 2020.

Hayes, Karen. "Veterans Day Observances to Mark War's End." *Boston Globe*, November 5, 1995.

Haythorn, Trace. "Conclusion: What We Learned and Next Steps." *Journal of Pastoral Care & Counseling* 75, no. IS (2021): 53–54.

"'He Was Truly One of Us.'" MIT News. April 24, 2013. https://news.mit.edu/2013/officer-sean-collier-memorial-0424.

Healy, Robert. "'Wait Rioters Out . . . for Now,' Says Warden." *Boston Globe*, January 20, 1955.

Hicks, Allison. "Role Fusion: The Occupational Socialization of Prison Chaplains." *Symbolic Interaction* 31, no. 4 (2008): 400–421.

Hicks, Allison M. "Learning to Watch Out: Prison Chaplains as Risk Managers." *Journal of Contemporary Ethnography*. 41, no. 6 (2012): 636–67.

Hicks, Douglas. *Religion and the Workplace: Pluralism, Spirituality, Leadership*. Cambridge: Cambridge University Press, 2003.

Hilsman, Gordon. *How to Get the Most Out of Clinical Pastoral Education: A CPE Primer*. Philadelphia, PA: Jessica Kingsley, 2018.

Hochschild, Arlie Russell. *The Managed Heart: The Commercialization of Human Feeling*. Berkeley: University of California Press, 1983.

Hohler, Bob. "Faith Binds Many on Sox: Evangelical Christians Give Sport a Spiritual Context." *Boston Globe*, August 31, 2005.

Holifield, E. Brooks. *A History of Pastoral Care in America: From Salvation to Self-Realization*. Nashville: Abingdon Press, 1983.

Holifield, E. Brooks. *God's Ambassadors: A History of the Christian Clergy in America*. Grand Rapids: Eerdmans, 2007.

Holst, Lawrence. "The Hospital Chaplain between Worlds." In *Health/Medicine and the Faith Traditions*, edited by Martin E. Marty and Kenneth L. Vaux, 293–309. Philadelphia: Fortress Press, 1982.

Holst, Lawrence, and Harold P. Kurtz. *Toward a Creative Chaplaincy*. Springfield: Charles C. Thomas, 1973.

Howell, Frank M., John P. Bartkowski, Lynn M. Hempel, and Jeremy R Porter. "When Faith, Race, and Hate Collide: Religious Ecology, Local Hate Cultures, and Church Burnings." *Review of Religious Research* 60, no. 2 (2018): 223–45.

"Hub Police to Honor Deceased Members." *Boston Globe*, May 31, 1983.

Hufford, David J., Matthew J. Fritts, and Jeffrey E. Rhodes. "Spiritual Fitness." *Military Medicine* 175, no. 8 (2010): 73–87.

Hughes, Everett C. "Good People and Dirty Work." *Social Problems* 10, no. 1 (1962): 3–11.

Hughes, Everett C. *The Sociological Eye: Selected Papers*. Chicago: Aldine-Atherton, 1971.

Jacobsen, Douglas, and Rhona Hustedt Jacobsen. *No Longer Invisible: Religion in University Education*. New York: Oxford University Press, 2012.

Jenkins, Jack. "For Hospital Chaplains, Being Vaccinated First Brings a Mix of Emotions." *Religion News Service*, December 23, 2020, sec. News. https://religionnews.com/2020/12/23/for-hospital-chaplains-being-vaccinated-first-is-a-mix-of-emotions/.

Jenkins, Jack. "'Protest Chaplains' Shepherd at Protests." *Religion News Service*, October 11, 2011, sec. Politics. https://www.ncronline.org/news/politics/protest-chaplains-shepherd-protests.

Jeuland, Jane, George Fitchett, Dena Schulman-Green, and Jennifer Kapo. "Chaplains Working in Palliative Care: Who They Are and What They Do." *Journal of Palliative Medicine* 20, no. 5 (February 1, 2017): 502–8.

"John Dugan Is Assigned to Be the Catholic Chaplain at Cushing General Hospital, Framingham." *Boston Globe*, May 27, 1945.

Johnson, Marilynn. *The New Bostonians: How Immigrants Have Transformed the Metro Area since the 1960s*. Amherst: University of Massachusetts Press, 2015.

Johnson, Marilynn. "'The Quiet Revival:' New Immigrants and the Transformation of Christianity in Greater Boston." *Journal of Religion & American Culture* 24, no. 2 (2014): 231–58.

Jones, Vanessa. "A Study in Comfort: More Muslims Hear the Call to Chaplaincy as a Way to Share Their Faith yet Minister to All." *Boston Globe*, March 7, 2007.

"Kansas campus minister to go to Antarctica." *Associated Press*, December 29, 2018.

Kapp, Deborah. "I'll Think of Something: Improvisation in Small Church Service Programs." *Review of Religious Research* 54, no. 2 (2012): 197–215.

Katz, Jack. "Jazz in Social Interaction: Personal Creativity, Collective Constraint, and Motivational Explanation in the Social Thought of Howard S. Becker." *Symbolic Interaction* 17, no. 3 (1994): 253–279.

Kauffman, Christopher J. *Ministry and Meaning: A Religious History of Catholic Health Care in the United States*. New York: Crossroad, 1995.

Kaufman, Sharon R., and Lynn M. Morgan. "The Anthropology of the Beginnings and Ends of Life." *Annual Review of Anthropology* 34 (2005): 317–41.

Kestenbaum, A., M. Shields, J. James, W. Hocker, S. Morgan, S. Karve, and L. B. Dunn. "What Impact Do Chaplains Have? A Pilot Study of Spiritual AIM for Advanced Cancer Patients in Outpatient Palliative Care." *Journal of Pain and Symptom Management* 54, no. 5 (2017): 707–14.

Knickerbocker, Wendy. *Bard of the Bethel*. Cambridge: Cambridge Scholars, 2014.

Konieczny, Mary Ellen, and Megan C. Rogers. "Religion, Secular, Humanism and Atheism: USAFA and the Cadet Freethinkers Group." *Journal for the Scientific Study of Religion* 55, no. 4 (2017): 821–38.

Kopacz, Marek S., April L. Connery, Todd M. Bishop, Craig J. Bryan, Kent D. Drescher, Joseph M. Currier, and Wilfred R. Pigeon. "Moral Injury: A New Challenge for

Complementary and Alternative Medicine." *Complementary Therapies in Medicine* 24 (February 2016): 29–33.

"Kosher Kitchen at Devens Brings General a Citation." *Daily Boston Globe*, September 18, 1955.

Kowalski, Mumina. "A New Profession: Muslim Chaplains in American Public Life." Master's thesis May 2011. Hartford, CT: Hartford Seminary.

Kowalski, Mumina, and Wendy S. Becker. "A Developing Profession: Muslim Chaplains in American Public Life." *Contemporary Islam* 9, no. 1 (January 1, 2015): 17–44.

Kraut, Alan M. "'No Matter How Poor and Small the Building': Health Care Institutions and the Jewish Immigrant Community." *In Religion and Immigration: Christian, Jewish, and Muslim Experiences in the United States* edited by Yvonne Yazbeck Haddad, Jane I. Smith, and John L. Esposito, 129–58. Walnut Creek: Alta Mira Press, 2003.

Kronus, Carol L. "The Evolution of Occupational Power: An Historical Study of Task Boundaries between Physicians and Pharmacists." *Work and Occupations* 3 (1976): 3–37.

Kuruvilla, Carol. "Hospital Chaplains Grapple With COVID-19's 'Tsunami' Of Grief." HuffPost, June 23, 2020. https://www.huffpost.com/entry/hospital-chaplains-coronavirus-patients_l_5ed15ab8c5b6520bd9fb5501.

Kurzman, Dan. *No Greater Glory: The Four Immortal Chaplains and the Sinking of the Dorchester in World War II*. New York: Random House Books, 2004.

Kwak, Jung, Soyeon Cho, Brian P. Hughes, Sami S. Hasan, and Albert Luu. "The Role and Activities of Board-Certified Chaplains in Advanced Care Planning." *American Journal of Hospice and Palliative Medicine*, 38, no. 12 (January 28, 2021): 1495–502.

Labuschagne, Dirk, Alexia. Torke, Daniel. Grossoehme, Katie. Rimer, Martha Rucker, Kristen Schenk, James E. Slaven, and George Fitchett. "Chaplaincy Care in the MICU: Examining the Association Between Spiritual Care and End-of-Life Outcomes." *American Journal of Hospice and Palliative Medicine*, 38, no. 12 (January 19, 2021): 1409–16.

Lamont, Michele, and Virag Molnar. "The Study of Boundaries in the Social Sciences." *Annual Review of Sociology* 28 (2002): 167–95.

"Latent Violence, Courtsey Weird Riot Bedfellows." *Daily Boston Globe*, January 20, 1955.

Lawrence, J. M. "Rev. James Lane, Police Chaplain, Pastor." *Boston Globe*, August 1, 2007, sec. Obituaries.

Leehey, Patrick. "A History of Mariner's House, 11 North Square, Boston, MA." 1995.

Legath, Jenny Wiley. *Sanctified Sisters: A History of Protestant Deaconesses*. New York: New York University Press, 2019.

Levenson, Michael. "For Heroes, Tributes and Treats; Bomb-Sniffing Dogs Honored for Service in Iraq." *Boston Globe*, August 11, 2007.

Levey, Robert L. "Clergy Interrupt School Board Meeting." *Boston Globe*, June 8, 1965.

Levinson, Marc. *The Box: How the Shipping Container Made the World Smaller and the World Economy Bigger*. Princeton: Princeton University Press, 2006.

Lewis, Bobby. "Local chaplain serves Team USA in Pyeongchang." *Tampa Bay's 10*, February 17, 2018.

Lichterman, Paul. "Religion in Public Action: From Actors to Settings." *Sociological Theory* 30, no. 1 (2012): 15–36.

Lloyd-Williams, Mari, Mark Cobb, Chris Shiels, and Fiona Taylor. "How Well Trained Are Clergy in Care of the Dying Patient and Bereavement Support?" *Journal of Pain and Symptom Management* 32, no. 1 (2006): 44–51.

"Logan Airport—a City within a City." *Boston Globe*, August 14, 1984.

Long, Ibrahim J., and Bilal Ansari. "Islamic Pastoral Care and the Development of Muslim Chaplaincy." *Journal of Muslim Mental Health* 12, no. 1 (August 2, 2018): 109–21.

Long, Jeffrey. "Hindu Chaplaincy as Karma Yoga in the Tradition of Sri Ramakrishna and Swami Vivekananda: An Interview with Swami Tyagananda." In *Hindu Approaches to Spiritual Care: Chaplaincy in Theory and Practice*, edited by Vineet Chander and Lucinda Mosher, 157–66. Philadelphia: Jessica Kingsley, 2020.

Long, Tom. "Msgr. J.J. Keating, Was Chaplain with Boston Firefighters; at 83." *Boston Globe*, November 17, 1995, sec. Obituaries.

Lonsway, Francis A. "Profiles of Ministry: History and Present Research." *Theological Education* 41, no. 2 (2006): 111–25.

Loveland, Anne C. *American Evangelicals and the U.S. Military: 1942–1993*. Baton Rouge: Louisiana State University Press, 1996.

Loveland, Anne C. *Change and Conflict in the U.S. Army Chaplain Corps since 1945*. Knoxville, TN: University of Tennessee Press, 2014.

Maas, Steve. "Healing Mind and Soul: Chaplains Say More Hospice Patients Look Harder for Spiritual Care as Their Bodies Are Failing." *Boston Globe*, May 11, 2014.

MacCormack, Matthew. "Antiviolence Ministry Ordains First Group of Chaplains: 7 Members Train in Prevention." *Boston Globe*, June 22, 2015.

MacQuarrie, Brian. "For Longtime Chaplain, a Duty That Never Gets Easier." *Boston Globe*, March 29, 2014.

Mahoney, Frank. "In Boston: Ceremonies in the Rain." *Boston Globe*, May 29, 1984.

Maia. "The Protest Chaplains: A New Paradigm in Chaplaincy during a Time of Social Transformation (Part 1)." *The Jizo Chronicles* (blog), March 24, 2012. https://jizochronicles.com/2012/03/24/the-protest-chaplains-a-new-paradigm-in-chaplaincy-during-a-time-of-social-transformation-part-1/.

"Maj Dugan Assigned as Cushing Chaplain." *Daily Boston Globe*, May 27, 1945.

Marshall, Joey, and Daniel V. A. Olson. "Local Religious Subcultures and Generalized Social Trust in the United States." *Journal for the Scientific Study of Religion* 57, no. 3 (2018): 473–94.

Mass Live. "Massachusetts State Employee Salary Database 2015." March 4, 2015. https://www.masslive.com/politics/2015/03/massachusetts_state_employee_salary_database_2015.html?appSession=.

Mass Live. " "Massachusetts State Employee Salary Database 2019." January 7, 2020. https://www.masslive.com/news/2020/01/massachusetts-state-employee-salary-database-2020.html.

Massari, Paul. "A Joyful Sorrow." Harvard Divinity School, May 5, 2020. https://hds.harvard.edu/news/2020/05/05/joyful-sorrow.

Massey, Kevin, Marilyn J.D. Barnes, Dana Villines, Julie D. Goldstein, Anna Lee Hisey Pierson, Cheryl Scherer, Betty Vander Laan, and Wm. Thomas Summerfelt. "What Do I Do? Developing a Taxonomy of Chaplaincy Activities and Interventions for Spiritual Care in Intensive Care Unit Palliative Care." *BMC Palliative Care* 14, no. 10 (2015). doi: 10.1186/s12904-015-0008-0

McCarroll, Pamela, and Angela Schmidt. "The Present and Future of Spiritual Care and Chaplaincy in Canada." In *Multi-Faith Perspectives in Canadian Religious and Spiritual Care* edited by Mohamed Taher, 699. Toronto, ON: Canadian Multifaith Federation, 2019.

McCauley, Bernadette. *Who Shall Take Care of Our Sick?: Roman Catholic Sisters and the Development of Catholic Hospitals in New York City*. Baltimore: Johns Hopkins University Press, 2005.

McGrath, Edward G. "'Berlin Rope' Falls in Selma." *Boston Globe*, March 13, 1965.

McMorrow, John P. "What People Talk about: Chaplain's Prayer in House Calls for Love of Neighbor." *Daily Boston Globe*, September 13, 1955.

McRoberts, Omar M. *Streets of Glory: Church and Community in a Black Urban Neighborhood*. Chicago: University of Chicago Press, 2005.

McWilliams, Frances. "Voices Crying in the Wilderness: Prophetic Ministry in Clinical Pastoral Education." *Journal of Pastoral Care* 51, no. 1 (1997): 37–47.

Mealer, Bryan. "'You're Not Alone. I Am with You': The Chaplains Tending to Those Dying from Covid-19." *The Guardian*, May 6, 2020. http://www.theguardian.com/world/2020/may/06/coronavirus-covid-19-chaplains-christian.

Meier, Levi, and Robert P. Tabak. "Hospitals." In *Encyclopaedia Judaica*, edited by Michael Berenbaum and Fred Skolnik, 9:562–65. Detroit: Macmillan, 2007.

"Memorial Services Held for Boston's Firefighters." *Boston Globe*. June 9, 1975.

Menzies, Ian. "Prisoner Welfare Continued Story for Fr. Hartigan." *Daily Boston Globe*, January 23, 1955.

"Miami Hoping for a Miracle." *Boston Globe*, December 19, 2007.

Mieth, Jennifer. *All Hand Herald: Massachusetts Department of Fire Services*, 2016.

Mieth, Jennifer. *All Hands Herald: Massachusetts Department of Fire Services*, 2014.

Miller, David W. *God at Work: The History and Promise of the Faith at Work Movement*. New York: Oxford University Press, 2007.

Miller, David W., Faith Wambura Ngunjiri, and James Dennis Lorusso. "'The Suit Cares about Us:' Employee Perceptions of Workplace Chaplains." *Journal of Management, Spirituality & Religion*, 15, no. 5 (2018): 399–97.

Mills, Alexa. "Tirelessly, the Minister Goes to Where the Need Is: From Church to Shelter to Jail to Graveside, Rev. Laura Ahart Follows a Midlife Calling." *Boston Globe* January 30, 2014.

Molna, Alejandra. "As Americans Become Less Religious, the Role of Chaplains May Grow." *Religion News Service*, November 27, 2019.

"Money Not 'Be-All, End-All,' Abp. Cushing Tells Guild." *Daily Boston Globe*, May 16, 1955.

Monfalcone, Wesley R. "General Hospital Chaplain." In *Dictionary of Pastoral Care and Counseling*, edited by Rodney J. Hunter, 456–57. Nashville: Abingdon Press, 2005.

Morison, Samuel Eliot. *The Maritime History of Massachusetts 1783–1860*. Boston: Houghton Mifflin, 1921.

"Mrs. Roosevelt Will Address Seniors." *Boston Globe*, May 29, 1955.

Mueller, Collin W. "Civil Religion in the Congressional Chaplaincy: Prayer Rhetoric and Signaling Behavior in the United States Legislature." 2012.

Muhammad, Bahiyyah M., and Melanie-Angela Neuilly. *Mothering from the Field: The Impact of Motherhood on Site-Based Research*. New Brunswick: Rutgers University Press, 2019.

Myers-Shirk, Susan E. *Helping the Good Shepherd: Pastoral Counselors in a Psychotherapeutic Culture 1925–1975*. Baltimore: Johns Hopkins University Press, 2008.

National Center for Education Statistics. Table 104.10.

Rates of High School Completion and Bachelor's Degree Attainment among Persons Age 25 and over, by Race/Ethnicity and Sex: Selected Years, 1910 through 2019. https://nces.ed.gov/programs/digest/d19/tables/dt19_104.10.asp?current=yes.

See National Center for Education Statistics. Table 104.88. Number of Persons Age 25 and over and Rates of High School Completion and Bachelor's Degree Attainment among Persons in This Age Group, By Sex and State: 2018. https://nces.ed.gov/programs/digest/d19/tables/dt19_104.88.asp?current=yes.

Nelson, Laura J. "Farewell to Trooper Who 'Saw the Good in Everything': More Than 600 Attend Funeral." *Boston Globe*, June 7, 2011.

Nicas, Jack. "Boston's First Black Officer Receives His Long-Overdue Honors." *Boston Globe*, June 27, 2010.

"'Night of Panic' on WBZ Next Wednesday Marks 17th Anniversary of Grove Fire." *Daily Boston Globe*, November 22, 1959.

"Nine N. E. Chaplains among 88 Graduated at Fort Devens School." *Boston Globe*, May 5, 1945.

Nolan, Steve. "'He Needs to Talk!': A Chaplain's Case Study of Nonreligious Spiritual Care." *Journal of Health Care Chaplaincy* 22, no. 1 (2016): 1–16.

Nolan, Steve. "Hope beyond (Redundant) Hope: How Chaplains Work with Dying Patients." *Palliative Medicine* 25, no. 1 (January 1, 2011): 21–25.

NORC. "National Survey of Religious Leaders (NSRL)." University of Chicago. N.d. https://www.norc.org/Research/Projects/Pages/national-survey-of-religious-leaders.aspx.

O'Connor, Thomas. *The Boston Irish: A Political History*. Boston: Back Bay Books, 1997.

O'Connor, Thomas. *Boston Catholics: A History of the Church and Its People*. Boston: Northeastern University Press, 1998.

O'Connor, Thomas. *Building a New Boston: Politics and Urban Renewal 1950 to 1970*. Boston: Northeastern University Press, 1993.

Open Payrolls. "52 Employee Records for Massachusetts Chaplain in 2010." N.d. https://openpayrolls.com/state/massachusetts/2010-chaplain.

Olsen, Jon C., Michael L. Buenefe, and William D. Falco. "Death in the Emergency Department." *Annals of Emergency Medicine* 31, no. 6 (1998): 758–65.

Otis, Pauletta. "An Overview of the U.S. Military Chaplaincy: A Ministry of Presence and Practice." *Review of Faith & International Affairs* 7, no. 4 (2009): 3–15.

Paget, Naomi K., and Janet R. McCormack. *The Work of the Chaplain*. Valley Forge: Judson Press, 2006.

Parks, Sharon Daloz. *Big Questions, Worthy Dreams: Mentoring Emerging Adults in Their Search for Meaning, Purpose and Faith*. San Francisco, CA: Jossey-Bass, 2011.

Perry, Samuel L., and Cyrus Schleifer. "Are Bi-Vocational Clergy Becoming the New Normal? An Analysis of the Current Population Survey, 1996–2017." *Journal for the Scientific Study of Religion* 58, no. 2 (2019): 513–25.

Pew Forum on Religion and Public Life. "Religion in Prisons: A 50 State Survey of Prison Chaplains." 2012.

Pew Research Center. "Adults in the Boston Metro Area." N.d. https://www.pewforum.org/religious-landscape-study/metro-area/boston-metro-area/.

Pew Research Center. "Why Americans Go (and Don't Go) to Religious Services." August 1, 2018.

Piderman, Katherine M. "On These Holy Mountains." *Journal of Health Care Chaplaincy*, 28, no. 1 April 6, (2020): 63–68.

Piderman, Katherine M. et al. "The Feasibility and Educational Value of Hear My Voice, a Chaplain-Led Spiritual Life Review Process for Patients with Brain Cancers and Progressive Neurologic Conditions." *Journal of Cancer Education* 30, no. 2 (2015): 209–12.

Piderman, Katherine M. et al. "Hearing and Heeding the Voices of Those with Advanced Illnesses." *Journal of Palliative Care* 35, no. 4 (2020): 248–55.

Potter, John. "Hero Priest at Club Fire Tells of 'Terrible Sights.'" *Daily Boston Globe*, December 1, 1942.

Power, Bridget. "What It's Like to Help Families Say Goodbye." *WBUR*. June 19, 2020.

PRRI. American Values Atlas. N.d. http://ava.prri.org/home#religious/2019/States/religion/16 and http://ava.prri.org/#religious/2019/MetroAreas/religion/m/2.

Puchalski, Christina, Robert Vitillo, Sharon K. Hull, and Nancy Reller. "Improving the Spiritual Dimension of Whole Person Care: Reaching National and International Consensus." *Journal of Palliative Medicine* 17, no. 6 (2014): 642–56.

Purvis, Taylor E., Thomas Y. Crowe, Scott M. Wright, and Paula Teague. "Patient Appreciation of Student Chaplain Visits during Their Hospitalization." *Journal of Religion and Health* 57, no. 1 (February 1, 2018): 240–48.

"Rabbi Ira Korff, 25, Has Been Appointed Chaplain of the Boston Fire Dept." *Boston Globe*, February 25, 1975.

Radin, Charles A. "A Fire with Faith." *Boston Globe*, May 1, 2006.

Raskins, Hanna. "Chaplain experienced in crisis counseling now tends to restaurant workers' mental health." *The Post and Courier*, July 4, 2018.

Rawlings, Deb, Jennifer Tieman, Lauren Miller-Lewis, and Kate Swetenham. "What Role for Death Doulas Play in End-of-Life Care? A Systematic Review." *Health and Social Care in the Community* 27 (2019): 82–94.

Regan, James H. "Marine Sheds Uniform for Tights to Perform in Shrine Circus Here." *Daily Boston Globe*, October 1, 1945.

Reich, Jennifer. "Pregnant with Possibility: Reflections on Embodiment, Access, and Inclusion in Field Research." *Qualitative Sociology* 26, no. 3 (2003): 351–67.

Reimer-Kirkham, Sheryl, and Lori G. Beaman. 2020. "Creating an Inclusive Public Sphere: Healthcare and the Role of Prayer." In *Prayer as Transgression: The Social Relations of Prayer in Healthcare Settings*, edited by Sheryl Reimer-Kirkham, Sonya Sharma, Rachel Brown and Melania Calestani, 37–53. Montreal: McGill University Press.

Reimer-Kirkham, Sheryl, Sonya Sharma, Rachel Brown, and Melania Calestani. *Prayer as Transgression? The Social Relationship of Prayer in Healthcare Settings*. Montreal, QC, and Kingston, ON: McGill-Queens University Press, 2020.

"Religion Bolsters Freedom, M.I.T. Seniors Are Told." *Daily Boston Globe*, June 10, 1955.

"Religion in Prisons: A 50 State Survey of Prison Chaplains." Pew Forum on Religion and Public Life, 2012.

"Religious Responses to Boston Bombings." PBS, April 13, 2013. https://www.pbs.org/wnet/religionandethics/2013/04/19/april-19-2013-religious-responses-to-boston-bombing/15986/.

"Rev. H.E. Pomeroy Protestant Chaplain of Fire Department." *Boston Globe*, January 1, 1945.

"Rev. Pomeroy." *Boston Globe*, February 12, 1975.

Ribadeneira, Diego. "A Times of Testing, Affirmation Rosh Hashanah a Renewal for Many Jewish Students." *Boston Globe*, September 25, 1995.

Ribadeneira, Diego. "Diverse College Crowd Is Catching the Spirit: Religious Activism Is Back on Campus." *Boston Globe*, September 18, 1995.

Richard, Ray. "The Unusual Becomes the Norm at Boston Waterfront Chapel." *Boston Globe*, September 11, 1981.

Richman, Alan. "Rare Breed of Officer." *Boston Globe*, December 20, 1984.

Ridderbusch, Katja. "For Hospital Chaplains, Coronavirus Has Shifted Spiritual Care." *U.S. News & World Report*, April 22, 2020.

"Rioters' Grievances Told Priest, Doctor." *Daily Boston Globe*, January 20, 1955.

Risse, Guenter B. *Mending Bodies, Saving Souls: A History of Hospitals*. New York: Oxford University Press, 1999.

"RNS Circus Chaplain." October 18, 2011.

Roberts, Oliver Ayer. *History of the Military Company of Massachusetts Now Called the Ancient and Honorable Artillery Company of Massachusetts, 1637–1888*. Boston: Alfred Mudge & Son, 1895.

Roberts, Stephen B., and Williard W. C. Ashley. *Disaster Spiritual Care: Practical Clergy Responses to Community, Regional and National Tragedy*. Woodstock, VT: Skylight Paths, 2008.

Rosenberg, Charles E. *The Care of Strangers: The Rise of America's Hospital System*. New York: Basic Books, 1987.

Rousmaniere, Leah Robinson. *Anchored within the Veil*. New York: The Seamen's Church Institute of New York and New Jersey, 1995.

Ruggiero, Erica. "The Chaplain's Job." *Chronogram Magazine*, May 6, 2020. https://www.chronogram.com/hudsonvalley/the-chaplains-job/Content?oid=10496040.

"Sacred Places." Center for Spiritual Life, Brandeis University. N.d. https://www.brandeis.edu/spiritual-life/sacred-places/index.html.

Sampson, Helen, and Bin Wu. "Compressing Time and Constraining Space: The Contradictory Effects of ICT and Containerization on International Shipping Labour." *International Review of Social History* 48, no. S11 (2003): 123–52.

Sanford, Monica. "The Practice of Dharma Reflection among Buddhist Chaplains: A Qualitative Study of 'Theological' Activity among Nontheocentric Spiritual Caregivers." PhD diss., Claremont School of Theology, 2018.

Sarna, Jonathan D., and Ellen Smith. *The Jews of Boston*. Boston: Combined Jewish Philanthropies of Greater Boston, 1995.

Schleifer, Cyrus, and Wendy Cadge. "Clergy Working Outside of Congregations, 1976–2016." *Review of Religious Research* 61 (2019): 411–29.

Schmalzbauer, John. "Campus Prophets, Spiritual Guides, or Interfaith Traffic Directors? The Many Lives of College and University Chaplains." *Journal of College and Character* 22, no. 2 (2021): 156–62.

Schmalzbauer, John. "Campus Religious Life in America: Revitalization and Renewal." *Society* 50, no. 2 (2013): 115–31.

Schmalzbauer, John, and John S. Mahoney. *The Resilience of Religion in Higher Education*. Waco: Baylor University Press, 2018.

Seigler, Carolina, and Wendy Cadge. "How Leaders Negotiate Religious Differences: Frameworks of Mandate and Interpersonal Care." Under review.

Sells, Heather. "Hospital Chaplains Report Uptick in Questions about Eternity, Fight through Their Own Tears to Help the Grieving." CBN News, May 7, 2020. https://www1.cbn.com/cbnnews/us/2020/may/hospital-chaplains-report-uptick-in-questions-about-eternity-fight-through-their-own-tears-to-help-the-grieving.

Seltz, Johanna. "Easton Church to Honor Town's Police, Fire Departments." *Boston Globe*, September 30, 2015.

Shapiro, Leo. "Feasts in Homes, Rites Usher in Passover Tonight." *Boston Globe*, April 6, 1955.

Shapiro, Leo. "Wakefield to Honor Four Chaplains." *Boston Globe*, May 29, 1955.

Sharma, Vanshdeep, Deborah M. Marin, Xiaobo Zhong, Madhu Mazumdar, Maggie Keogh, Zorina Costello, and Lina Jandorf. "Using the Taxonomy: A Standard Vocabulary of Chaplain Activities." *Journal of Health Care Chaplaincy* 27, no. 1 (2021): 43–64.

Shaw, Richard Denis. *Chaplains to the Imprisoned: Sharing Life with the Incarcerated*. New York: Haworth Press, 1995.

Shinzawa, Fluto. "Return Engagements Pay Off; Cuts Overcame Sticky Situations." *Boston Globe*, January 14, 2005.

Shipman, Asha. "Hindu Chaplaincy in US Higher Education: Summary and Guidelines." 2019.

Shipman, Asha. "Hinduism and Chaplaincy: Relating Core Concepts to Spiritual Care." *Convergence Magazine*, May 2020.

Sikora, Chris. "The Case for Music in Times of Loss." *New York Times*, May 21, 2020, sec. Well. https://www.nytimes.com/2020/05/21/well/mind/music-grief-coronavirus.html.

Sims, Rayna. "Truck Stop Chapels Provide Place of Worship for Truckers." *Columbia Missourian*, April 17, 2018. https://www.columbiamissourian.com/news/local/truck-stop-chapels-provide-place-of-worship-for-truckers/article_8c0b584e-4191-11e8-9cb9-8f1027e032e4.html.

"Sitting in with Ted Ashby: Only One America." *Daily Boston Globe*, April 11, 1955.

"Sketches of Those Who Settled Revolt." *Daily Boston Globe*, January 22, 1955.

Slomovitz, Albert Issac. *The Fighting Rabbis: Jewish Military Chaplains and American History*. New York: New York University Press, 1999.

Smalley, Suzanne. "Amid Turmoil, Davis Takes Police Reins." *Boston Globe*, December 5, 2006.

Smith, Gregory A. et al. "U.S. Decline of Christianity Continues at Rapid Pace." Pew Research Center, 2019.

Snowden, Austyn. "What Did Chaplains Do during the Covid Pandemic? An International Survey." *Journal of Pastoral Care & Counseling* 75, no. IS (2021): 6–16.

Spillman, Lyn, and Sorcha A. Brophy. "Professionalism as a Cultural Form: Knowledge, Craft, and Moral Agency." *Journal of Professions and Organization* 5 (2018): 155–66.

Stack, James. "Memory Dies Hard: Cocoanut Grove—Visions of Hell." *Boston Globe*, November 26, 1967.

Stahl, Ronit. *Enlisting Faith: How the Military Chaplaincy Shaped Religion and State in Modern America*. Cambridge: Harvard University Press, 2017.

Stanley, Lauren R. "Standing Rock Chaplains Attended to Needs after Joyful News." *Episcopal News Service* (blog), December 15, 2016. https://www.episcopalnewsservice.org/2016/12/15/standing-rock-chaplains-attended-to-needs-after-joyful-news/.

Starr, Paul L. *The Social Transformation of American Medicine*. New York: Basic Books, 1982.

Stavig, Alissa, Lynn Bowlby, John P. Oliver Min, J. Dillard, and E. Nickolopoulos. "Patients, Staff, and Providers' Factual Knowledge about Hospital Chaplains and Association with Desire for Chaplain Services." *Journal of General Internal Medicine* 37 (2022): 697–699.

https://www.tandfonline.com/doi/abs/10.1080/2194587X.2021.1939721?journalCode=ujcc20.

Sudnow, David. *Passing On: The Social Organization of Death*. Englewood Cliffs, NJ: Prentice-Hall, 1967.

Sullivan, Winnifred Fallers. *A Ministry of Presence: Chaplaincy, Spiritual Care and the Law*. Chicago: University of Chicago Press, 2014.

Sullivan, Winnifred Fallers. *Prison Religion: Faith-Based Reform and the Constitution*. Princeton: Princeton University Press, 2009.

Sundt, Jody L., and Francis T. Cullen. "The Correctional Ideology of Prison Chaplains: A National Survey." *Journal of Criminal Justice* 30, no. 5 (2002): 369.

Sundt, Jody L., and Francis T. Cullen. "The Role of Contemporary Prison Chaplain." *Prison Journal* 78, no. 3 (1998): 271.

Sundt, Jody L., Harry R. Dammer, and Francis T. Cullen. "The Role of the Prison Chaplain in Rehabilitation." *Journal of Offender Rehabilitation* 35, no. 3–4 (2002).

Swain, Storm. "The T. Mort. Chaplaincy at Ground Zero: Presence and Privilege on Holy Ground." *Journal of Religion and Health* 50 (2011): 481–98.

Sweeney, Kathy. "Chaplain lays out plan for homeless shelter in Cape Girardeau." *KFVS2*, February 10, 2010.

Sweeney, Patrick, Jeffrey E. Rhodes, and Bruce Boling. "Spiritual Fitness: A Key Component of Total Force Fitness." *Joint Force Quarterly* 66, no. 3rd quarter (2012): 35–41.

Swift, Christopher. *Hospital Chaplaincy in the Twenty-First Century*. 2nd ed. Surrey, UK: Ashgate, 2014.

Tabak, Robert. "The Emergence of Jewish Health-Care Chaplaincy: The Professionalization of Spiritual Care." *American Jewish Archives Journal* 2 (2010): 89–109.

Tan, Heather, Cheryl Holmes, Eleanor Flynn, and Leila Karimi. "'Essential Not Optional:' Spiritual Care in Australia during a Pandemic." *Journal of Pastoral Care & Counseling* 75, no. IS (2021): 41–45.

Tanner, Tom. "Four Trends That May Portend the Future for ATS Enrollment: What the Last Decade Says about the Next Decade." *Journal of Christian Ministry*, 6 (2017): 22–26.

Tata, Beba, Daniel Nuzum, Karen Murphy, Leila Karimi, and Wendy Cadge. "Staff-Care by Chaplains during COVID-19." *Journal of Pastoral Care & Counseling* 75, no. IS (2021): 24–29.

The Economist. "Civil Rites: As Fewer Americans Go to Church, Chaplains Are Finding Work Elsewhere." *The Economist*, July 11, 2020. https://www.economist.com/united-states/2020/07/11/as-fewer-americans-go-to-church-chaplains-are-finding-work-elsewhere.

Thomas, John Rea. "A "Snap Shot" History (1975–2000) of the Association for Clinical Pastoral Education, Inc.: A Celebration of the 75th Anniversary of CPE." Association for Clinical Pastoral Education, 2000.

Thurston, Angie, and Capster ter Kuile. "How We Gather." 2015. https://caspertk.files.wordpress.com/2015/04/how-we-gather.pdf

Timmermans, Stefan. "Death Brokering: Constructing Culturally Appropriate Deaths." *Sociology of Health and Illness* 27, no. (2005): 993–1013.

Tobak, Phyllis Brooks. "A Theological Reflection on Baptism by a Jewish Chaplain." *Journal of Pastoral Care & Counseling* 47, no. 3 (n.d.): 315–17.

Tolfree, Christine. "Working to Curb Violence, One Youth at a Time." *The Pilot*, September 3, 2004. https://www.thebostonpilot.com/article.asp?ID=1633.

Transforming Chaplaincy. "Phase 1 Final Report." June 30, 2019. https://www.transformchaplaincy.org/wp-content/uploads/2019/06/TC-Phase-1-Final-Report-June-2019.pdf.

Trickey, Erick. "Has Boston Given Up on God?" *Boston Magazine*, December 18, 2018. https://www.bostonmagazine.com/news/2018/12/11/boston-given-up-on-god/.

Turco, Catherine J. *The Conversational Firm*. New York: Columbia University Press, 2016.

Turner, Robert L. "Bludgeon Falls Lightly on Legislature's Budget." *Boston Globe*, September 25, 1975.

U.S Air Force. "Chaplin Corps." N.d. https://www.afrc.af.mil/About-Us/Chaplain/.

U.S. Army. "Army Chaplain." N.d. https://www.goarmy.com/chaplain/become-an-army-chaplain/candidate-program.html.

U.S. Navy. "Navy Chaplain." N.d. https://www.navy.com/careers/navy-chaplain.

Vandenhoeck, Anne. "The Impact of the First Wave of the Covid-19 Pandemic on Chaplaincy in Health Care: Introduction to an International Survey." *Journal of Pastoral Care & Counseling* 75, no. IS (2021): 4–5.

Vandenhoeck, Anne, Cheryl Holmes, Cate Michelle Desjardins, and Joost Verhoef. "'The Most Effective Experience Was a Flexible and Creative Attitude'—Reflections on Those Aspects of Spiritual Care That Were Lost, Gained, or Deemed Ineffective during the Pandemic." *Journal of Pastoral Care & Counseling* 75, no. IS (2021): 17–23.

Vaters, Karl. "The New Normal: Realities and Trends in Bivocational Ministry." *Christianity Today*, 2017. https://www.christianitytoday.com/karl-vaters/2017/december/new-normal-9-realities-trends-bivocational-ministry.html

Veiga, Manny. "For I Have Sinned; with Guidance from Boston College Volunteers, Inmates at the State Prison in Norfolk Find a Path from the Past to Spirituality and 'Internal Freedom.'" *Boston Globe*, March 6, 2008.

Viser, Matt. "Revere Bids Farewell to Fallen Officer: Five-Year Veteran Recalled as 'Best We Have to Offer.'" *Boston Globe*, October 7, 2007.

Vrabel, Jim. *The People's History of the New Boston*. Boston: University of Massachusetts Press, 2014.

Waggoner, Ed. "Taking Religion Seriously in the U.S. Military: The Chaplaincy as a National Strategic Asset." *Journal of the American Academy of Religion* 82, no. 3 (2014): 702–35.

Wakenshaw, Clare. "From a Good Death to a Better Bereavement? The Impact of the End of Life Experience on Bereavement Adjustment, a Thematic Analysis." *Bereavement Care* 37, no. 3 (2018): 109–17.

Walker, Christina. "Hospital Chaplains Are Bridging the Gap between Patients and Grieving Families Who Can't Stay by Their Bedside." CNN, April 26, 2020. https://www.cnn.com/2020/04/26/us/hospital-chaplains-coronavirus/index.html.

Walsh, Colleen. "Dust in the Wind." *Boston Globe*, April 3, 2005.

Wangsness, Lisa. "Interfaith Group Rallies on Beacon Hill vs. Anti-Muslim Rhetoric." *Boston Globe*, September 8, 2010.

Wangsness, Lisa. "'You Are Not Forgotten About': Behind Bars, a Cardinal's Quiet Prison Ministry." *Boston Globe*, December 26, 2010.

Warner, R. Stephen. "Work in Progress: Toward a New Paradigm for the Sociological Study of Religion in the United States." *American Journal of Sociology* 98, no. 5 (1993): 1044–93.

Weiss, Bari. "The Men and Women Who Run toward the Dying." *New York Times*, April 3, 2020. https://www.nytimes.com/2020/04/03/opinion/coronavirus-hospitals-chaplains.html

Whalen, Jack, Marilyn Whalen, and Kathryn Henderson. "Improvisational Choreography in Teleservice Work." *British Journal of Sociology* 53, no. 2 (2002): 239–58.

Wheeler, David R. "Higher Calling, Lower Wages: The Vanishing of the Middle-Class Clergy." *The Atlantic*, July 22, 2014.

White, Kelsey B., Ryan M. Combs, Hallie R. Decker, and Brandon M. Schmidt. "Gender-Based Perspectives on Professional Healthcare Chaplaincy Board Certification." *Journal for the Scientific Study of Religion* 60, no. 4 (July 24, 2021): 871–89.

White, Kelsey B., Patricia E. Murphy, Jane Jeuland, and George Fitchett. "Distress and Self-Care among Chaplains Working in Palliative Care." *Palliative & Supportive Care* 17, no. 5 (2019): 542–49.

Whitt, Jazqueline E. *Bringing God to Men: American Military Chaplains and the Vietnam War*. Chapel Hill: University of North Carolina Press, 2014.

Wilcox, W. Bradford, Andrew Cherlin, Jeremy Uecker, and Matthew Messel. "No Money, No Honey, No Church." *Research in the Sociology of Work* 23 (2012): 227–50.

Winship, Christopher. "End of a Miracle? Crime, Faith, and Partnership in Boston in the 1990s." In *Long March Ahead: African American Churches and Public Policy in Post-Civil Rights America*, edited by R. Drew Smith, 171–92. Durham, NC: Duke University Press, 2002.

Wittenberg-Lyles, Elaine, Debra Parker Oliver, George Demiris, Paula Baldwin, and Kelly Regehr. "Communication Dynamics in Hospice Teams: Understanding the Role of the Chaplain in Interdisciplinary Team Collaboration." *Journal of Palliative Medicine* 11, no. 10 (2008): 1330–35.

Wuthman, Walter. "For Nearly 140 Years, a Seaside Mission Has Offered Ship Workers Small Comforts And Spiritual Support." wbur, September 3, 2020. https://www.wbur.org/radioboston/2020/09/03/new-england-seafarers-mission-sacred-spaces.

Wuthman, Walter, "For Seafaring Workers, the Pandemic Could Mean Even More Time Away from Home." wbur, July 9, 2020. https://www.wbur.org/radioboston/2020/07/09/cargo-ship-workers-coronavirus-extended-voyages.

Zollfrank, Angelika A. "Chaplaincy in a Free-Standing Psychiatric Hospital during the COVID-19 Pandemic." *Journal of Pastoral Care & Counseling* 75, no. IS (2021): 49–52.

Index

For the benefit of digital users, indexed terms that span two pages (e.g., 52–53) may, on occasion, appear on only one of those pages.

Tables and figures are indicated by *t* and *f* following the page number

agnosticism, 12, 14–15, 82. *See also* demographic shifts *under* Religion
American Red Cross, 3, 59
animals, 43–44, 111
atheism, 12, 14–15, 23, 82, 110, 145–46. *See also* demographic shifts *under* Religion
authenticity (in the work of chaplaincy), 16–17, 129, 145
authority of chaplains and its sources, 71, 84–91

Beth Israel Deaconess Medical Center, 2–3, 184n.75
bi-vocationality, 151, 156
Boisen, Anton, 24–25, 136–37. *See also* Cabot, Richard *and* clinical pastoral education (CPE)
Boston, 8–11, 14–15, 154
Boston City Hospital (now Boston Medical Center), 26, 27, 31, 45–46
Boston Logan Airport, 9–10, 28–29, 36, 37–38, 41, 115–16. *See also* airports *under* sectors of chaplaincy
Boston Marathon bombing, 2–4, 89, 154
Boston Medical Center, 2–3, 188n.148, *See also* Boston City Hospital
"Business Model" supporting chaplaincy, 13–14, 15, 21–22, 24, 46, 89–90, 94–95, 97–105, 156, 161

Cabot, Richard, 136–37. *See also* Boisen, Anton *and* clinical pastoral education (CPE)
certification (chaplaincy credential), 59–60, 64, 67, 149, 159, 161, 170*t*, 173, 174, 190n.38
chaplaincy
  alternate language for (e.g., "spiritual advisor"), 8, 45, 154–55
  barriers to entering the profession, 17, 25, 45, 159, 161
  defined, 5, 7–8, 11, 15–16, 17–18, 22–25, 30–31, 36–37, 39–40, 43–45, 50–52, 64, 67, 84–85, 87–88, 94–95, 100–1, 115, 149–52, 154–55, 160–62, 165, 177n.30, 179n.8
  paths into the work, 52–55, 62, 63–64
  relationship to government, 7, 11, 50
  who chaplains serve, 95–97, 98–102, 118, 122–23, 125–26, 127–29, 165
Chaplaincy Innovation Lab, 158, 161, 170, 172–73
clinical pastoral education (CPE), 14*f*, 24–25, 60, 61, 67, 136–37, 140, 146–47. *See also* Boisen, Anton *and* Cabot, Richard
civil rights movement of 1960s, 33–34
code switching, 15–17, 77, 82, 105, 107–8, 109–10, 129, 142–43. *See also* neutralizing
compensation of chaplains, 57, 86, 137, 155–57, 171*t*, 186n.111
congregational clergy, 15, 17–18, 21–22, 24, 25, 26–27, 31–32, 37, 45–46, 53, 65–66, 67, 114, 122–23, 149, 153, 156–60, 189n.23
COVID-19, 4–5, 11, 68, 114, 148, 171–72, 176n.20, 198n.13, 206n.14

Cushing, Richard (Archbishop of Boston), 1, 20–21, 28–30, 31, 37–38, 47, 137

death, 16, 84, 151–52. *See also* grief
  and bereavement care, 124
  and life review, 119–21, 199n.36
  preparation for (personal and societal), 118–19, 124–26, 197n.8
  and ritual, 121–23
  when unexpected, 16, 112–13, 114, 116–18, 125, 126, 151–52
demand for chaplaincy, 4–5, 18, 20, 22, 87–90, 94–97, 148–49, 157–58
demographics of chaplains, 5, 10, 12, 15, 20–22, 26, 36–37, 38, 39, 40, 45–46, 65–66, 67, 69, 129–30, 137–38, 149–51, 168, 169*t*, 191n.6, *See also* denominations within chaplaincy; gender; race

education, 7, 10, 13–14, 15, 17, 24–25, 27, 44–45, 50, 52–55, 59–64, 67, 136–37, 139–40, 154, 157–60, 170–71, 170*t*, 190n.38, 190n.53. *See also* master of divinity (MDiv)
  specific to sectors in which chaplains work, 61–62
endorsement (of chaplains by religious / philosophical organizations), 7, 24–25
entrepreneurship (religious) 5, 10, 17–18, 50, 68, 150–51, 156, 161

Faith Matters, 17, 25, 156, 159, 176n.15, 193n.61
first amendment, 6–7, 11, 47, 70–71, 74, 85, 141, 142

gender (as subject of chaplaincy work), 43
  as demographic in chaplaincy, 5, 15, 21–22, 149, 150–51, 169*t*, 174, 189n.10, 204n.7
grief, 121. *See also* death

hegemony (Christian), 146
history of chaplaincy, 6–8, 9–10, 14–15, 130–31, 133–37, 167, 168, 175n.13, 179n.8, 182n.42, 185n.84, 188n.7
holding space, 108–10, 152
humanism. *See* atheism

improvisational work, 81–83, 114
institutions / organizations (chaplains' relationships to) 6–7, 10, 15–16, 17, 46, 50–51, 57–58, 65, 72–73, 77, 83–84, 89–91, 97–105, 139, 140–42, 153–54, 158, 161, 165
interfaith work, 38–39, 40–41, 42, 49, 52, 114, 127–28, 137–38, 139, 140, 141, 144, 145, 146–47, 165
International Fellowship of Chaplains, 44–45, 62, 63*f*, 64, 67, 170*t*

language used in chaplaincy, 51, 52, 77, 95, 105–10, 127, 143–44, 203n.57
Legal issues, 11, 58–59
liminality (aspect of chaplaincy work), 22, 72, 93–94, 109, 113–14, 149–50, 152, 154, 162, 163
listening (as chaplaincy skill), 75, 76

Massachusetts General Hospital, 24–25, 26, 29–30, 42, 136–39
master of divinity (MDiv), 25, 44–45, 60–61, 170*t*, *See also* education
meaning-making, 98–100, 158
media coverage of chaplaincy, 4–5, 114, 148, 154–55, 168, 198n.13
mediating and bridging, 77, 113–14, 120, 122–25
ministry of presence. *See* presence (as chaplaincy skill)
models of chaplaincy, 128–29, 132–33, 136, 137, 138–39, 146
moral injury, 195–96n.29

neutralizing, 142–44. *See also* code switching

outcomes, 89–90, 100–1, 102, 179–80n.13

pastoral and prophetic, 95, 97–98, 103–5, 109
pets. *See* animals
presence (as chaplaincy skill), 79–80, 98, 100–1, 152, 161, 193n.45

professional associations, 10, 168–69
public understanding of chaplaincy, 4, 8, 18–19, 160–61, 162, 163, 176n.16

race
as demographic of chaplaincy, 15, 21–22, 23, 36–37, 38, 150–51, 159, 169*t*, 170–71, 173, 204n.7, 205n.11
as subject of chaplaincy work, 4, 16, 34, 36–37, 38, 114, 186n.104
racism, 101–2. *See also* race
relationality, 72, 74–76, 81–82, 90, 104–5, 114
religion
congregations (social unit of religious gathering), 12, 13–14, 17–18, 20–21, 27, 35–36, 37, 40, 41–42, 45, 46, 50–51, 57, 62, 65–66, 69–70, 93, 130–31, 133–34, 151, 153, 156–58, 160, 177n.30, 186n.111, 190–91nn.57–58
deinstitutionalization, 12–14
demographic shifts, 4–5, 10–11, 12–15, 17, 18–19, 20–21, 28–29, 38–39, 129–30, 136, 146, 154–62, 165
and physical space, 167
pluralism, 16–17, 31
religious diversity, 127–29, 131–32, 136, 139, 140–42, 144, 145–46, 165, 193n.58
unaffiliation, 12, 14–15, 146, 165–66
religious traditions within chaplaincy
Buddhist, 39–41, 45–46, 137–38, 169*t*
Catholic, 1–2, 9–11, 15, 20–22, 24, 26, 28–31, 35–38, 39–40, 41–42, 45–46, 47–48, 50–51, 53, 54–55, 60–61, 65–66, 68, 70, 73–74, 86–87, 121–22, 128, 133–35, 136, 137, 138–39, 146, 150, 156–57, 168, 169*t*, 170*t*, 182n.48, 183n.57, 184nn.70–71, 185n.89, 188n.7, 191n.58, 202n.33
Episcopalian, 15, 21–22, 26, 27, 31–34, 35–36, 37, 39, 40–41, 51, 53, 86, 137
Hindu, 24, 184n.74
Jewish, 24, 25, 29–31, 35–37, 38–39, 45–46, 54, 122, 128, 133–34, 136, 137, 138–39, 144, 169*t*, 170–71, 183n.63, 185n.89, 186n.103
Muslim, 24, 41–42, 48, 169*t*
Orthodox (Christian), 137, 169*t*
Protestant (non-Catholic and non-Orthodox) 1–2, 5, 8–10, 12, 17–18, 20–21, 24–25, 26, 27, 29–31, 35–37, 43–44, 45–46, 48, 53, 58, 68, 69, 86–87, 105–6, 127, 128, 130–31, 132–34, 136–37, 138–39, 142, 144, 146, 149, 156–57, 169*t*, 185n.89, 191n.58
Quaker, 169*t*
Unitarian / Unitarian Universalist, 43–44, 53–54, 108, 169*t*
United Church of Christ, 15
ritual work, 16, 50, 73–74, 83–84, 87–88, 114, 117–18, 121–22, 192n.11

scholarship on chaplaincy, 4, 11–14, 20, 22, 162, 165–66, 167, 169–70, 173, 179–80n.13
sectors of chaplaincy (discussed), 55–59, 65–66, 67, 83–84, 161, 165, 166, 167, 168–69, 170–71, 171*t*
airports, 9–10, 37–38, 41, 115–16, 166–67, 178n.39
animals, 43–44
community, 2, 10, 15, 20, 39–40, 43–45, 55–58, 61–62, 63*f* Photo 3.3, 67, 83–84, 89, 90–91, 92, 95, 96, 103, 105, 116–17, 140, 142–43, 171*t*, 176n.22, 192n.11, *See also* Boston Marathon bombing
corporate / industrial, 10, 28, 201n.9
corrections (*see* prison *under* sectors of chaplaincy)
disaster, 3, 10, 55–56, 59, 63*f* Photo 3.3, 88, 160, 168–69, 175n.11 (*see also* American Red Cross; Boston Marathon bombing)
fire, 9–10, 29–30, 35, 36, 38, 42, 117–18, 133–36
government, 3–4, 9–10, 30–31, 35–36, 37, 38, 69–70, 115–16, 166, 180n.14, 183n.61, 184n.70, 185n.89, 187n.126
and number of chaplains in federal service, 10

sectors of chaplaincy (discussed) (*cont.*)
healthcare, 4, 7, 8, 10, 15–16, 22, 23–25, 26–28, 29–30, 35, 37, 38–39, 55–58, 59, 60, 61, 64, 67, 68, 71, 72, 74, 77, 78, 81–82, 83, 85–86, 89–91, 95, 96–97, 102, 104, 105, 107, 120–21, 124, 128–29, 136–39, 140, 142, 149, 151, 152, 153, 155, 160, 165, 169–71, 171*t*, 179–80n.13, 181n.31, 183n.63, 189n.10, 190n.38, 191n.58, 193n.62, 194–95nn.5–6, 194n.85, 195n.16, 195–96n.29, 198n.13, 199n.30
and number of chaplains working in healthcare, 10
higher education, 3–4, 10, 15–16, 18, 22, 23–24, 26–28, 31–34, 35–36, 37, 39, 40–41, 52, 55–57, 65–66, 67, 68, 72, 83, 89, 90–91, 93, 116, 144, 152–53, 167, 168, 170–71, 177n.35
hospice, 3–4, 10, 18, 41–42, 43–44, 51, 55–58, 66, 67, 68, 76–77, 81–82, 83, 84, 85–86, 95–96, 98, 100–1, 105, 107–9, 110, 118–19, 124, 155, 203n.57
mental health / psychiatric care, 26, 37, 195–96n.29
military, 3–4, 6–7, 10, 22–23, 28, 41, 55–58, 60–61, 85, 103, 115, 141–42, 155, 180n.17, 190n.43
Dorchester sinking, 30–31
and number of chaplains in federal service, 10, 23
National Guard, 2, 53, 55–57, 58, 60–61, 85, 140–41, 177n.35
palliative care, 42, 119, 124, 197n.8, 198n.22, 203n.57
police, 10, 35, 36, 42, 61–62, 185n.84
prison, 1–2, 3–4, 6–7, 10, 12, 15–16, 22, 23–24, 26–28, 29–30, 35, 38, 41–42, 47–48, 51–52, 55–56, 66, 70–71, 74, 85, 142, 155
protest (*see* social justice and movements *under* sectors of chaplaincy)
retirement centers / nursing facilities, 10, 29–30, 38–39, 65, 75, 76, 80, 96, 122, 124–25, 154, 156, 160
seaports, 10, 26, 35, 39, 41, 42–43, 130–33, 160, 166, 170–71, 171*t*, 201n.16
social justice and movements, 10, 17, 25, 33–34, 35–36, 39, 43–44, 48–50, 52–55, 60, 83–84, 101–2, 149, 156 (*see also* Civil rights movement of 1960s)
occupy movement, 3–4
Standing Rock, 3–4, 176n.15, 193n.61
sports, 10, 43
truck stops, 7, 43
Veterans (including the Veterans Administration), 3–4, 6–7, 10, 28, 37, 41, 53, 60, 61, 65, 67, 74, 84, 95, 150–51, 171*t*, 177n.35, 204n.7
and number of chaplains in federal service, 10
self-care, 161–62
spiritual but not religious, 12. *See also* demographic shifts *under* religion
staff support, 4–5, 19, 23–24, 41, 43, 72, 73, 77, 78, 89, 90, 95, 96–97, 102, 109, 112, 114, 118, 121, 123–24, 128, 142, 148, 151–52, 155–56, 195n.16, 198n.13
Still Harbor, 48–49
supply of chaplains. *See* education

teaching (as chaplaincy skill), 76
theodicy, 15–16, 95, 110, 168, 195n.9
Thurman, Howard, 33–34. *See also* Civil rights movement of 1960s
trauma, 10, 66, 69–70, 118, 171–72